The Diary of Hamman Yaji

HAMMAN YAJI. From Kurt Strümpell, "Die Geschichte Adamauas nach mündlichen Überlieferungen." Hamburg: L. Friederichsen, 1912.

The Diary
of
Hamman Yaji

Chronicle of a
West African
Muslim Ruler

Edited and Introduced by
James H. Vaughan and
Anthony H. M. Kirk-Greene

Indiana University Press
BLOOMINGTON AND INDIANAPOLIS

©1995 by James H. Vaughan and Anthony H. M. Kirk-Greene

The paper used in this publication meets the minimum requirements
of American National Standard for Information Sciences—Perma-
nence of Paper for Printed Library Materials, ANSI Z39.48-1984.

MANUFACTURED IN THE UNITED STATES OF AMERICA

Library of Congress Cataloging-in-Publication Data

Yaji, Hamman.
    The diary of Hamman Yaji : chronicle of a West African Muslim
ruler / edited and introduced by James H. Vaughan and Anthony
H. M. Kirk-Greene.
        p.   cm.
    Includes bibliographical references and index.
    ISBN 0-253-36206-7 (alk. paper)
    1. Yaji, Hamman—Diaries. 2. Kings and rulers—Nigeria—Diaries.
3. Sokoto State (Nigeria)—History. I. Vaughan, James H., date.
II. Kirk-Greene, A. H. M. (Anthony Hamilton Millard). III. Title.
DT515.77.Y35A3 1995
966.96'2—dc20   94-27840

1 2 3 4 5 00 99 98 97 96 95

This publication is dedicated to all of the people of Madagali District, with the hope that their future will be one of harmony and mutual cooperation.

C O N T E N T S

6. *The Later History of the Diary: An Archival and Autobiographical Note* ANTHONY H. M. KIRK-GREENE **146**

Foreword

PAUL E. LOVEJOY

The diary of Hamman Yaji records the unusual story of a notorious slave raider. Initially appointed emir of the small Muslim territory of Madagali in northeastern Adamawa by the Germans in 1902, he subsequently served under the French and then the British as the region of northern Cameroon successively changed hands during World War I. The diary, which covers the period of his reign as emir from 1912 to 1927, was among over 100 documents seized at the time of his arrest and deposition in 1927. According to Hamman Yaji's own testimony, he was responsible for enslaving over 2,000 people in the hills surrounding Madagali from 1912 to 1920. Given such a record, it is not surprising that he is remembered locally as a particularly brutal tyrant. The diary contains other information besides a record of slave raiding under colonialism, including observations on the daily activities of the palace, the relationship of Hamman Yaji to his concubines, slaves, relatives, and court officials, and his dedication to Islam.

In their introduction, James Vaughan and A. H. M. Kirk-Greene explain how Hamman Yaji came to power after the Germans executed his father and how he was able to consolidate his rule under three different colonial regimes. Relying on extensive archival and oral documentation, their introduction is a major contribution in scholarship in its own right. Kirk-Greene first became aware of the diary while serving as a colonial officer in Yola in the 1950s: he is widely regarded as one of the foremost authorities on the history of Adamawa and colonial Northern Nigeria. Vaughan learned of Hamman Yaji during his extensive field work as an anthropologist among the very people who had suffered from the slave raiding. The oral traditions he has collected help to balance the impressions gleaned from the diary itself.

Specialists and nonspecialists alike will find the diary a fresh and revealing documentary source for studying the colonial era in Africa. Clearly not intended for public view, the diary offers a rare opportunity to examine the mind of a man who was caught between two worlds, one that continued the commitment of Muslims in the Sokoto Caliphate and its many dependencies to slavery and the slave trade in the name of Islam and one that imposed new forms of exploitation and different laws under colonialism. Hamman Yaji engaged in actions that were illegal under European rule, whether German, French, or British, but the location of Madagali on the distant frontier enabled the continuation of practices and activities that at times were conveniently overlooked, even if disapproved of. Hamman Yaji fell from grace only when the League of Nations began to search for cases of abuse in the mandated territories of the former German empire. British officials then removed him from office to avoid public embarrassment. Until the publication of the diary by Vaughan and Kirk-Greene, the Hamman Yaji affair has remained a carefully guarded secret of the colonial state.

Department of History
York University
North York, Canada

Acknowledgments

In addition to the persons mentioned in the text who so generously helped us in this publication, we would like to acknowledge the assistance of several others. Dahiru Dan Galadima was District Head of Madagali throughout Kirk-Greene's tour and greatly helped in collecting local history. He also welcomed Vaughan to Madagali and introduced him to the late Alhaji Mohammed Sanusi, then a young man of 18 who became Vaughan's first field assistant and who subsequently became the first Margi District Head of Madagali. Sanusi was an enthusiastic supporter of this project, and it is unfortunate that his untimely death prevented him from seeing its completion. Field work in Madagali was greatly facilitated by Muhammadu S. S. Gulak and Usman Ibrahim Jalingo. Vaughan's first working index was compiled by Dr. David Coplan, then a graduate student at Indiana University.

This copy of Hamman Yaji's diary was taken from a photocopy which the Nigerian National Archives authorized the University of Ibadan to release to Anthony H. M. Kirk-Greene with the provision that the source be acknowledged (DNA 20/10/Vol. 111/266, 8 September 1970). We are very grateful for this authorization.

Preface

In 1959 I began field research among the Margi in Madagali District, in what was then Northern Cameroons, at the suggestion of Tony Kirk-Greene, whom I had met at Northwestern University. Almost immediately I was regaled with tales of Hamman Yaji, the former District Head. He had been deposed in 1927 because of his tyrannous behavior toward the non-Muslim peoples, the montagnards,[1] who constituted 80 percent of the district's population. I talked to men who had fought against his soldiers and to widows of his victims; I was shown the walls built to defend against his raids and the sites of some of his far-flung palaces. His memory was still vivid to aged montagnards, many of whom had suffered under his regime. They recounted how he raided their hamlets, stole their livestock, killed those who resisted, and enslaved those he captured.

I soon discovered that Hamman Yaji was more than a historic figure, for during both a United Nations plebiscite (the first of two, which ultimately transferred the region to Nigeria) and the area's first local government election, his name was prominently used to forge alliances (Vaughan 1964:1087–1091). Stories of his exploits abounded among the montagnards who so feared him, among his Fulbe compatriots who, while rejecting the cruelty of which he was charged, admired his celebrity, and among administrators, whose records documented some of his behavior. Soon, without being aware of the process, I had adopted the Margi attitude and regarded him as an oppressor, though I knew very little about him that could be confirmed by anything other than legend.

Madagali is a district of about 400 square miles with a population at that time of about 90,000, a majority of whom were still pagan and largely concentrated in the rugged Mandara Mountains, which ran along the eastern edge of the district. Rule was still in the hands of the Muslim Fulbe (Fulani)[2] minority, though no longer in the hands of heirs of Hamman Yaji. My family and I settled in a Margi hamlet near Gulak, the seat of the district, and I concerned myself with those remarkable people—not the Fulbe or Hamman Yaji.

1. Most frequently the indigenous peoples of the Mandara Mountains have been collectively referred to as "pagans" (Hausa: *arna*; Fulfulde: *kirdi*), and this appears extensively in Reed's translation of the diary. In the context of Muslim vs. non-Muslim, the term has relevance, but as a general term I prefer "montagnard," which is used extensively in writing about the Mandara populations in Cameroon.

2. In Nigeria, the Fulbe have traditionally been referred to as "Fulani," as will be noted in many of the quotations and citations that follow. However, modern practice seems to call for the standardization of terminology.

To aid me in my study of the history of the district, Derek Mountain, the District Officer, very generously loaned me the District Note Book, and from it I learned more about Hamman Yaji's reign. It was also from Mountain that I first heard of Hamman Yaji's diary, though he had not seen it nor was he sure that it still existed. Later, I learned that Kirk-Greene had a copy, and when I visited him in 1974, he very kindly made an additional copy for me. It is that diary, chronicling events between 1912 and his arrest in 1927, which is here presented.

Initially my interests were restricted to correlating Margi accounts of events with Hamman Yaji's, though I was aware that the diary had general historical value. For example, his references to events during World War I not only shed light on battles fought in the area but raise interesting questions about the nature of colonial administration. At times it is impossible to tell whether he was dealing with German, French, or British administrators—or whether he cared—and in 1917, well after the defeat of the Germans, he inexplicably refers to the French and German borders (*Diary*, July 6, 1917). But, perhaps because I am an anthropologist rather than a historian, I saw no compelling reason to press for the diary's publication.

Over the next years, I read the diary many times. With each reading, a more complete person emerged, and gradually I have come to see someone other than the man I thought I "knew." The raids are so dramatic that it is tempting to concentrate on them to the exclusion of all else, but it must be said that the diary is much more than a chronicle of enslaving, killing, and plundering; much of it is less explicit, and all of it is less dramatic. It reveals a troubled man, a victim of forces he could neither understand nor control. It is an extraordinary document for the picture it presents of a man, whose cultural values are so different from our own and from those of contemporary Fulbe, struggling to control the world he knew. For one with my commitment to the Margi—his victims—it is a difficult document to read, first in the sense that it is painful to read of their suffering, but second because I discover that I have some feeling for their oppressor. As an anthropologist I should have known that villains are best kept two-dimensional characters.

I have come to regard the diary as more than history, for I find an even broader value to reading it, one which I would urge upon any serious student of culture. The process of viewing a person from *that person's* perspective, particularly one whose behavior is so reprehensible to us, is an important educational experience. It is not unlike the challenge of field work; when you read Hamman Yaji's diary, you enter another world.

Hamman Yaji's values were those of nineteenth-century Muslim Fulbe society, which had established suzerainty over the pagans of the area in a complex arrangement with the much larger emirate of Adamawa. But the montagnards were themselves the products of proud cultures, and they resisted their loss of freedom with both force and cunning. Moreover, the colonial powers represented a third set of values. The British, who emerged as rulers of Madagali, struggled with an evolving policy of "indirect rule" whereby local rulers were granted considerable autonomy so long as it did not interfere with basic colonial goals. It was a balancing act; the British had conquered the Fulbe, yet they used them as local rulers. It was a situation made more difficult by the memory of the catastrophe in Sudan, wherein Muhammad Ahmad, the proclaimed Mahdi, had defeated their forces and wrested independence for a time.

We have provided an introductory section which places Hamman Yaji in this historical and cultural context. The conflict in Madagali gradually intensified as events unfolded, events which, in part, were only revealed to me some thirteen years after I first read the diary. I hope that a sense of that revelatory character is captured in our introduction.

The Diary of Hamman Yaji

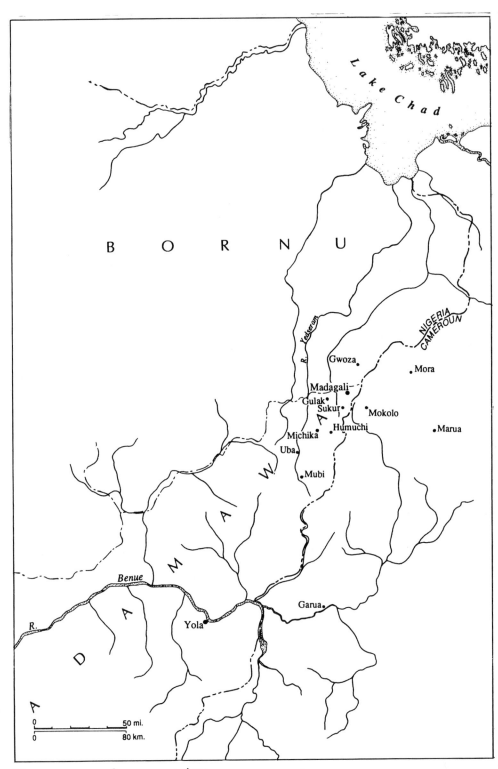

MADAGALI AND THE SURROUNDING AREA.

1. *The Context*

JAMES H. VAUGHAN

INTRODUCTION

In August of 1927, the British Touring Officer of the Northern Area of Adamawa Province of Northern Nigeria, with a detachment of Nigerian police and a half company of the West African Frontier Force, moved on the remote town of Madagali, where on the 26th they arrested the District Head, Muhammad Yaji, the most famous Emir of the Fulbe of Madagali, better known as Hamman Yaji.[3] An explanation of this unusual action was offered in a report to the League of Nations (Madagali had formerly been a part of German Kamerun) in which it was charged that he "would not carry out fairly the orders of Government towards the primitive hill tribes who live adjacent to [him]. . . . [and that] he persisted in malpractices until he could be tolerated no longer" (Great Britain Colonial Office 1928).

In Hamman Yaji's own diary, which had been seized when he was arrested, there was indisputable evidence that he had raided, killed, and enslaved hundreds of montagnards. The evidence of repression would be difficult to diminish, though it must be acknowledged that the conflict between Hamman Yaji and the montagnards was a continuation of a struggle in which his reign may be distinguished only because it is better documented. The contemporary reader will find much more in his diary, for it also reveals much about his daily life and the friction between Madagali and its Fulbe neighbors, including the overruling emirate of Adamawa. Certainly, one of the most interesting threads to follow is the increasing difficulty he had with colonialism and especially his conflict with the British—ostensibly—over his admin-

---

3. In the introduction to the diary and on its first page, Reed spelled the name "Haman." Other government documents also spell the name this way. However, on the title page and when the name occurs in the text, it is spelled "Hamman," which is the common spelling. Under British administration, the title *Emir* was reserved for the heads of provinces, and our use of that title for Hamman Yaji is irregular. However, the diarist referred to himself as "the Emir of Madagali, Muhammad Yaji" (*Diary*, January 5, 1926), and he typically referred to other Fulbe rulers by that title, so we continue his practice.

istration of the local populations. Thus, an understanding of the diary must be sought in the context of Hamman Yaji's milieu, Madagali: its history and its diverse population.

THE PEOPLE OF MADAGALI

Madagali is the northeasternmost district in Adamawa State, Nigeria. It is bounded on its west by the Yedseram River, which flows northward into Lake Chad, and on its east by the Mandara Mountains rising abruptly and dramatically from the river basin. The area is beautiful, peaceful, and remote. Until 1949, it was officially designated by the authorities as "Unsettled Territory," and there was not an all-season road through the district until 1959. But the isolation belies a turbulent and complex history. In its time, Madagali has been a simple Margi hamlet, an independent Fulbe emirate, and a vassal state of the great Emirate of Adamawa; it has been a part of German Kamerun, of French Cameroun, of British Northern Cameroons, and, finally, of Nigeria.

The Emirate of Madagali—which designation we shall use for its precolonial existence—was not a homogenous ethnic unit. It was a conquest state composed of a large majority of non-Muslim montagnards and a minority of settled Muslim Fulbe rulers (with an even smaller transient group of nomadic Fulbe, called Mbororo, who are occasionally mentioned in the diary). With the coming of colonialism, it became a conquest state within a conquest state, as European powers asserted their authority.

This is an area in which the overused term "culture conflict" is entirely appropriate, for three historical streams—the indigenous montagnard, the intrusive Fulbe, and the even more intrusive European—converged with calamitous results. Each was often ignorant and disdainful of the others, and each, to some extent, used the others to gain its own advantage.

The Montagnards

Although one may speak of the montagnards as though they are an entity, and Hamman Yaji probably thought of them in that way, they are a notably heterogeneous population. Today there are eight named montagnard groups comprising about 80 percent of the population of Madagali District, and it is doubtful that they have ever composed less. The Margi,[4] the district's largest population, the Wagga, Sukur, Tur, and Vemngo are each virtually native to and contained in the district. The three remaining populations are parts of groups principally found outside the district; the Kapsiki and Matakam are largely located in Cameroon, while the Higi[5] are the major

4. The name first appears as "Marghi" in the work of Heinrich Barth (1857, 2:117), who journeyed through the area in 1851, and it is likely that he got the term not from the people themselves but from the Kanuri (Rowling 1930:2).
5. Although the Kapsiki and Higi may be considered a single cultural unit (van Beek 1992:39), they are differentiated in the censuses of Madagali.

population of Cubunawa District to the south. The boundaries of the emirate have extended east at times into what is now Cameroon and slightly farther south into Cubunawa.[6] During such periods, it included larger proportions of Kapsiki, Matakam, and Higi.

These ethnic labels imply unity that does not exist, a fact that has made the montagnard easier—if not easy—to rule. There are not even indigenous general histories of the montagnard ethnic units, only histories of the various clans which have independently populated a given area.[7] Communities are often little more than groups of patrilineally related men and their wives and families, though in the larger settlements there may be representatives of two or three lineages. Even today, when ethnic labels are much more commonly used, identity is still largely in terms of clan or locale. This provincial orientation is a significant cultural characteristic and, in the context of this work, critical in explaining both the Fulbe's inability to incorporate the montagnards or the montagnards' inability to use their superior numbers to repulse the Fulbe.

However, some of the montagnards of Madagali have one distinction which sets them apart from all the other montagnards of the Mandara Mountains and which has had consequences for the history of Montagnard-Fulbe relations. Sukur and the several Margi units have complex political organizations—small kingdoms—unlike anything found in the rest of the mountains. More to the point, these units were able to resist the Fulbe, and they never acceded to Hamman Yaji's rule. Further, they were established well before the advent of the Fulbe at Madagali. The Sukur dynasty dates from the mid-sixteenth century; the Margi kingdom at Gulak[8] dates from the mid-seventeenth century and those at Maiva and Dluku from the last quarter of the eighteenth century.[9]

Although these kingdoms had ideological foundations (Vaughan 1980b), they were not conquest states and never attempted any broader political integration. The failure of a broader identity, which might have facilitated an

6. There are brief claims in the diary to Gwoza in the north (March 1, 1919) and to some of the lands of Isge beyond the Yedseram in the west (October 19 and November 18, 1918; July 18 and May 28, 1920), but there is no internal evidence that he ever administered these areas.

7. There is a brief and superficial history of the Margi in Meek (1931:214–216), but I have relied upon my field notes for the material herein.

8. There is confusion between Margi names and those used today, which derive from Fulbe usage. The name *Gulak,* which is common on all maps, is a corruption of *Gulagu,* a Margi word and the name of their kingdom, which Hamman Yaji referred to as "the pagans of Gulak." Herein I use *Gulak* as the place name for the town which is the principal settlement in the old kingdom. Similarly, *Dluku* refers to a kingdom, *Duhu* as its principal settlement.

9. There was another dynastic tradition in Madagali—though by Hamman Yaji's time its influence and power were much diminished—descended from the Pabir on the Biu plateau in the west. Shortly after the founding of Sukur, they settled east of the Yedseram at Madi-Kangkang, a site which is today only an archaeological midden. After two generations, they moved eastward to the mountains and settled upon a foothill called Mazhinyi, by which name the tradition is known today. From there they moved north to another low hill, Hymbula, leaving Mazhinyi, with its impressive ruins, to become a ward of Gulagu. Hymbula is also known as Chambula and was referred to by Hamman Yaji as Zu, the name of its principal settlement.

even more concerted resistance to the Fulbe, is related to the same parochial tendencies which characterize the smaller and less well organized montagnards. Even the Margi of Gulagu, who developed an aggressive state, did not acquire the lands of its victims. Margi political units maintained their mutual political independence and were often at war with one another. In fact, they entered the historical record when, in 1851, Heinrich Barth recorded that Gulagu raided a Margi village on the west bank of the Yedseram (Barth 1857, 2:118).

It is also true that within kingdoms the political rivalry sometimes became so intense that exterior action was precluded. During virtually all of Hamman Yaji's reign and for the entire period covered by the diary, Gulagu, the strongest montagnard state, was riven by dynastic disputes in which one side or the other used the Fulbe (as well as the Europeans) to its advantage. This is documented in part in oblique references in the diary in June and July of 1923.

Even had these political units achieved a larger base, it seems unlikely that they would have been a match for the cavalry and guns of Hamman Yaji's soldiers. Nonetheless, they refused to acquiesce and remained capable of organizing attacks. From their isolated mountain abodes they mounted forays against Fulbe, to the point of attempting to kidnap a high official who was visiting from the emirate of Adamawa in 1872 and killing Hamman Yaji's son in 1916 (*Diary*, August 27, 1916).

The Fulbe

The immigrations of the Fulbe[10] into Madagali, as to all of Adamawa, were a consequence of their transhumant pastoralism. Each year they moved south as the rains ended and pasture desiccated, then journeyed north as rains—and the tse-tse fly—returned. Gradually they pressed eastward across the Western Sudan. In this fashion the principal clans arrived in the basins of the Benue and Yedseram rivers.

The main Fulbe occupation of the Yedseram basin did not occur until the eighteenth century, during which lineage encampments belonging to

10. There are three primary sources on the history of the Fulbe in Madagali: Kurt Strümpell (1912), who was the German Imperial Resident of Adamawa; the Madagali District Note Book; and Kirk-Greene (1954b). Strümpell is the earliest source on the Fulbe of Adamawa including the earliest history of Madagali, and of the three sources, it is the only one published. The District Note Book is an unpublished collection of notes and comments by various administrative officers over many years. Typically, each section on a "village area" begins with historical and ethnographic information compiled by D. F. H. Macbride who was Assistant District Officer in the 1930s and had first-class honors in anthropology and classics from Cambridge. The section on the founding of the emirate at Madagali has additional comments by W. R. Shirley. Kirk-Greene's unpublished manuscript is the most detailed history of Madagali, particularly for the period after 1800. Although Macbride and Kirk-Greene had access to Strümpell and Kirk-Greene to Macbride, each did enough original research that his document must be regarded as a primary source. Two other sources are sometimes cited: Lemoigne (1918), who translated Strümpell into French, and Migeod (1927); but, they are entirely secondary and only important in that by poor translations they created erroneous "traditions" which still plague the unsuspecting researcher.

Mohammadou (1981) is an excellent source for the history of Camerounian Adamawa.

several clans moved seriatim into the valley from the north, where they had entered the Kingdom of Bornu by at least the sixteenth century (Strümpell 1912:52). These were not mass movements; they were the uncoordinated migrations of camps or at most of lineages.[11] In the process, where the water was abundant and the tse-tse absent, some would settle, often after acquiring permission from the indigenous sedentary farmers.

South of Bornu, where the Fulbe were subject to the rule of the Shehu of Bornu, there was a string of independent Fulbe settlements along the Mandara Mountains southward into the basin of the Benue River. The first of these was Madagali. It was founded by members of the Wolarbe clan[12] during their migration southward between the Yedseram River and the western slopes of the Mandaras. The District Note Book describes the founding of Madagali as follows:

> Tradition has it that the original leader of the Fulani clan now found in Madagali—the Wolarbe—was Ardo Kin. He led his men out of Malle and is said to have died at Damaturu. The clan then moved to Gamargu and again to Lokadisa under the leadership of Ardo Mutaru. At the latter place he died being succeeded by Ardo Hammanjamri who took the clan to Disa, Jaje and finally Damada, where he died. From Damada the clan moved to Gori under Ardo Bubu and then to Rumirgo, just north of Madagali, under Ardo Jidda [modern Njidda, the grandfather of Hamman Yaji].
>
> Ardo Jidda appears to have come to Rumirgo in c. 1800 or a little earlier. He settled with the consent of the pagans of Madagali. . . .
>
> At this time the Mandara [the sultanate] sphere of influence is said to have extended as far south and west as Uba. The Mandara forces raided annually in this area, though the most southerly of their posts seems to have been Kamboro. In this sphere the Fulani maintained themselves precariously, at first merely grazing their flocks within it between Mandara expeditions, retiring hurriedly when necessary, but later in stockaded towns such as Madagali, which were always liable to be sacked and burnt. . . .

11. An excellent sense of the heterogeneity of these migrations is portrayed in Frantz (1981:89–90).

12. This assertion is at variance with Strümpell, who attributes the founding to the "Baewue" (modern Mbewe) (1912: 87–88). But contemporary Madagali informants as well as the District Note Book are in agreement that the founders were Wolarbe. The section on the town of Madagali includes the following parenthetical remark: "The notes given below are based partly on Mr. Macbride's notes and partly on notes made by Mr. Shirley in June 1935 at a meeting of old men of both Fulbe and Marghi extraction in Madagali Town." It might be added that no authority on this area has proven more reliable than Macbride, who traveled extensively in the mountains, drew the first reliable map of the montagnard communities, and made notes of incomparable value. However, it cannot be said that Strümpell's information was hearsay, for he visited Madagali and includes the Margi story of the founding of the hamlet before the coming of the Fulbe (1912:87). The most compelling link between Strümpell and Madagali is a photograph he took of the "Lamido Madagali" (*Ibid.,* facing p. 87), which has been identified by sons of Hamman Yaji. Strümpell notes the possibility that the Mbewe came with the Wolarbe, but he places greater credence in "reliable informants" (1912:55–56). In any event, the versions, including local lore, are not significantly different after the accession of Ardo Njidda, the grandfather of Hamman Yaji.

It must be remembered that the Fulbe were not moving into unoccupied land; Madagali was a Margi community, named for the spear (gali) of a Margi named Madu. Nonetheless, until the nineteenth century, it is unlikely that montagnards were concerned with the movements of the Fulbe or their settlement at Madagali, beyond a guarded hostility between the two based on mutual suspicion.[13] It is less that they were indifferent than that they occupied different ecological niches. The montagnards terraced the slopes and tilled the plateaus and valleys of the mountains, while the Fulbe needed the expanses of the basal plains for their cattle. Each was introverted and maintained its distinct identity despite—perhaps because of—friction and occasional conflict.

This mutual isolation was not, however, typical of the whole area. In the basins of the Yedseram and the Benue, physical separation was less easily maintained, and as a consequence there were developments which came to affect all Fulbe-pagan relationships, including those in Madagali. In the plains, the Fulbe, as late-comers and pastoralists, needed permission to pasture or traverse the fields of the local farmers, and this was sometimes a source of conflict. Although the farmers welcomed the manuring of their fields, occasionally it is reported that they exploited the peaceful pastoralists. The Benue valley farmers, notably the Bata and the Verre, were far less accepting and tolerant of the Fulbe than the insular montagnards. The Fulbe, as Muslims, particularly resented acceding to the demands of pagans, including the often cited instance of the demand of *jus primae noctis* (Barth 1857, 2:175n, Strümpell 1912:53, Kirk-Greene 1958:128, Njeuma 1978:12), and by the beginning of the nineteenth century, the Fulbe in the Benue valley had developed a sense of ethnic/religious militarism.

However, these were times of ferment for all Fulbe, as evidenced by the rise of Sokoto. When it emerged as a center of political authority, disparate Fulbe emirates were attracted to it as a righteous way of remedying their plight. In 1808, Modibbo Adama, a pious noble of the Ba lineage of the Benue Fulbe, led a delegation to Sokoto to ally themselves with the jihad against the heathen. Their emirate came to be called Adamawa after Adama, and Yola became its capital. It became the rallying point for the nearby autonomous emirates, and through it Fulbe rule was coordinated over the area. As a part of the agreement, Adama received the title *Lamido* (leader),[14] a flag and commission to wage a jihad in the east,[15] with the obligation to send an annual quota of slaves to Sokoto—which were, of course, taken from the non-Muslim population.

13. Strümpell offers tales "wrapped in complete darkness" of Fulbe raids upon the montagnards (1912:57), including one at an unspecified time led by one Bautschi-Gordi into the heart of what became Madagali. Today there remains no record, oral or otherwise, of such.

14. Emirs of Adamawa have been characteristically called *Lamido*, a Fulfulde word.

15. A letter from Usman dan Fodio to Adama dated March 5, 1809, offers instruction and advice in the conduct of the jihad. Acknowledging that the Bata and Verre have oppressed the Fulbe, it nonetheless enjoins Adama not to conquer them, an injunction which was not followed (Njeuma 1978:247–249).

It is not evident that the slave quota had any immediate impact upon the montagnard pagans, for they, unlike the farmers in the basins, remained largely inaccessible. Even when the Fulbe adopted military tactics, they relied upon horses, which were ineffective in the rugged mountains.

The problems that the Fulbe at Madagali faced were not primarily with the montagnards but with the Sultanate of Mandara, which had never accepted the presence of the Fulbe in what it considered its territory. Around 1809, Ardo Njidda of Madagali, the grandfather of Hamman Yaji, struck an alliance with Adama. Consequently, in 1815, when the forces of Sultan Illiyasa defeated Njidda and sacked Madagali,[16] Adama responded with a full campaign, which resulted in the defeat of Mandara in 1823. According to Strümpell, Adama took Njidda to Madagali, where he planted a tree and said, "As I plant this tree, so I now place you in Madagali. If Mandara attack you in the morning, I will be here in the evening, and if he attack you in the evening, I will come in the morning" (1912:88). Mansur, Adama's son, remained in Madagali for two years, fortified the town, and built a mosque. The defeat of Mandara finally limited its power in the area, but it established Madagali as a true dependant of Adamawa, a relationship which it has not always been content to accept.

Around mid-century, an aging Ardo Njidda resigned in favor of Bakari, a 14-year-old son by his only legitimate wife. (Bakari was to become the father of Hamman Yaji.) He was, however, soon replaced by Buba Ciuto, an older son of Njidda by a concubine, on the authority of Lamido Lawal of Adamawa. Some light is shed upon this transition by Barth, for at this point Madagali first appears in history recorded by Europeans. On June 17, 1851, Barth wrote that he met the two sons of Njidda, "to whom belongs the country between Segúr and Wándalá or Mándará," and he remarks:

> I now learned that the young men were already mixing in politics; the younger brother, who was much the handsomer, and seemed to be also the more intelligent of the two, had, till recently, administered the government of his blind father's province, but had been deposed on account of his friendly disposition toward Wándalá, having married a princess of that country, and the management of affairs had been transferred to his elder brother. (1857, 2:159)

This fixes the date of Buba Ciuto's accession as earlier than mid-year 1851, and undoubtedly it reveals the reason for the deposition of Bakari. An alliance with Mandara would have been strongly opposed by the Lamido of Adamawa.

---

16. Strümpell reports that once again the Madagali Fulbe sought refuge among the Sukur (1912:88), but this legend is not noted in the District Note Book. Indeed, none of the legends of support by Sukur for the Madagali Fulbe reported in Strümpell seems to be known today at either Madagali or Sukur.

Although Buba Ciuto was successful in repulsing another Mandara attack, his was a disastrous administration. His problems began when Sudi, a son of Lamido Lawal of Yola, waged an unsuccessful campaign against the Matakam, a montagnard society located just east of Madagali. He blamed his failure upon a lack of support from Buba Ciuto, who was summoned to Yola to answer the charge. Buba Ciuto was alleged to have said, "If I skinned Sudi and stuffed his hide with gold, the Lamido would forgive me" (Kirk-Greene 1954b:2). The remark was reported to the Lamido, Buba Ciuto was arrested upon his arrival in Yola, and Bakari was reinstated in 1870. Buba Ciuto escaped and, after the death of Lamido Lawal in 1872, asked the new lamido, Sanda, to return his domain.

When the request was refused, Buba Ciuto returned to Madagali and opportunistically made common cause with a concurrent rebellion by the Margi of Gulagu, who had attempted to kidnap the Waziri of Yola as he returned from Madagali. This impertinence was countered by an attack which is known in the history of Yola as "the Gulak Campaign" and in Margi legend as "the Wazhiri's war." Neither the stories of Gulagu nor the Adamawa version (East 1935:91) mention Buba Ciuto. However, with Yola's forces already in the area to deal with the rebellion at Gulak, Buba Ciuto was pursued and captured at Hosere Baji, a small hill south of Madagali. He was taken back to Yola, where he died in 1874. In the main assault of the campaign, Gulak was attacked with a ferocity and thoroughness which still prompts tales from the descendants of those involved. It was sacked along with other Margi hamlets at Chambula, Midlu (modern Mildu), and Maiva-Palam, although they were not involved with Gulagu, and for measure the totally unrelated villages of Vemngo and Wula were burnt. Perhaps Buba Ciuto's flight exacerbated the campaign; if so, it was not the only time that montagnards would be caught in struggles between Madagali and its adversaries. During later battles between Madagali and Yola, montagnards were often drawn into the conflict, to their sorrow and never to their gain.

Europeans, Fulbe, and Montagnards

The European partition of the area, which began at the end of the nineteenth century, brought radical changes to both the Adamawa Emirate and Madagali. Adamawa was divided by the boundary which was established between German Kamerun and British Nigeria. Its capital, Yola, became the headquarters of Yola Province in Nigeria, while Madagali fell to the Germans.

Adamawa resisted the incursion and the partition, but the British captured Yola in 1901. Lamido Zubeiru fled eastward only to run into the Germans at Marua, where in 1902, he made a stand in a legendary battle in which 424 of his soldiers were killed by machinegun fire (Kirk-Greene 1958:59–60). He then fled into the mountains, taking refuge at Mabas-Wandai, an outpost of Madagali. The Lamido then summoned help from Ardo Bakari. When Bakari refused on grounds of age, Zubeiru warned him that the Germans would punish him as an associate of Yola. Although Bakari sent some sheep with his son Haliru as a gift for the Germans at Garua, the warning proved accurate: the Germans beat the boy and sent him back to Madagali. Alarmed, some of the Fulbe joined Zubeiru and fought for him against the Germans, but Bakari fled south, only to be caught near Mildu by a German patrol and brought before a German officer remembered as "Dan Kasko" or "Dumnuki."[17] Declaring that Bakari was too old to rule effectively—he would have been approximately 67 years old—Dumnuki sent him back to Madagali with the proposal that he resign in favor of his son, Hamman Yaji.

It was not a popular proposal with the Fulbe of Madagali, though whether this was by reason of support for Bakari or opposition to Hamman Yaji is impossible to say. Bakari sent word to the Germans that Hamman Yaji would not be acceptable as Ardo, but wary of the Germans, he evacuated the town. He sent his Fulbe to hide at Sukur, while he stayed in the plains at the base of the mountain. Dumnuki pursued the Madagali Fulbe, arrested the Tlidi of Sukur and brought the Fulbe refugees back to Madagali.

Bakari was found and promised that his life would be spared if he would return to Madagali. Kirk-Greene, relying upon eyewitness testimony, relates the dramatic events:

> Ardo Bakari asked what day it was. On being told it was Tuesday, he replied, with characteristic Moslem resignation: "It has been foretold that on a Tuesday I shall die—let us return to Madagali." As his cavalcade reached the District Head's compound, where the German troops were drawn up, Dumnuki gave the order to open fire. In the panic that ensued Bakari quietly dismounted and prostrated himself in silent prayer, alone save for his algaita [a horn] player, Mbico, who refused to join in the general flight: if his master died, he said, there would be nobody left he could play for. Bakari was shot in cold blood and then apparently beheaded, for when the townspeople returned that evening the head was found severed from the body. He was buried at the foot of the bald, black rock to the south of the town. (1954b:4)

HAMMAN YAJI

Hamman Yaji, who was 35 years old, was installed on the day following Bakari's death;[18] he ruled from 1902 until August 26, 1927, when he was deposed. During this period there were sweeping changes, requiring that he successively adapt to German, French, and British administrations.

When he assumed power, much of his orientation was toward Kamerun. He often sent messengers to the government centers at Marua, Garua and Mora, and he claimed Mokolo approximately 15 miles from Madagali along the route to Garua. In 1916 he sent a son to school in Garua (*Diary,*

---

17. Kirk-Greene believes that this was probably the celebrated Herr Dominik, Resident at Garua (1954b:4).

18. There are those who claim that it was Hamman Yaji who betrayed his father, but there is no credible evidence for that allegation.

December 9, 1916). Representatives were exchanged with Fulbe regimes at Rei and Ngaundere, the latter being more than 300 miles from Madagali.

Although he was not involved in any fighting during World War I, he was armed by the Germans, and both the British and the French made appearances in Madagali. Following the war, the French took control, and Hamman Yaji appeared to enjoy good relations with them. In 1920, however, the former Kamerun was formally partitioned between the British and the French;[19] Madagali fell to the British, coming once again under the administration of Yola. That was to be an uneasy relationship, for it had been the last Lamido of Yola whom Bakari had refused to support. Furthermore, the British administration was much more interventionist than either the German or the French.

The British established a system of rule composed of a hierarchy of colonial officers supervising an African administration which, consistent with the philosophy of indirect rule, roughly approximated preexisting local authority. The African administration was called the Native Authority (NA), and in Northern Nigeria, the provincial Native Authorities were headed by Emirs. In this case, the province was initially called Yola and headed by the Emir of Yola, who had formerly been the head of the Adamawa emirate, the greater portion of which fell to the Germans. (In 1926, the province was merged with Muri Province and reorganized as Adamawa Province.) The Native Authority was divided into Districts with African rulers as District Heads; Hamman Yaji was the District Head of Madagali District. Under the District Head there were numerous Village Heads, who were often montagnards, some of whom were non-Muslim. The village was the smallest unit of administration recognized by authority.[20]

In the overruling British hierarchy, the Province was divided into Divisions, each the responsibility of a District Officer (DO) or Senior District Officers (SDO) accountable to the Resident. Under the DO there were Assistant District Officers (ADO) based at Divisional Headquarters but who spent a good deal of their time on tour. In the case of Adamawa Province, which had an unusually large north-to-south span, one ADO was permanently posted to Mubi (approximately 50 miles south of Madagali) in charge of the Northern Cameroons and adjacent districts. Over time this officer became known as the Touring Officer of the Northern Area or TONA. Above the Resident was the Lieutenant-Governor—who, during the period covered in the diary, was located in Kaduna—and above him was the Governor in Lagos.[21]

---

19. Although the official establishment of the boundary was not until 1922, British administration began from this earlier date.

20. In the case of the Margi kingdoms, there was a further breakdown into "hamlet" administration, though hamlet headmen were not paid by the government nor was their authority sanctioned.

21. It is likely that, in at least some of Hamman Yaji's references to "the Governor" in the diary, he means the lieutenant-governor.

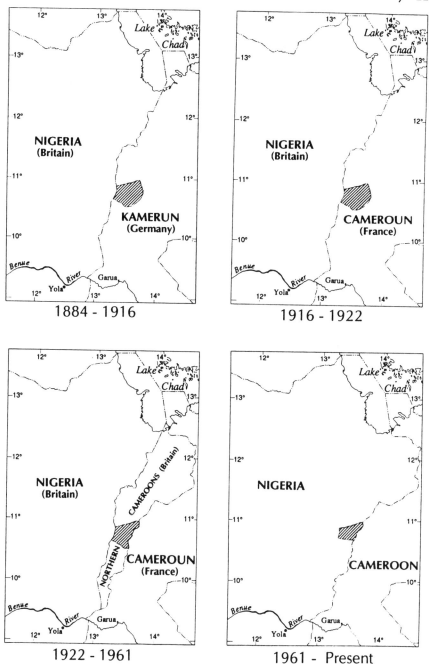

MADAGALI AND THE INTERNATIONAL BOUNDARIES.

The new international boundary took away a portion of the eastern edge of the emirate. Mabas-Wandai, where Hamman Yaji had been photographed by Strümpell sometime prior to 1912, was lost, as was the more distant Mokolo, which seems never to have been effectively ruled. In time, there were also changes to the southern border. There were four small independent Fulbe settlements south of Madagali: Kircinga, Moda, Michika, and Duhu. Kircinga, near the Yedseram, had long had difficulties maintaining its independence from Bornu and was amalgamated into Madagali. (Since there are no references to this in the diary, one may presume it occurred prior to 1912.) Moda, the chief of which was referred to as Emir in 1918 but as Ardo in subsequent references, enjoyed relatively cordial relationships with Madagali, and Hamman Yaji's daughter married a son of the Ardo of Moda (*Diary,* February 19, 1918). Nonetheless, Moda was placed under Michika in 1927, and one person was given the rule of both (*Diary,* June 6, 1927). This reflected the increasing importance of Michika, which was on the road to Mubi. The mountains east of Michika and Moda remained the responsibility of Madagali, though they were later transferred to Cubunawa District, administered from Michika.

Relations with Duhu were a source of difficulty throughout Hamman Yaji's reign. It was a small independent enclave within Madagali's borders, and disputes are frequently mentioned in the diary, but these were not disputes to be resolved like those with the montagnards; his values would not let him attack a legitimate Fulbe emirate. As a result, there were many formal cases against the various leaders of Duhu which had to be resolved by the colonial administrators. To judge by what is recorded in the diary, he won virtually all disputes with Duhu: in 1922, 1924, and 1925, he writes that the colonial administration had given him control of Duhu or the Duhu pagans. In each case, however, Duhu reappears as an independent emirate with its own pagans. It finally became a part of Madagali District in the 1930s,[22] after Hamman Yaji's demise.

These were problems external to his realm and probably of no great concern to the colonial administrations. It was his relations with the pagan montagnards which came to characterize and ultimately plague his administration. Although slavery had been outlawed by the colonial powers, it is important to note that the institution of slavery was accepted in traditional Fulbe culture, as it was in the cultures of the montagnards.[23] Furthermore, in some instances Hamman Yaji converted pagans to Islam and must have believed that he was doing the correct thing. Note the entry for July 21, 1927: "A letter came from the Christian Mr. Wilkinson, saying that Ghamiri

22. Duhu still appears on maps and is the name of one set of the sheets of maps published by the Nigerian government, but by 1988 it had all but disappeared. The road no longer passes through the village and virtually all of its Fulbe have moved away, most to the town of Gulak. There is, however, on the outskirts of the old village the ruin of one of Hamman Yaji's houses, which probably is the oft cited house at Maradi.

23. The status of slave (*mafa*) was still recognized among the Margi in 1960 (Vaughan 1977).

had made a complaint against me. He ordered me to return the girl to her mother, but she rejected her parents and said to them that she would never return to the pagans." In most instances, though, enslavement was vigorously opposed by the Madagali montagnards.

Although references to slavery and slaves abound in his diary, and one comes to understand just how central the institution was to Fulbe society, it is the raids which so haunt the reader. Undoubtedly, they were more horrible than suggested by the antiseptic descriptions in the diary. The montagnards must have known little safety, and their lives were surely filled with uncertainty and terror. His soldiers had obtained rifles of European manufacture from the Germans (though the diary reveals that getting ammunition was a problem), and the montagnards were no match. The pages are filled with accounts of attacks upon montagnard villages[24] with lists of the numbers killed and captured and the livestock stolen. Approximately 100 raids are recorded, in which 2016 captives are enumerated, and there are instances in which the numbers are unspecified. In each of two raids, one upon Mokolo and the other upon Tekem (probably Tukum or Tahum, on the Maiva massif), Hamman Yaji took 120 slaves. To be sure, raids were sometimes in retaliation for attacks upon his people—indeed, one of his sons was attacked and killed by montagnards (*Diary,* August 27, 1916)—but in every instance the counterattack exceeded the provocation. There is a horrible banality to the document; the same phrases ("I raided . . ." "I attacked . . ." "I sent my soldiers . . .") are stated over and over, as are the references to the numbers captured and killed. One can become quite inured to the suffering behind the words.

Sukur, the mountain kingdom, received his special attention. It is no more than 10 miles from the town of Madagali, and perhaps that proximity and the awe with which its traditions were viewed by virtually all of the montagnards challenged him. Whatever the reason, he raided it often and mercilessly. The first raid recorded in the diary was upon Sukur; so, too, was the last. Some of the most reprehensible charges against Hamman Yaji were collected twenty-five years later at Sukur by Anthony H. M. Kirk-Greene, who was then an Assistant District Officer:

> On one raid Hamman Yaji's soldiers cut off the heads of the dead pagans in front of the Llidi's [Tlidi's or King's] house, threw them into a hole in the ground, set them alight and cooked their food over the flames. Another time they force the wives of the dead Sukur men to come forward and collect their husbands' heads in a calabash; on yet another occasion, to take all the heads down to Madagali for the Fulani to see. One witness told me how he had seen children have a coil of wire hammered through their ears and jaws by the soldiers, while another related how, when Hamman Yaji learned of the

---

24. With few exceptions, Hamman Yaji only raided the montagnards within his domain, for example, when he raided into the Uba hills (March 13, 1919), he shared the captured slaves with the Emir of Uba.

great significance attached to the Sukur burial rites, he ordered his troops to cut up the bodies of the dead so that they could not be given a decent burial. (Kirk-Greene 1960:75)

Let it be acknowledged that the montagnards were always recalcitrant and that, though he retaliated against their slightest assertions, he never conquered nor controlled them. Despite raids, killing, and enslavement, the montagnards continued their guerrilla war against Madagali and all Fulbe. Such resistance was more destructive to the montagnards than to the Fulbe, but, with the increasing presence of the British, an alternative to rebellion emerged. The montagnards began to lodge formal complaints against Hamman Yaji. The diary reveals that initially he was generally supported by the colonial authorities, but as administrators learned more about the history of the area and of Fulbe-montagnard relations, the complaints had their effect.

On August 26, 1927, he was finally arrested and deported to Sokoto (for more detail see "The Arrest" in chapter 2). His local property was sold, his debts paid, the balance restored to him, and he was given a pension. It was claimed in the Colonial Office's report to the League of Nations for the year 1927 that his arrest was a consequence of his relations with the montagnards. Even the Fulbe of Madagali say that he was arrested because of his treatment of the montagnards.

Yet that explanation long seemed unsatisfactory; the British had known of Hamman Yaji's behavior well *before* taking over the administration of the area. In the Bornu Annual Report for 1913 there was a report of slaving in "German territory at Madagali" (SNP 10/2 95p/1914) and in a Yola Province report in 1916 there was the statement ". . . chaos reigns in the North East. Slaves are openly sold now in Madagali and Mubi, and the chiefs are indulging in a orgy of oppression and confiscation" (SNP 10/3 373p/ 1916).[25] But the most immediate evidence came from T. F. Carlyle, an experienced District Officer who accompanied S. H. P. Vereker, the leader of the "Madagali Patrol," which was sent to reconnoiter the area in 1921 while it was still under the French. Carlyle wrote: "Among the hillmen Madagali's name is an object of such dread and loathing as I have never seen in this country before, as was illustrated by the pagans in a manner fantastic but for its intensity" (quoted in Kirk-Greene 1954b:4). In a previous publication, I concluded "that data from the period show ambivalence and expediency on the part of British administrators" (1980a:101). But, in point of fact, the situation was even more puzzling than I realized at that time.

From the beginning, Hamman Yaji had viewed British administration with disfavor. In August 1920, he wrote, ". . . a letter arrived from the Captain saying that the English were coming. . . . Then on Wednesday another letter arrived saying that my land has been transferred from the

---

25. We are grateful to Paul Lovejoy and Jan Hogendorn for drawing our attention to these sources.

French to the English. Let us hope that the French are telling lies." The next mention of an administrator is two and one-half months later. On December 19, he refers to "Judge Mai Madubi," a nickname for a European who wears eyeglasses; though not one Reed identified, it seems probable that it was either Vereker or Carlyle, who were in the area at this time. It is stylistically a peculiar and, I believe, most significant entry. "I welcomed the Judge Mai Madubi. He spent the night and then on Monday I met him and he told me what he had to say."

The expression *told me what he had to say* is unlike any other description of interaction in the diary, and in this oblique fashion he calls attention to the importance of the transaction. His behavior on subsequent days indicates that it was a message which displeased him very much. On December 25, he refused to accompany the "Judge," who redrew the boundary giving a portion to Bornu. Two days later he wrote, ". . . I left the Judge Mai Madubi in view of his evil words and conversation and his mischief-making in cutting off my land."

Indisputably, one element of his displeasure concerned the adjusted boundary with Bornu. But the reference to "the evil words and conversation" and the fact that he was upset *before* the boundary was re-drawn, refusing to accompany Mai Madubi, suggest that there was some other point of contention—something that Mai Madubi had told Hamman Yaji which had seriously angered him. What this may have been can be deduced from Hamman Yaji's radically changed behavior. *After this meeting, there is not a single instance of Hamman Yaji's forces raiding a village or taking a slave.* The last raid recorded in the diary was on October 23, 1920, before the meeting with the English, at which time he took 39 slaves from Sukur. I conclude that "the evil words and conversation" which so upset him were a prohibition against raiding and taking slaves.

Thus, the most commonly accepted reason for his arrest, i.e., that he was raiding and enslaving montagnards, had not been the case for seven years before his deposition. He had, as the diary makes clear, radically altered his behavior after his first contact with the British. Nonetheless, by 1927, he was clearly out of favor, and entries from the manuscript of the touring officer's political diary give evidence of the attitude toward him just before his arrest. For example, the entry in the Touring Officer's Political Diary for March 3, 1927 reads:

> Arrived at Sukur accompanied by D. H. (District Head). He said he did not wish to come to these pagan towns. I told him he *must* come with me unless he was too sick to travel. This D. H. has never toured before [*sic*]. He had never been to Sukur before [*sic*]. It is quite obvious he is afraid to go among the pagans: he knows too well what trouble he has given them in the past. I noticed he made his camp away from the village. (Kirk-Greene 1953)

Hamman Yaji's diary indicates that he was often involved in disputes, and especially towards the end, he was the subject of complaints that the British had to arbitrate. A complaint from the king of Sukur and an ensuing dispute in June 1927 is regarded by many as central to his arrest. It is apparent that his relationship with the various District Officers was never cordial, yet the diary reveals no awareness on his part of serious troubles with the administration. It seems improbable that he believed that he was in any danger of being deposed or in any other substantial difficulty with the administration.

The gist of my argument is that none of the evidence to this point quite explains the sudden arrest and exile of Hamman Yaji. Could there have been something other than—or in addition to—his treatment of the montagnards which led to this drastic act? From papers deposited in Rhodes House, Oxford, it is apparent that another scenario was being played out, unknown to all but a few.[26]

To Europeans, one of the galvanizing events at the end of the nineteenth century was the siege and massacre in 1885 of the British garrison at Khartoum under C. G. Gordon. That uprising is attributed to the actions of a Muslim fundamentalist movement under Muhammad Ahmad ibn al Said Abdullah, who proclaimed himself to be the *Mahdi*, the prophesied leader destined to establish a reign throughout the world. The defeat of Gordon, a popular figure in Great Britain, was largely the result of governmental indecision and procrastination. The revolt was eventually crushed in 1898 by H. H. (later Lord) Kitchener in a battle as famous as the siege which had lost Khartoum.

Mahdism was, however, more than a Nilotic movement. It had many of the elements of those revitalization movements which so frequently arise under conditions of cultural suppression—in this instance African Muslims dominated by Christian colonialism. Other Mahdist movements emerged in Islamic Africa, including a rebellion at Satiru in Northern Nigeria in 1906 which was ruthlessly crushed (Lovejoy and Hogendorn 1990). But military suppression of ideological movements has always been ineffective, and Mahdism survived in Nigeria.

In 1915, a Mahdist disciple appeared in Cameroun and Nigeria, and once again the administration reacted with alacrity and moved vigorously against the sect. They captured its leader, Shaikh Sa'id ibn Hayatu, in 1923,[27] and the formal aspects of the movement collapsed without a major public impact. But as it happened, Madagali played a role in that short-lived drama, for on March 15, 1915, Hamman Yaji wrote:

> . . . I took on the devotional practices of the Mahdist sect under Malam Muhammad's instruction.

26. In 1987, I enjoyed a term as Senior Associate at St. Antony's College, Oxford and worked on the diary with Kirk-Greene. It was while searching through the personal papers of former administrators in Rhodes House, in the vain attempt to find one who would report on a meeting with Hamman Yaji which was also reported in the diary, that I came across these papers and learned the "real" reason for his arrest. These papers were the property of W. O. P. Rosedale, a former district officer who is mentioned in the diary (Mss. Brit. Emp. s. 276).

27. For a full discussion of Sa'id and his movement see Ubah (1976) and Saeed (1982–85), who mentions the connection with Hamman Yaji.

Thereafter there are four references to Mahdism: in the first, he indicates that he will fine anyone leaving the sect (April 26, 1919); in the second, he says that he is going to attempt to convert a man named Adamu (June 11, 1921); in the third, he reports the arrest of seven members of the sect in Michika (August 24, 1923); and in the fourth, he instigates a Mahdist prayer (March 24, 1924). There is no reference to Mahdism after that date. Significantly, in Reed's translation there are lines drawn in the margins beside each of the references to Mahdism (lines which remained unnoticed until I was making a final check of Reed's translation against my computer-generated copy).

If the marginalia are but subtle evidence of the Government's concern about Hamman Yaji's Mahdism, their true apprehension is revealed in the papers mentioned above. There are two almost identical papers marked "Confidential." One is an "Address by His Honour the Acting Lieutenant-Governor to the Emir of Katsina, at Katsina, on 16th August 1927"[28] and the other is a memorandum (K. 5621/4, dated 29 September 1927) from the Secretary of the Northern Provinces to all Residents. In the former there is the statement, "You will remember that [when] the seditious Mallam Said was arrested in Dumbulwa it was found afterwards that he had adherents or sympathizers far and wide." Correspondence with Hamman Yaji was found.[29] In both papers there is the following passage:

> There is also now to be chronicled the deposition, with probable deportation to follow, of the District Head of Madagali in Adamawa. . . . There is unfortunately no room for doubt that his intransigence was largely accentuated as a result of his strong "Mahdist" leanings, the active propaganda of "Mahdism" in his district, and the frequent passage of "Mahdist" itinerant mallams in the region. He had been himself a correspondent of Mallam Said of Dumbulwa. . . .

Clearly, the principal reason for Hamman Yaji's arrest was his Mahdist devotion and fears of what it might precipitate. It seems probable that this was not made public because the administration feared that it might have made a martyr of Hamman Yaji.

The diary, which was seized because an illiterate servant hid the wrong document, must have been disappointing in its failure to provide evidence of a Mahdist conspiracy or even of activities which had been "accentuated as a result of his Mahdist leanings." Nothing of the sort is revealed in the diary. As Lovejoy and Hogendorn indicate, not all Mahdism is revolutionary (1990:219), and Ubah (1976) has convincingly demonstrated that Shaikh Sa'id, the leader of the Mahdist movement to which Hamman Yaji was affiliated, was not of the revolutionary tradition. The diary did, however,

---

28. There is a curious problem with this document in that its date, 16 August, *precedes* the date of Hamman Yaji's arrest, 26 August. Apart from suggesting a typographical error, I am unable to resolve this.

29. Correspondence was also found with the Emir of Yola, but as he had only recently been made an officer of the British Empire (OBE), he was merely reprimanded (Ubah 1976:181–2).

document Hamman Yaji's earlier raids and slaving, and it is that knowledge which has been passed down in the lore of Madagali.

One should not attempt to diminish the tragic consequences of Hamman Yaji's reign, but, as mentioned earlier, there is more to the diary than his undoubted cruelty to the montagnards. He was a man of personal honor who took his obligations seriously: on the last page of the diary he reports repaying a personal debt to a pagan (August 20, 1927). Like many in authority, he could not understand why others did not see things as did he, whether the person be another Fulbe, a slave, a montagnard, or a colonial official.

The behavior of slaves seems always to have puzzled him. Consider the following:

> February 4, 1913 . . . I found that my slave girl in the absence of her fellow slaves had said that she would not prepare my food for me. Why she would not cook my food I do not know, but anyway the result was that I got no food from her and was obliged to buy it.

But he could be compassionate, as illustrated in the following two passages:

> May 27, 1924 . . . My young slave Samaki and Jauro quarrelled in front of me. Samaki shouted at me and made me angry. So I took some things away from him, namely my horses and my pagans and gave them to Jauro Bamgel. Then I sent him before the Court, but nothing was proved against him.

> May 29, 1924 . . . While I was sitting with my female slave Kujji talking to her, she said: "Poverty has oppressed him," as though she said: "His property is destroyed." So the same day I returned to Samaki his property.

There are numerous references in the diary to punishments which are meted out to Fulbe for unjustified treatment of pagan montagnards, including one against his favorite son, Bello (April 10, 1922). His sons gave him considerable cause for worry, as for example, "I heard that my son Musa is suspected of having killed his son" (April 11, 1921), and the following somewhat humorous report: "I said to [my son Abd al Rahman]: 'Listen: I am not going to clothe you any more'" (April 1, 1924).

He was fascinated—almost to the point of being obsessed—by the automobile, and greatly wanted one, with no thought of its practicality:

> June 12, 1925 . . . Then I took my leave of the Emir of Yola, who said to me: "I will give you a motor car."
> September 30, 1925 . . . He brought the news that the Emir al Yemen [the Emir of Yola] promised to sell me a motor car.
> April 30, 1926 . . . I also mentioned the matter of a motor car.
> May 21, 1926 . . . As regards the matter of the motor car, he [Captain Reed] said I should inform the Emir al Yemen, and ask whether he also would permit me to have one.

He worried about his health and obviously had chronic stomach problems. Who would not sympathize with the entry for June 15, 1924? "I remembered that I had been free from stomach trouble for some days, and I therefore ate a meal such as I had not eaten for some time."

We may even gain some understanding of his relations with pagans if we remember that he lived in a sea of montagnards. He once intercepted a force led by two young princes of Gulagu as they stealthily scaled Mount Gulak to kill the king, their father's brother. It is *their* testimony that he was puzzled and persuaded them only to force the king into exile. To Hamman Yaji the montagnards were an uncontrollable ilk who fought among themselves and outsiders alike. And above all, he saw them as worshipers of false gods and the practitioners of bizarre rites. They were pagans, beyond understanding, viz: "My people were looking at the wheels of the motor car, both the Fulani and the pagans. So I made the Fulani go away, but I allowed the pagans to behave in their accustomed fashion" (December 5, 1924).

He wrote religious verse; he was pious, converted pagans and built mosques. Yet the mundane did not escape his attention. The very last entry in the diary fascinates for its mixture of imperviousness to slavery and its attention to routine: "I sent Tataraktu a slave girl from my house, who belonged to the Webengo pagans. His wife gave me 32s as her ransom. . . . On the same day Sarkin Lifida ruined the onions." And on the next day Hamman Yaji was arrested.

CONCLUSION

It is not known why he kept the diary; so far as we know, it is a document unique for its time. We may infer that it was a chronicle of events he thought important. One of the striking features of the diary is how meticulously Hamman Yaji recorded gifts and obligations. It so assiduously records gifts that it is virtually impossible to index the word since it appears on almost every page. This fact alone emphasizes just how important gifts and reciprocity were in his society. The diary also catalogs his "journeys"— what we might think of as administrative tours. An administrator must move through his territory, and District Officers similarly went on tours, staying at rest houses much as he stayed at his houses. Other values of his may be noted as less conscious, perhaps: for example, reference to cattle, a hallmark of Fulbe culture, appears on virtually every page, and his frequent references to religious belief give some indication of life in a Muslim culture.

The greatest challenge the diary presents the modern reader is that of entering Hamman Yaji's world. Obviously we read it with the values of Western culture in the twentieth century, and consequently we are repulsed by the cruelty he visited upon the "pagans." But the same values which permit us to view the montagnards benignly should also require us to attempt an understanding of his culture and contemplate our own acceptance of the cruelty inherent in colonialism.

Colonialism has been so much a part of Western culture that it is difficult for us to grasp what must have been his sense of violation and confusion as Europeans intruded into what he regarded as his rightful domain. With this in mind, it is revealing to read of his contact with Europeans. What is he to conclude about the montagnards from French behavior he reported on February 28, 1920? viz: "I received a letter from the Captain saying he had raided the pagans of Kuhum and had captured a large quantity of cattle and sheep and had also taken 70 prisoners and killed 10." And surely he must have been confused when, after having altered his practices toward the montagnards, he observed the ADO burn the houses of two of "the Humuchi pagans" (*Diary*, March 20, 1927) and was told by the ADO "that he did not forbid the pagans to cultivate my farms" (*Diary*, June 6, 1927). We can sense his frustration and exhaustion in the entry for February 5, 1927: "A Christian arrived at Madagali, named Mr. Wilkinson. Derebe made a complaint and recovered his daughter, and Umaru Adda made 7 complaints, which were not proved. This was all a waste of time." One of the most tantalizing passages occurs early in his contact with Europeans: "I made arrangement with my scribe Amin by which if I do a certain thing the Christian will not stop at Madagali. I gave him a slave for this, and if God does prevent him from staying here I will give him two slaves" (*Diary*, March 1, 1919). Finally, the long hidden evidence of his Mahdism, the real reason for his arrest, reveals him to have been a victim of colonialist repression of religious expression.

Hamman Yaji's is a complex story, set amidst competing cultures in a radically changing Africa. The diary reveals the increasing effects of colonialism as it evolved from largely meaningless contacts to intrusive management. It is a micro-history of tyranny and slavery practiced one hundred years after these things were presumably controlled and eliminated, and it is a tangible reminder that not all imperialist exploitation was European. Above all it is a personal, internal view of a man in his time and, by its end, perhaps, a man out of his time.

It would surely be incorrect to judge anyone's character by his diary, for there seems ever to be a self-justificatory quality in them. (In one touching passage, Hamman Yaji reaches through time and space to address an unknowable audience: "Let him who pauses to regard this writing know . . ." [*Diary*, January 5, 1926].) But, in this case, he made no attempt to hide his raids and his slaving, which may be an indication of how he felt about these acts. On the other hand, the charges of the government, of which much more will be learned in the next chapter, are not corroborated. It is not possible to read the diary and find evidence of bribery and corruption—though there is behavior which an anxious government could call corruption.[30] Finally, the diary in no way supports the allegation that his Mahdism was a threat to the region. We are left to wonder if it was all a "witch hunt," the opportunistic charges of ambitious administrators anxious to further their careers (see "The Aftermath" in chapter 2).

In the end, the Hamman Yaji who emerges from the diary is both villain and victim. Unquestionably the persecutor of montagnards, but also a man who, with Fulbe aloofness and devout Muslim values, is caught between rebellious pagan montagnards and encroaching Christian Europeans. I believe that he was finally brought down less by his actions than by changing standards and colonialist intrigue, though readers may reach their own conclusions.

In the 1950s the offices of the District Headquarters were moved from the town of Madagali to Gulak, but it was largely through the ballot that the era ended. In a United Nations plebiscite in 1959, the montagnards firmly rejected Fulbe rule. Quickly, concessions were made, and in 1960, Risku Zidiku Madziga, a montagnard from Wagga, became both the first elected head and the first non-Fulbe to lead the district (Vaughan 1964). He was succeeded in 1971 by Alhaji Mohammed Sanusi, the son of the late Margi Village Head at Shuwa and, thus, of Sukur/Gulagu/Dluku descent.

Today, Hamman Yaji's palace at Madagali is a ruin. So too are the numerous residences he had scattered throughout the emirate—ruins which montagnards point to with tales of that terrible past. They are hardly more than mute middens with one exception: in 1987, at Wuro Alhamdu, an aged Matakam, blind and unable to walk, spoke with increasing enthusiasm about the days of the emirate. Although himself a slave, brought as a boy from Mokolo, he remembered only the emirate's glory and Hamman Yaji's celebrity.

---

30. It is evident that the administration simply failed to understand the nature of reciprocity in the African cultures, both Muslim and montagnard. There are innumerable examples of Hamman Yaji receiving gifts in money or kind after appointing an individual to an office. This, however, is standard custom persisting to the present time. The allegation that he bribed Allah Kyauta, an employee of the administration (see chapter 3), is curious in the light that in one transaction he presented the gift to the ADO to pass along to Kyauta (*Diary*, February 7, 1925)—hardly the way to offer a bribe.

2. *The View from Yola: 1927*

ANTHONY H. M. KIRK-GREENE

On September 2, 1927, in the middle of the rainy season—which at Yola, the headquarters of the new Adamawa Province of Northern Nigeria, often caused the River Benue to rise from its low-water depth by 20 feet, making the Jimeta waterfront look more like a lake than a riverside settlement—three prisoners and an escort of West African Frontier Force (WAFF)[31] soldiers crossed from Namtari on the north bank in a canoe and disembarked at the foot of the cantonment escarpment. At last the senior colonial official in the Province, the Resident, could see with his own eyes—and, doubtless, with a deep sigh of relief—evidence that the turbulent reign of the Fulbe chief of Madagali District in Northern Cameroons was over. The worrisome Hamman Yaji affair had been brought to an end . . . though, as it turned out, not yet concluded.

ANXIETY: THE GATHERING CLOUDS

What impression, the researcher and the reader of the Hamman Yaji story inescapably asks, had this remarkable local chief made on the mind of the Yola provincial administration in the ten years since Madagali District had been seized from the Germans in 1915 and then, after a short and shadowy spell under French government, handed over to the British, an act finally confirmed by the formal award to Great Britain of the League of Nations mandate over the former German Kamerun in 1922?[32]

31. The title of Royal was not granted until the following year. The soldiers were, in fact, from the 2nd Nigeria Regiment.

32. For Hamman Yaji's own description of how this international exchange of territory was viewed at the grassroots level, see the diary, entries for August 2, August 7, and September 10, 1920. Of the earlier handover from German to French occupation: although news of the fall of Garua reached Hamman Yaji on June 17, 1915, it was another eight months before he was officially confirmed in his fiefdom by the French (*Diary*, February 12, 1916).

The original Royal Commission to administer "such parts of the Cameroons as may from time to time be occupied by the British Forces" was dated March 23, 1916. For a summary of the wartime and immediately post-war partition of the former German territory in this area, see Kirk-Greene (1958:chap. 6). Fuller standard studies in English are in Rudin (1938) and Le Vine

Among the earliest reports is a note by the Political Officer attached to the Madagali Patrol of October 1921, S. H. P. Vereker. He had been in Yola since before the war. This patrol was not a standing body of troops but an *ad hoc* force dispatched as escort to the first resident British political officer in that part of Northern Cameroons allocated to the administration of Yola Province (as Adamawa was then known). The initial District Officer, who had been specially selected "for the purpose of bringing the Madagali and adjoining districts under administrative control" was E. A. Brackenbury. A year later, his successor, T. F. Carlyle, had "secured the establishment of order in a part of the area" after having disarmed "the followers of the Chief of Madagali" (Reports on the British Sphere of the Cameroons, 1922 [dispatch from the Governor of Nigeria to the Secretary of State dated May 8, 1923] para. 67).[33] Vereker's assignment was now to visit the untoured districts, many of which had never been visited previously "by any French or German officers" (ibid.: para. 70; see also Reports on the British Sphere of the Cameroons, 1923, paras. 71–73); to ensure its "complete pacification," a mission accomplished, though not without armed resistance and casualties at Bazza Tillijo, including the chief; and to select a site for a new administrative headquarters (he chose Mubi). "The District Head [DH]," ran his approving conclusion, "appears to be naturally energetic."[34] He added that Hamman Yaji did seem to suffer considerably from rheumatism, a condition which frequently necessitated his using a hammock for getting around the district. However, the DH was in no way to be taken for an old man (he was, in fact, only in his forties). The report ended on a note nearer the truth than the freshly-posted colonial official realized:

> No doubt [Madagali town] has been a prosperous slave center in bygone days, being ideally situated for such a purpose hidden away as it is in a valley among high mountains. ("Report to Resident, Yola," November 1921 [Kirk-Greene 1954b]. See also Kirk-Greene 1958)

(1964). While some of the best campaign accounts are in German or in fiction like the short stories of Joyce Cary, useful accounts in English are Moberly (1931) and Gorges (1927), and, in French, Aymèrich (1931).

33. At the time of the formal handover in 1922, Madagali District comprised some 400 square miles and was believed to have a population of 8,907.

34. Vereker's "Report to Resident, Yola" was submitted in November 1921; that by Carlyle is dated July 18, 1921. As with these two reports, most of the data on the narrative in part 2 is based on field notes made when I was Touring Officer Northern Area (TONA) in the Cameroons districts of northern Adamawa Emirate (principally Mubi, Michika, and Madagali) in 1953–54. While some oral history was involved, the largest part of my field notes consisted of extensive summaries, often with detailed material copied in manuscript *in toto* (e.g., the whole of the diary which now forms Part V), of the contents of the TONA files, Political and Touring Diaries, and the District Note Books (DNB) for the years 1921–1927, extant in the DO's Office, Mubi. I still have my field notebooks; their condition today is fragile. Quotations in the text from TONA's correspondence with the Resident, Yola, are taken from the former's files unless otherwise attributed. For ease of reference, the shorthand "Field Notes 1953" is used here to indicate the source as my handwritten field notes. On their regrettable lack of file numbers, pages, etc., see chapter 6.

One of the very first reports by the Governor of Nigeria, on what was still referred to in 1922 as "the British Sphere of the Cameroons," was frank enough about the vagueness and remoteness of the Uba-Michika-Madagali conclave not only to reply in some detail to the League of Nations' leading questionnaire on the prevalence of slavery but also to describe the Madagali region as being under such "very shadowy control" that "slave dealing, with its attendant evils of kidnapping and raiding, have become rampant and the country rendered unsafe for traders and caravans."[35] Hamman Yaji himself has recorded, somewhat ominously, his first encounter with the new British district officer, Jojin Mai Madubi, "the Judge with the Spectacles," in December 1920, to take over what was called Northern Cameroons (Yola section) (see chapter 1).[36] One of Vereker's first reports[37] was a vigorous indictment of the area as a lawless paradise for slave trading and dealing (again, see chapter 1). Within the week, Hamman Yaji was to refer to Vereker's "evil words and conversation, and his mischief-making. . . ." (*Diary*, December 27, 1920). Seven years later, these two were to find themselves locked in a firm, final, and fatal encounter.[38]

In 1924, the Touring Officer Northern Area or TONA—the political officer responsible for the eleven new Northern Cameroon districts, comprising 200 square miles and a population reckoned at some 67,500—was ordered to investigate the reported increase of Mahdism in the area.[39] An entry in his touring diary (January 24, 1924) referred to his perception that the District Head was "very reticent." This, he surmised, was because "secret instruction" in Mahdism was almost certainly a feature of daily life in the

35. Supra p. 25. The diary confirms this picture, with nearly every entry for 1912–13 recording some slave raid or another. See index under "slavery."

36. When the French first appeared in Madagali, at the outbreak of the war, Hamman Yaji recorded that "The people of Madagali all ran away" (December 12, 1914). Significantly, there is no mention of any German official visiting Madagali until August 23, 1913.

37. Dated June 14, 1922 and contained in SNP 17 12577, "Slave Dealing in Nigeria and Cameroons" (now in National Archives, Kaduna).

38. The two political officers who dominated the Hamman Yaji story from 1921 to 1927 were Standish Harry Prendergast Vereker, who in 1922 was the first district officer Yola emirate responsible for the Madagali District (having been one of the first British officials ever to visit the area) and was the Acting Resident during the final showdown with Hamman Yaji in 1927; and Harold Howard Wilkinson, who was in charge of the Northern Touring Area from the end of 1926 and was personally responsible for the District Head's arrest in 1927. Vereker was born in 1878 and, after service in the South African War and a period as vice-consul at Cherbourg, was appointed to Northern Nigeria as Assistant Resident in 1906. He retired in the rank of Resident (1929) soon after the Hamman Yaji affair. Like many of the newer generation, Wilkinson came into the Colonial Service in 1921, at the age of 27, with the wartime rank of Captain, having gone to Trinity College, Dublin shortly before the outbreak of war. He spent his first eight years in Adamawa (Yola) Province. He continued in the Nigerian service until the 1940s, reaching the rank of Resident in 1941. I recall that when I was DO Bida in 1954, Wilkinson's name was mentioned in connection with the witchcraft riots in 1931, but S. F. Nadel does not mention the names of the officials concerned (1942). There are many references to Wilkinson in the diary.

39. From internal evidence in the diary throughout 1924, this was probably W. O. P. Rosedale. This would tally with the remarks by his younger predecessor, Captain R. R. Oakley, in his memoir (1938:189). Oakley makes no reference to Hamman Yaji in his three chapters on the Northern Touring Area, but Hamman Yaji mentions his name in the diary during the second half of 1923.

Bawo Hosere ward of Madagali. Two months on, the TONA's (Rosedale) suspicions had firmed: "The District Head is very secretive. He tells me nothing and allows no information from his District to leak out" (TONA report to Yola, March 11, 1924 [Kirk-Greene 1953]). This was a hardening of his superior's comment in the official report to the League of Nations, which confidently spoke of the Madagali DH exercising good control over his people and of the progress under his jurisdiction, qualified only by the general rider that

> It would be too optimistic a view to take that all the district heads . . . have entirely given up their malpractices; but they have nothing like the scope they had before the British occupation, and they know that the chances of discovery, with the attendant results, are great. (Report on the Cameroons, 1924, para. 68)

The British authorities were now beginning to think that Madagali town had developed into a Mahdiya center right from the moment when the German administration collapsed towards the end of the Cameroons campaign, leaving an unsupervised vacuum until the British took over and established a tangible political presence in 1920–21.[40] According to the evidence of Hamman Yaji's diary, his conversion to Mahdism was ten years earlier (see chapter 1 and *Diary*, May 15, 1915).

From a perusal of the secret reports submitted to the governor by such senior officers as G. J. F. Tomlinson and G. J. Lethem,[41] it is clear that for the Nigerian administration the 1920s was the era of the Mahdist scare. First, Sokoto itself had been dominated by the Hayatu affair at Dumbulwa in 1923 (Tomlinson and Lethem 1927:5–18 and Al-Hajj 1971).[42] Now came the suspicion of an underground outbreak of Mahdism in the northeast of Nigeria. Indeed, in the aftermath of Hamman Yaji's final removal in 1927,

40. The diary entry for April 26, 1919 mentions "a fine for every one who leaves the Mahdist sect." Two years later, Hamman Yaji recorded his adoption of "the new ceremonial ablution" (April 3, 1921), and on March 24, 1924, he decided to "institute the prayer of the Mahdist sect on the following Friday." Given the likely motivation of the government and the marginal markings in the original translation against every passage in the diary referring to Mahdist activity, it is surprising that the official index has no entry for "Mahdism," only to "religious observance."

41. See, in particular, their confidential report, *History of Islamic Political Propaganda in Nigeria* (1927), along with its appendices in a separate and "secret" volume. The accompanying letter forwarding it to the governor of Nigeria was signed by Sir Richmond Palmer, the lieutenant-governor of the Northern Province, not in Kaduna but from his London club, the Travellers. There is a certain irony in Tomlinson's report, which was largely derived from the "voluminous" files in the Secretariat (against Lethem's account of his personal visit to Chad, Sudan, and Egypt): dated May 17, 1927, Palmer was able to confirm his officials' conclusion that "the religious excitement of exaltation, which was so marked during the years 1923–24 in the Muhammadan provinces, had died away." Yet in the same year there had been a recrudescence of Islamic fervor just across the border at Tassawa, and at the very moment of Palmer's dispatch a fresh crisis was about to erupt in Northern Adamawa—the arrest of Hamman Yaji on grounds of Mahdist activity.

42. The most recent research into the colonial administration's "stormy petrel," Hayatu Sa'id, is that currently being undertaken by Asma'u Garga Saeed in her thesis for Bayero University, Kano.

one Madagali informant named Abba was to declare that the District Head had on one occasion threatened to bury his son alive if he ever dared to betray to the white man his secret adherence to Mahdism.

Evidence was now also coming in from across the border, in French Cameroun, with rumors and reports of what the TONA labelled "flagrant oppression" by Hamman Yaji. "The District Head" he now assessed, "is a great intriguer." This evaluation coincided with the impression of dishonesty that Vereker had had when he found Hamman Yaji trying to conceal £100 of *jangali*, a tax levied on the herds of the nomadic Fulbe. Vereker had reported that each time he queried the District Head over some alleged peculation or extortion which had come to his ears, the reply was always the same: he needed to save money to purchase a motor car. The same excuse was made to subsequent political officers. For instance, when H. O. Leonard ADO, was investigating a complaint that the Madagali *talakawa* (peasantry) had been obliged to pay an additional three shillings on top of their *haraji* or poll-tax, with a higher levy for craftsmen and artisans, they told him that the District Head had said it was to help him buy a motor car.[43] In the event, there was very little in the way of motorable roads in the district; at best they were dry-season, unmade tracks. If Hamman Yaji's excuse was poor health and the need to spare his rheumatic legs,[44] his ambition was interpreted by officialdom as simply the desire to display the panoply of prestige.

Piece by piece, an unprepossessing portrait of Hamman Yaji began to emerge in the mind of the provincial administration from the reports submitted by successive TONAs and read by their seniors in Yola. It took a whole four years for the colonial administration, in the course of its annual tax investigation, to "discover" nine villages (including the settlements of Kojiti, Juyel, and Kamburo) in 1925 and add them to the emirate's population records. They were found to have land which was farmed by the villagers exclusively for Hamman Yaji. Indeed, after his arrest in 1927, more villagers testified to the TONA that Hamman Yaji himself had never dared visit such major settlements as Sukur, Wua, or Kurang.[45] Such a "general attitude of aloofness" was attributed by the TONA partially to Hamman Yaji's well-grounded fear of showing his face in villages which he had consistently raided for slaves during the eras of German and French rule, and partly to the fact that, once the British assumed control, he had everything to gain from keeping a slave resource, secreted in his domain, from the knowledge of his

43. This may be the tax referred to in the diary on November 14, 1925. The diary has many references to the rare sight of a motor car in the Northern Touring Area, both the Resident's (March 27, 1924) and the Lamido's (December 5, 1924). Significantly in this context, Hamman Yaji recorded that on one occasion, the Lamido, after giving him a ride in his automobile, had promised him a car (June 12, 1925; September 30, 1925; and also April 30 and May 21, 1926).

44. Like many diarists, Hamman Yaji frequently refers to his ill-health (June 15, 1924; February 11, August 7, and October 30, 1925; and September 1, 1926). The original index carried the subheading "Hamman Yaja [*sic*]: Domestic Events - health and well being."

45. For example, the entry for May 12, 1913 refers to sending his soldiers to Sukur, rather than leading them.

liege lord, the Lamido or Emir of Adamawa.[46] Subsequently, on Hamman Yaji's undoing and eventual downfall, the Lamido declared that he had never heard in his Native Administration of any official known as the *Arnado* or Village Head of Sukur. Not until the dry season of that fateful year of 1927 was the TONA able to "persuade" the District Head to accompany him to the fortified hilltop village that was Sukur (*Diary*, March 3, 1927; see also June 6, 1927). It was a similar story at "unknown" Sina Gali (*Diary*, March 25, 1927).[47] The Northern Touring Area tax records are instructive here. In 1926–27, Sukur showed ten adult male taxpayers; in 1927–28, with Hamman Yaji out of the way, this figure rose to 480. In 1926–27, £292-10-0 was collected in haraji from the whole of Madagali District. In the following year, the haraji totalled £520-12-0: little wonder that the disbelieving assistant district officer promptly called for a recount!

By the middle of 1927, the suspicious scents from the Northern Touring Area had taken on the unmistakable odor of an administrative bad smell to a law-and-order-conscious colonial administration in Yola. To allegations of deceit, disdain, and dishonesty—with Gordon, Khartoum and Omdurman all comfortably in the past—was now added a whiff of danger riding on the insurrectionist air of Mahdism.

THE STORM BREAKS

Towards the end of February 1927, the Resident (A. C. Francis?[48]) decided it was time he went on tour to Madagali to speak to the District Head himself (*Diary*, February 18 and 25, 1927).[49] His record of the interview and official warning is critical, in pointed contrast to Hamman Yaji's laconic entry of February 25 that "On the same day the Resident entered

46. It was not until 1923 that the Emir (Lamido) of Yola was allowed to play a role in the administration of the mandated territories.

47. Oral testimony given to me in 1953 claimed that when Wilkinson finally managed to persuade Ngande (Gande), the village head of Sina Gali, to come down off the mountain and be officially "robed" by the District Head in Madagali, he threw the robe (*riga*) into Hamman Yaji's face.

48. The original index names the Resident in 1926–27 as "Mr. Francis," though the name does not—unlike the scrupulously listed names of other political officers—appear in the diary other than in the translator's own correction, from Browne to Francis, to the entry of October 6, 1926, which survived all readings. Official sources show that George Sinclair Browne, who had been promoted as Secretary, northern provinces in 1921 after only sixteen years' service, was appointed Resident of Yola Province in July 1926 and did not proceed on leave until the following June. Augustus Claude Francis, who started his career with the British South Africa Company, was appointed to Northern Nigeria in 1905 and became a Resident in 1920, acting as Senior Resident in 1924. Elsewhere in the diary there is a manuscript correction in October 1924 of the name of a British official from [illegible] to "Mr. Lyon," though it is possible that the original may have been no more than the typo "Lony."

49. The pace was clearly heating up. The Resident had thought it prudent to visit Madagali less than a year earlier (*Diary*, April 18, 1926). Additionally, the lamido had summoned Hamman Yaji to Yola in February, "urgent without delay" (February 12, 1926), and yet again in July. This time the Resident decided to delay him in the Provincial headquarters for several days. Altogether this kept Hamman Yaji out of Madagali for seven weeks (*Diary*, August 16, 1926).

Madagali." He stressed to Hamman Yaji that times had changed and that he could no longer continue on the lines that he had been able to follow during the period of German rule. The British had been extremely patient in the last six years, taking the attitude that tolerance was in order for a District Head who was not accustomed to the close supervision of British administration. Yet he was constrained to observe to Hamman Yaji that, despite this lenient understanding, there had not been a trace of any visible improvement in his conduct. The Resident took the opportunity to reiterate the British administration's prohibition on peasants, especially "pagans" (i.e. non-Muslims), being forced to farm for a District Head without payment. Instead, the colonial government favored a policy whereby District Heads encourage their subjects to farm cash crops, trade and earn an income. This last point may well have had its origin in a report by the TONA that Hamman Yaji consistently took care to drive out any trader wishing to travel among the pagan villages of Madagali District, allegedly to prevent the peasant farmers from getting to hear about the justice of British rule and the contrasting corruption of Hamman Yaji's. It was even said that on one occasion he had tied up for fifteen days a group of youths setting off to visit the market at Gwoza in neighboring Bornu Province. In an oral interview in 1953, the Imam of Madagali told me that the District Head of Gwoza was looked on by Hamman Yaji as one of his enemies. The Resident's record of his 1927 interview with Hamman Yaji does not make it clear whether he reminded him of another report, two years earlier, of how a gang of thirteen chained men had been found working on his private farms, eleven of whom had been sentenced to periods of imprisonment ranging from 25 to 45 days, all without trial.

Such complaints to the provincial administration became, of course, much more common after their subject had been removed from the scene. Especially damaging—and damning—was the testimony of one of Hamman Yaji's own sons, the telltale Abba. In detail he recounted—once his father was safely in detention—how, when four female slaves of his father's favorite son, Bello, attempted to run away, Hamman Yaji ordered each to receive one hundred lashes administered by three slaves, with a fourth holding them down (*Diary,* March 15, 1921). They were then deprived of food for three days. One of the women, Asta Jumba, died from this treatment, while according to Abba, Dudu and Muradu retained marks of the whipping for the rest of their lives. Abba's hatred of his father was such that even in remote Yola it was said that there was only one thing that would prevent Hamman Yaji from killing Abba—for the son to murder the father first. The Lamido himself was reported to have commented in 1926 that "the people fear the District Head of Madagali more than they fear Allah."

The Political Officer in the Mubi area was convinced that the local people were too frightened to bring complaints to him when he went on tour in Madagali District. Hence he could only report incidents that he had heard about indirectly, stories such as the one about the eight chickens collected by certain villagers for sale to the TONA when he camped there for the night and then seized by the District Head's *jekadu* or official agents as soon as the ADO had left the resthouse, or the time a peasant was held for ransom by Hamman Yaji and freed only in exchange for his daughter. In another village, Hamman Yaji was alleged to have collected two pence from every householder so as to be able to offer a present to the ADO when he came on tour. Again, when the Lamido visited the northern districts of his emirate, Hamman Yaji was said to have extracted sixpence from every pagan and a sack of corn from every Fulbe male, explaining that such was his traditional welcome to his overlords.

TIME FOR ACTION

By May 1927, then, the mind of the provincial adminis-tration had hardened. The Resident was now convinced that Hamman Yaji was both corrupt and—a double threat—a fanatic in the bargain. Looking back on his twenty years' experience in the Nigerian Administrative Service, he concluded:

> I have met no one in this country who has so completely impressed me as a really dangerous man, who would not hesitate to murder a Political Officer if he thought the game was up. (Kirk-Greene 1953)

In support of this, he referred to the file notes of one of the very first reports on Hamman Yaji, written by the District Officer in charge of the Yola Emirate, T. F. Carlyle (see chapter 1). In the ensuing six years there had been neither improvement in the eyes of the colonial government nor, let it be conceded, much official reproof or reform by the provincial administration—an omission in duty which, in due course, was to catch the watchful eye of the Lieuten-ant-Governor in Kaduna. For one reason or another, often as commendable as it was condemnable, the grindstone of colonial administration moved extremely slowly. When it did move, however, it could, like its proverbial counterpart, grind exceedingly finely. Now, in the steamy atmosphere of another Mahdist scare (and he had to hand a secret report on Islam in Adamawa prepared by his Assistant Commissioner of Police, Capt. G. Callow, the previous year) Hamman Yaji's cumulative record of official distrust and disaffection pointed him out as a risk to law and order that could no longer be tolerated. The Resident's mind was made up: Hamman Yaji must go.

Doubtless sensitive to the fact that, after his dressing down from the Resident in person, the snare was closing around him, Hamman Yaji played what may have seemed to him to be his trump card. In the event, it turned out to be his last trick. It is possible to argue that at the back of the Nigerian colonial government's mind was the fact that, with "French" territory on three sides, there was always the shaming fear that should Nigerians, be they peasants or princes (e.g., the Sultan of Sokoto in 1931), find British rule too harsh, all they had to do was to up sticks and decamp overnight, over the border to Dahomey, Niger, Chad, or French Cameroun. The propaganda value of such voluntary emigration would have been embarrassing: for a peasantry, contented under the caring eye of a benign system of Indirect Rule closely supervised by British officers, to flee across the border to a French colony, with all its well-known injustices of forced labor—chiefly tyranny and power of instant imprisonment conferred upon the *Commandant de Cercle* by the infamous *indigénat*—would be an instant sign to Lagos that there must surely be something very wrong with the state of the Resident's administration. Having served, almost uniquely, under all three colonial administrations, Hamman Yaji was well aware of this dilemma. Accordingly, in June—a sensibly decent period after his painful interview with the Resident—he confided as a loyal District Head, to the new TONA, Capt. H. H. Wilkinson, that he had heard that the Fulbe administrative elite of Madagali feared that the upright British administration might one day decide to bring them to justice for the way they had treated their pagan subjects both during the German era, when administrative supervision was light, and in the French period when it was lax. He went on to say that they were now secretly deciding whether the best course might not be to emigrate across the border to Marua in French territory. The files suggest that when the Resident reported this potential defection of his subjects to the Lamido of Adamawa, the Lamido was so incensed that he called for the instant deposition of Hamman Yaji, sinisterly adding that there were enough serious complaints about his administration of Madagali since 1924 to preclude any investigation of the pre-British period (*Diary*, August 12, 1927). With such supportive concurrence—a *sine qua non* of Indirect Rule at its most theoretical, including encouragement from a First-Class Chief of the senior stature of the Lamido[50]—the way was now clear for the Resident to initiate action for the removal of Hamman Yaji.

In June, S. H. P. Vereker, Second Resident acting for G. S. Browne, who had only recently departed for Kaduna en route to Lagos for home leave after his first tour as Resident of Adamawa Province, addressed a secret letter to the Secretary, Northern Provinces (SNP), in Kaduna, advising the Lieutenant-Governor that

> unless we take some drastic action we are going to have continual trouble in this area [Madagali]. . . . I think it is better to face the risk of the District Head going to French Territory than to risk an attack on Captain Wilkinson (TONA), with his escort of police only. (Kirk-Greene 1953)[51]

50. He ranked no less than sixth in the official order of precedence among first-class chiefs in the northern provinces.

51. It has been generally assumed that H. R. Palmer, who had been a prime mover in the Sa'id affair of 1923, was then in Government Lodge, Kaduna. In fact, as a private letter from G. J. Lethem to Palmer substantiates, the latter was on leave in England in the summer of 1927, and the acting Lieutenant-Governor was C. W. Alexander. In his letter written from Kaduna on July 17, 1927, under the heading "Madagali," Lethem tells Palmer that "Alexander had approved the deposition of Mai Yaji [*sic*]" (Lethem Papers, Rhodes House Library, Brit. Emp., s.276).

There followed a recommendation which was bound to trouble Kaduna and would certainly have to be referred to the Governor in Lagos:

> Should the situation become serious, I think Madagali should be occupied by a Company [of WAFF].

Possibly to emphasize the gravity of the risks involved, the SNP reported to Lagos that Hamman Yaji had "a sinister reputation throughout the Northern Cameroons for ruthless cruelty," although he took care to ascribe such "buccaneering spirit" mostly to Hamman Yaji's days before the area came under British rule. That grave recommendation to call in the military was based on earlier advice to the District Officer in charge of Yola Division, to whom the TONA was responsible in the first place. H. H. Wilkinson, who had served in the war and emerged with the rank of captain, had told Vereker that, in his opinion as TONA, if it was ever decided to move against Hamman Yaji, the TONA would have to have at his disposal "a sufficient show of force" so as to enable him either to intimidate and order the District Head to accompany him down to Yola forthwith or to arrest him on the spot. It was suggested that a half company of the Nigerian Regiment would be the minimum necessary. Otherwise, as Vereker had minuted to the Resident,

> it would not surprise me if the present District Head, Madagali, collected all his supporters and attacked the Political Officer . . . would probably be made suddenly, and would be fraught with distinct risk to the officer and his native staff.

In now formally applying for the permission of the Lieutenant-Governor to arrest Hamman Yaji in Madagali, the Resident's plan was that he be immediately brought to Yola under police escort so that he could be formally deposed by the Lamido. For this operation, he pointed out, the TONA's escort of thirty policemen would not be enough to guarantee an arrest without disturbances of personal danger to the officer. He accordingly asked for a half company of troops to be deployed from the Yola garrison. In order not to arouse any suspicion in Madagali, it could be given out that the troops were being transferred from one provincial headquarters, Yola, to another, Maiduguri, 200 miles to the north, with Madagali just about halfway along that main road.

Following a warning order from the Resident, the officer commanding the Yola garrison of the Nigeria Regiment requested that the TONA collect between one and two tons of threshed corn as supplies for the two hundred men (including carriers in the proportion of approximately 3:1) likely to be involved in "the transfer" of his half company to Bornu Province. For the march to Mubi they would carry with them supplies from the Yola military granary, headloaded by forty extra carriers.

The stage was now set and the curtain poised to rise on the final act of the Hamman Yaji drama.

THE ARREST

Suddenly, Kaduna threw a spanner in the works. In a coded telegram, the Resident was informed that the use of troops would not be sanctioned. Instead, the Inspector-General of Police had agreed to draft thirty extra constables to Yola, ostensibly to relieve Wilkinson's escort in Mubi. With a force of sixty men at his disposal, the SNP felt that there would be no difficulty in effecting an arrest or in containing any opposition.

What now transpired between Yola and Kaduna, and in Kaduna itself, is not completely clear from the local files. However, four days later, on July 26, the SNP sent a priority message to the Resident informing him that there had been a change in plans. The Commandant of the Nigeria Regiment was now of the opinion that two platoons of troops should be deployed in support of the police reinforcements. They would march out of Yola one day in rear of the extra police, in case determined resistance was encountered in Madagali town. However, once arrested, the District Head was to be handed over to the military, not to the police, and escorted back to Yola as rapidly as possible. This was in keeping with the instructions strictly laid down by Kaduna that the military were to be used in aid of the civil power only under two possible circumstances: to execute a specifically identified offensive action or to act as escort for those arrested. As a further precaution, the Resident of neighboring Bornu Province had been instructed to dispatch the Dikwa Division DO and the Southern Marghi District ADO, both adjoining Madagali District, to "happen" to be out on tour at the provincial boundary. The SNP concluded by saying that they would also be letting the *Commandant de Cercle* at Mokolo in French territory know what was going on, but only on the day of the arrest. This would prevent any prior news leaking across the porous border. In the end, then, and after an about face in high places that has not been officially explained, a twin-force operation was sanctioned.

The police detachment left Yola on August 15—the middle of the difficult rainy season—and planned to reach Madagali within twelve days, proceeding via Song, Zumu, and Mubi. The military contingent marched out on August 16 and bivouacked a regular 24 hours behind the police all the way northwards. Pretending that it was because his relief police escort would be accompanied by an unusually large number of carriers, the TONA had arranged that stocks of food should be collected at every campsite between Kowogol and Mubi. At the final muster, the force was made up of, from the Nigeria Regiment, two British officers, 70 other ranks, eight camp-followers and 80 carriers, together with 40 more carrying emergency rations; and, from the Nigeria Police, one British officer, 30 constables and 50 carriers—a total of three Europeans and nearly 300 Africans. It is unlikely that such a substantial single force had been deployed in the area since the Cameroon Campaign of 1914–16.[52]

The advice consistently given by the TONA to the Resident was that as soon as Hamman Yaji had been arrested he must be evacuated from Madagali within the hour. Otherwise, he warned, if the District Head's more faithful and fanatical adherents should succeed in forcing his rescue while he was still in the town jail, the administration's chances of discovering his whereabouts somewhere in the inaccessible Mandara Mountains above Madagali was virtually nil.[53] Wilkinson also insisted that the police should, following the arrest, immediately and thoroughly search the District Head's compound for seditious literature and concealed firearms—this despite the fact that only a short while earlier his predecessor[54] believed that the rifles had been smuggled to Hamman Yaji's other houses at Womdeo, Mokolo, or Nyibango. The last-named cache was linked to a report by Abba, who told the DO that when his father's compound in Nyibango caught fire in 1927, Hamman Yaji had hurried there from Madagali. Even though the thatch roof and everything else was burned, his father had at once ordered water to be poured over the mud floor and then, driving Abba away, had entered the charred ruin alone. In support of Abba's allegation, we may note Hamman Yaji's oblique statement in the diary for May 12, 1927 that "nothing had been destroyed except the houses."

Wilkinson was understandably worried that a man as astute as Hamman Yaji would smell a rat in the story deliberately leaked that, unusually, the whole of the Northern Touring Area police escort was going to be relieved at one and the same time, thus doubling, however temporarily, the police presence in the area. He told the Resident that he was confident that, now that the use of two platoons of the Nigeria Regiment had been sanctioned, he could effect the arrest with his present force of 30 police. However, Vereker, as Acting Resident, was reluctant (perhaps understandably under the circumstances) to telegraph headquarters and try to alter His Honour's directive yet again. Subsequently the TONA changed his mind, explaining to Vereker that once he realized that the troops were to be held in reserve at a camp outside the town at Magar and not brought into Madagali itself, he would be glad to have the extra detachment of police alongside him in the town at the moment of arrest.

Back in Yola, Vereker issued the necessary movement order on August 9, authorizing Mr. Grantham, Commissioner of Police, and Capt. Taylor, Company Commander of A Co., 2 N.R., and O.C. Troops, Yola, to proceed according to plan. The details of precisely how the arrest was to be effected

52. Even the initial British "pacification" patrol, deployed in the immediate postwar breakdown of administrative control in 1921, consisted, after six years of political vacuum, of only two platoons and a Lewis gun.

53. How the Fulbe of Madagali would find haven among the montagnards was conveniently ignored.

54. Either L. N. Reed or H. O. Leonard.

were, as always in such civil-aid operations, to remain the responsibility of the TONA, Capt. H. H. Wilkinson, ADO.

With the police leaving Yola on August 15 and the troops a day later, this large force made good time despite the rains. Their route of march took them through prepared camps at Girei, Malam Madugu, Song, Wurode, Zumo, Kowagol, Pakka, Mubi (the TONA's headquarters), Uba and Michika, the two detachments rendezvousing at Magar, a village some six miles west of Madagali, on the evening of August 25. There they also met up with Wilkinson. All was now set for the climax the next day.

Contrary to common security practice, the arrest did not take place at dawn but at ten o'clock in the morning. This may have been so that the police would be in a better position, in the anticipated ensuing confusion, to spot anybody trying to make a run for it or to flush out anyone trying to hide in the District Head's labyrinthine compound. At an interview I conducted in 1953 at Madagali with Usman Madagali, who had been the Imam of the town's central mosque from 1924 to 1927, the following account was recorded:

> The ADO had spent five days in Madagali, the English Rest House then being on Wurdere Hill above the market place. On the sixth day, Friday, he ordered that the District Head and his party were to mount and ride out with him to meet another European at what was called the German Rest House, some distance away.[55] As the DH and his mounted retinue approached this Rest House, a laborer [carrier] stationed on a nearby hillock signalled to the ADO that the party was on its way. Thereupon the ADO set off along the road in the opposite direction with his Government messenger, Isa, and his interpreter, Audu, leaving the Lamido's Representative, Lawan, and a few policemen behind at the Rest House.
>
> Hamman Yaji now rode forward alone, leaving his followers, and went to talk with Lawan. While they were talking, Wilkinson suddenly reappeared from the other side, accompanied by more policemen and another European. They immediately entered the Rest House. Lawan followed them in. He quickly came out and called Hamman Yaji to come and greet the new European. This he did. The DH was accompanied by Alkali, Modibo Aminu, and Kaigama. These two then came out and left the place. A policeman took hold of Hamman Yaji's *riga* [gown], they all came outside together.
>
> Then the ADO went at once to the DH's compound and arrested the Ajia. He went into the house, he seized a small rifle [pistol?] and Hamman Yaji's book [diary]. This was always sat on by his slave Tayo so as to hide it. This time Tayo was so frightened that he sat on the Koran by mistake. The book was generally written by one Kaigama Saidu, the son of Hamman Yaji's former *ma-ga-takarda* [personal scribe]. Some other malams also wrote down what Hamman Yaji dictated to them.
>
> The book was not what the ADO was looking for. He wanted Hamman Yaji's favorite son, Yerima Bello. He was not in the compound. But as they were about to return to the Rest House they met him. Together they went

---

55. An entry for February 20, 1914, indicates that the Germans also had a rest house on Wurdere Hill.

to the Rest House, where the other European was. Nobody was handcuffed. This all took place at 10 o'clock on Friday. (Kirk-Greene 1953)

While the three prisoners (Hamman Yaji, his son Bello, and his head slave, Ajia) were being taken away, a crowd of some three or four hundred, mostly women, shouted and ululated, but beyond jostling the prisoners' escort they were sufficiently kept in check by the rest of the police. Wilkinson felt no need to call up the military, concealed but in readiness at Mayo Gang, some three miles away. The TONA was later to dismiss this demonstration as an insurance show of public loyalty, just in case—as was sometimes the case in Native Administration circles—the District Head later returned to his head-quarters after nothing worse than a reprimand from the Lamido. The official inventory spoke of a revolver, ammunition, and documents having been removed from Hamman Yaji's compound at the time of his arrest.

Keeping moving, the ADO, his prisoner and the police escort quickly reached Mayo Gang, where the troops were waiting. By 2:30 p.m. the Police Commissioner had formally handed over his prisoners to the O.C. Troops at Magar. The new escort and the prisoners at once set off on the long march to Yola, spending the first night at Duhu, a safe distance from Madagali town.

In the same interview (1953), the Imam recalled how it was Hamman Yaji's custom rarely to spend more than a week at a time in his headquarters at Madagali. His private army had worn a kind of khaki uniform, with red fezzes. In response to specific questions at the conclusion of his uninterrupted narrative, the Imam declared that he was convinced that Hamman Yaji's slave-raiding activities had declined markedly in the later years.

This time, being such a measurably smaller group, the journey south-ward was far quicker. Captain Taylor, O.C. Troops, was relieved to find that, in the villages they passed through, no animosity was shown to his soldiers. Once beyond Madagali District, more flour was brought in for sale each day than they required, still at only a penny a *tasa* (a measuring bowl), though the price rose to fourpence when they reached Girei, which served the semi-urban Jimeta-Yola complex. Fresh beef could be bought on the march without trouble, and at each halt a cow was purchased and slaughtered for the troops. On the first day a "truculent" *dogari* (Native Authority policeman) and eight other men had followed after them, but they were quickly "seen off" by the soldiers. When the party approached Zu, a small crowd of Hamman Yaji's slave laborers "wailed loudly" as they passed. Hamman Yaji himself refused to eat at all, but when a female member of his household turned up at Moda he agreed to eat the rice she had faithfully cooked for him, and Captain Taylor sent out for the honey and milk which he had particularly asked for.[56]

---

56. For Hamman Yaji's love for honey, see *Diary*, December 23, 1923.

The prisoners and escort reached Yola on September 2, a mere seven days after leaving Madagali.

THE EXILE

The Resident's recommendation to Kaduna had been unambiguous. On arrest, Hamman Yaji must be removed not only from Madagali District and from the Yola emirate, but also from Adamawa Province. Even if this turned out to be only a temporary measure, banishment from the whole of Adamawa had to be instant. Vereker's idea was to put Hamman Yaji on board one of the United Africa Company's steamers which, during the height of the rainy season, were regularly able to sail up the Benue as far as Yola and sometimes on to Garua, and transport him post-haste to Makurdi, 400 miles away to the west southwest. This unprepossessing river town, like Lokoja in the opening decade of British administration, was no stranger to the role of receiving exiled emirs and deposed chiefs. Vereker emphasized that Hamman Yaji's uncowed Fulbe followers in Madagali town were daily anticipating his triumphant return and warned that the naturally euphoric sense of relief throughout the district dared not find open expression until the peasantry were convinced that there was no likelihood of Hamman Yaji's return . . . and revenge.

Although the Lieutenant-Governor refused to sanction such an instantaneous and undignified shipping-out, the authorities in Yola nevertheless acted with unaccustomed celerity. Hamman Yaji was formally deposed by the Lamido's court (invested with Grade A powers) on September 19. He was awarded a monthly pension of £5. The charges, the proceedings and the defendant's replies were recorded in the court book, as was the judgement handed down by Muhammadu Bello, "Commander of the South [Sarkin Fombina]." The deportation order was served on October 3. It required Hamman Yaji to be out of Adamawa Province within 48 hours, on pain of imprisonment and a further order compelling him to reside in some specified Nigerian city. With the humiliating memory of his abrupt arrest now six weeks past, Hamman Yaji felt resolute enough to refuse to comply with the deportation order. Five days later, on October 8, he was briskly escorted aboard a Company steamer bound for Makurdi. With the Benue beginning to fall, the Resident must have uttered a sigh of relief as he saw the steamer round the point and head southward to Numan and Lau, and so safely out of his provincial jurisdiction. A further deportation order was applied for, restricting Hamman Yaji's movements for an unlimited period. On October 21, Hamman Yaji reached his asylum, Sokoto. His exile had begun.

THE AFTERMATH

Even with Hamman Yaji safely out of the way—or at least out of the Province—there were numerous loose ends to tie up in Yola. In reply to the eminently understandable and slightly pained query from SNP why, given Hamman Yaji's apparently long, dread and documented record of misrule, the Provincial Administration had taken no action to remove him from office earlier, the Resident explained to the Lieutenant-Governor, perhaps not quite convincingly or altogether self-convincedly, that "he was a fine type of Chief, a man of brain and strong character, of much prestige in every way" (Kirk-Greene 1953). On the Yola internal files, the DO went further still in admiration, recording that he had found Hamman Yaji "a man of charming address, civilized manner of living, strong character and great intelligence," and suggested that it might well be said of him *omnium capax impera nisi imperasset*.[57] Here, of course, was an example of the grim fallacy of the fundamental premise of indirect rule *pur sang*: How long did officials, following Lugard's dictum that "the *de facto* rulers who had been recognized by Government are to be supported in every way and their authority upheld" (Lugard 1970 [1917]: para. 3a), tolerate a "bad" chief in the hallowed name of non-interference ("it is obviously desirable that Government should be called upon as rarely as possible to intervene between the chiefs and people" [ibid.: para. 6])? The latter function was, in accordance with the principles of Lugardian indirect rule, solely the prerogative of the emirs and chiefs. Kaduna seemed sufficiently assuaged to overlook any administrative shortcomings in Yola and to focus on what it saw as the feather in the provincial administration's cap, the uncovering of a dangerous incidence of Mahdism in high places. In a confidential memorandum addressed to all Northern Residents on September 29, 1927 (SNP[K] 5621/4, 29 September 1927, para. 5)[58] on the topic of "Religious Propaganda," in particular Mahdism, in the North, the SNP (G. J. Lethem) drew attention to the proud and satisfactory fact that

> there is now also to be chronicled the deposition, with probable deportation to follow, of the District Head of Madagali in Adamawa. This chief, who had been independent in German times, had, after years of patient trial shown himself more and more irreconcilable to the directions of Government, and

57. Translated, the ready Latin (so characteristic of a Colonial Service generation recruited up to 1939, though *impera* should correctly read *imperii*) means "Everyone would have considered him competent to govern, had he never governed." The sentiment echoes the *capax imperii* judgement of Tacitus on the quality of Galba who overthrew Nero but was himself assassinated in A.D. 69.

58. A copy is retained in both the Rosedale Papers at Rhodes House Library, Oxford (Mss. Afr. s. 582) and the Lethem Papers (Mss. Brit. Emp. s. 276). The focus of the circular letter was prompted by the attack earlier in 1927 on the French post of Tassawa, where an official was killed, and the "murderous attack" on the District Officer, Minna, both by "a mallam." It urged Residents to see that native administrations "take a more definite line to ensure the discovery and suppression of this type of destructive propaganda" (para. 8). This letter was attached to SNP circular letter K.5621/12, dated October 4, 1927, which enclosed a copy of the lieutenant-governor's warning address about religious disorders delivered to the emir of Katsina on August 16, 1927 (see chapter 1). In the same year, the SNP issued a pamphlet (MP.K. 5669/3), *Introductory Notes on Mohammadanism,* to all administrative officers.

had deliberately neglected to put an end to many gross abuses of administration in his country taken over under the mandate.

Then came the triumphant conclusion:

There is unfortunately no room for doubt that his intransigence [*sic*] was largely accentuated as a result of his strong "Mahdist" leanings, the active propaganda of Mahdism in his district, and the frequent passage of "Mahdist" itinerant mallams in the region.

As a punchline, the SNP concluded that Hamman Yaji had been "himself a correspondent of Mallam Said of Dumbulwa and autograph letters from him were found in Dumbulwa in 1923."

In the end, of course, the Colonial Office's report to the League of Nations Mandates Commission, which, with Lugard as the British member, displayed a persistent interest in questions of slavery, was characteristically anodyne, if not somewhat economic with the truth:

During the past year it has been necessary to deport the District Head of Madagali . . . as it was quite evident, after a fair trial, that [he] would not carry out fairly the orders of Government. . . . [He] had been allowed much scope, and his undoubted gifts and strength of character had fostered the hope that he would eventually realize that it was to his interest to conform and to become a real pillar of the Administration. Adverse reports concerning him had been received for some years and he had received many warnings and reprimands, but in spite of all and in spite of many professions of repentance and promises to reform, he persisted in malpractices until he could be tolerated no longer. (Great Britain Colonial Office 1928)

No sooner had Kaduna been adequately—or at least apparently—appeased, if not completely satisfied, by Yola's self-exculpation than another query reached the Acting Resident's desk, this time from Mubi. A hot-under-the-collar Wilkinson, who had executed the arrest (with its potential for an ugly disturbance and loss of life) in a commendably competent fashion, now wrote to complain that he was at a loss to understand how he, the principal actor in the finale of the Hamman Yaji affair, was nevertheless, 26 days after the event, still completely in the dark as to what had happened once Hamman Yaji had been marched off under arrest. Why, he wondered reproachfully, had he heard not one word from his superiors? This querulous enquiry was quickly followed by another strongly worded letter, this time concerning the administration of Hamman Yaji's estate. Before leaving Yola, Hamman Yaji had changed his mind, it appeared, and nominated his Sarkin Bayi (chief slave), Ajia, as administrator instead of his favorite son, Bello. Ajia now proposed to move his principal's cattle and other property at Mubi, Yola, or Mayo Belwa. This was interpreted by Wilkinson as nothing less than a trick, giving out the impression that Hamman Yaji's departure was only a temporary move and that he would soon return to Adamawa. Wilkinson argued that

Hamman Yaji's claim to own in Madagali 40 cows, 60 horses, 40 sheep, five donkeys, five suits of *salsala* or chain armor, and 2000 bushels of corn should be challenged by the Lamido on the grounds that, since he had come by none of his wealth honestly, it all ought to be sold and the money credited to the *Beit-el-Mal* (Native Treasury) in compensation for the hundreds of pounds of tax money that Hamman Yaji had embezzled from the NA over the years. A subsequent entry in the TONA's records shows that 37 horses were sold off for £131-6-4, while two cows fetched £3-17-0.

No sooner had Wilkinson received a reassuring letter from Yola, with the news about Hamman Yaji's deportation to Sokoto, than he was once more up in arms. In his opinion, he wrote to the Resident, under no circumstances could Hamman Yaji be allowed to settle down in the heart of a fervidly Muslim community like Sokoto, historically the origin of the Caliphate and the symbol of Othman Dan Fodio's jihad. Hamman Yaji was, he maintained, "no ordinary man," rather one obsessed with the notion of his excessive superiority. Wilkinson instanced how, when talking with peasants in his district, they were forbidden to look at his face and had to sit on the ground with their backs to him.[59] In the *zaure* or courtyard reception hall of each of his houses in the district, the walls had apertures through which Wilkinson alleged that Hamman Yaji would address people without their being able to see him.

Such a forceful letter from a junior officer—the brusque overtones of "I cannot countenance . . ." more suited to the Lieutenant-Governor, or even the Governor than to an ADO addressing his Resident—was more than Vereker, understandably worn out by worry over the whole Hamman Yaji affair and its possible impact on his own reputation and approaching retirement in Kaduna, was prepared to take. Hitherto he had restricted his surprise and dismay to pencilling a series of exclamation and question marks on the incoming correspondence from the TONA. Now he let off steam officially. In a letter to Wilkinson he pointed out that neither the Governor in Lagos nor the Lieutenant-Governor in Kaduna had sought his (the Resident's) view on the place of deportation, and they were certainly not going to be interested in the unsolicited opinion of a junior ADO. To put it bluntly, he wrote, he found Wilkinson's ill-expressed remarks nothing less than "a criticism of the activities of both His Excellency and His Honour." Accordingly, would Wilkinson care to confirm that he still wished his letter to be forwarded to Kaduna for the Lieutenant-Governor's attention? Faced with such a neat bureaucratic trap, Wilkinson now had little choice. Writing on Christmas Day, when thoughts of peace on earth (or at least in Kaduna) and good will to all men (at least towards his Resident)

---

59. It is arguable that this was not as personal a conceit as Wilkinson had supposed; clearly he had not read Denham's account, a century earlier, of royal behavior in what was to become northeastern Nigeria, where the chief traditionally held audiences for his subjects who "took their places on the ground in front, but with their backs to the royal person, which is the custom" (Denham 1826:78 with accompanying illustration).

were possibly uppermost in his mind, he reiterated that while it was his belief that, as the man on the spot, he—like every Touring Officer—had an intimate and unique knowledge of the situation, nevertheless in view of the fact that his letter had unfortunately given rise to the erroneous impression that he was intent on criticizing his seniors, he now wished to request that no further action should be taken on that letter.

The experienced Vereker was a big enough man to write, in due course, to the Lieutenant-Governor saying that he thought that Wilkinson had handled the affair well. He had had a trying time during his posting to the Northern Cameroons, and he deserved credit for having been the first officer to unearth Mahdism in the Mubi area. In reply, the Lieutenant-Governor, H. R. Palmer, asked the Resident to convey his appreciation to Mr. Wilkinson. Historians of the controversy within the Colonial Service circles of Northern Nigeria at the time—over why Sir Donald Cameron had decided to post the senior and up-and-coming G. S. Browne to Kaduna (as SNP, 1920–26), after which the Lieutenant-Governor had then shunted him off to the backwater that was Yola—will be intrigued by the fact that Palmer added a personal congratulation to Mr. Browne on the progress achieved in the province since his appointment as Resident there.[60]

The story now takes an unexpected twist. Within twelve months G. S. Browne, now back in Yola from his home leave, had himself taken up with Kaduna the point that Sokoto was no place for a dangerous fanatic like Hamman Yaji. Shrewdly, Browne pointed out that it was uncomfortably close to the international border with both Niger and Dahomey: it would not be hard for such a clever man to slip across the frontier overnight, travel through French territory all the way eastward to Lake Chad, and then, still in French territory, settle down in southern Chad or northern Cameroun, from where he would once again constitute an awesome threat to the local Madagali population and represent an unwelcome thorn in the flesh of the British Administration. Now Kaduna paid immediate attention to a warning coming from such an able and experienced senior officer, and within no time an *ad hominem* ordinance was passed, the "Muhammadu Yaji (Detention) Ordinance," no. 4 of 1929.[61] Possibly in view of the Yola arguments, all the way from ADO Wilkinson to Senior Resident Browne, that French territory represented a real threat as a launching pad for reentry into the British Cameroons, care was taken to describe Hamman Yaji as the brother of Yakubu Yaji, chief of Mokolo in nearby French Cameroun since 1926. Under its provisions, Hamman Yaji was transferred from Sokoto to Kaduna, along with

60. The unfortunate Browne was looked on with superiority in Kaduna by senior officials like Sir Richard Palmer and considered to be Lagos's spy on the "Holy North." In 1930 Browne was rescued from his obscurity in the remote Adamawa Province and posted back to Lagos on promotion as Secretary for Native Affairs. He never realized his expectation of becoming lieutenant-governor of the northern provinces, for on his elevation in 1933 the Kaduna post was simultaneously downgraded to that of chief commissioner. The episode is best followed in Heussler (1968:77).

61. A copy is filed in the P.R.O., London, on CO.583/164/441/29.

the disgraced and dismissed Waziri of Sokoto, Macido. There they were provided with special accommodation well away from what was referred to as "the Native town." For his housing, Adamawa Native Authority was called on to pay £50.

The exiled Hamman Yaji did not enjoy his new abode for long. He died on May 8, 1929, from, to cite the official report, "primary cause septicaemia and secondary cause stricture of the urethra and extra-vasation of urine." His son Bello, five wives and womenfolk of his household, and two youths stayed in Kaduna. In the subdued Adamawa provincial report for 1927, the Resident found it necessary to state simply that the only person exiled from the Province was Hamman Yaji, the former District Head of Madagali, deported to Sokoto (National Archives Kaduna 28/A29: para. 146), quietly noting under the rubric of Native Administration in the emirate that "five District Heads were deposed" (para. 32). In 1928, this brief reference was repeated, with the additional comment that "His property has now been dealt with and the balance after payment of debts and expenses has been remitted to him" (NAK 30/A31: para. 74). The 1929 annual report was briefer and blunter yet: "There are now no exiles from Adamawa as Hamman Yaji, the ex-District Head of Madagali, died at Kaduna on the 8th of May" (NAK 31/A32: para. 100). However, his shadow was resurrected in the draft Adamawa provincial report for 1931, where the Resident commented on the progress made by the new DH of Madagali District "since the deposition of his predecessor, Hamman Yaji of evil reputation."[62]

Hamman Yaji features in no standard history of Nigeria,[63] and his mention in the published history of colonial Adamawa is solely in connection with an incident—"a small but pungent riot," in the meiotic idiom of officialdom (Provincial Annual Reports 1953: Adamawa, paras. 9–11)—which took place in Mubi and Madagali a whole quarter of a century later (see chapter 6).

62. Copy of draft report in the Lethem Papers, ibid.: box 5.
63. Even in the authoritative teaching aid drawn up by Nigerian scholars for the Historical Society of Nigeria, he merely appears in a brief footnote as an example of a Cameroons borderland chief, "a well-known Mahdist," who accepted subsidies from both colonial powers (Ikime, 1984:470, n. 89).

3. *The History of the Diary*

ANTHONY H. M. KIRK-GREENE

With Vereker's and Wilkinson's feathers at last de-ruffled and Kaduna as well as Yola relieved that 1927 had seen none of the feared bloodshed, attention could next be paid by the Provincial Administration to the documents which had been found in Hamman Yaji's house at Madagali. Given their likely significance in terms of Mahdist incitement, they had been sent down to Yola in a locked specie box. The TONA's contemporary records showed that they included a "portion" of a diary kept by the District Head, a "cover" (probably an office file-jacket) containing instructions on charms, and a book believed to be a commentary on Maliki law. Other papers incriminated both NA officials and government Native Staff (to use the official establishments and personnel terminology) as having received bribes, among them no less a person than Allah Kyauta, Wilkinson's Political Agent and right-hand at Mubi (See *Diary,* February 7 and October 15, 1925; April 1, 1926). Sixty-eight letters were found, none of them deemed to be of any real importance, though it was felt that some of the expressions used by the writers could be interpreted as being of "relevance" (presumably to Mahdism). Several of them addressed Hamman Yaji as *Sarkin Musulmi* or Leader of the Faithful (properly the title is reserved to the Sultan of Sokoto). His son Bello was said to have referred to him as "he who follows the Mahdi." Another form of address was "the slayer of the infidels" (*wanda ya kashe alkafirai*) and another wished him "victory over the pagans" (*nasara a kan arna*), while a third beseeched Hamman Yaji to use special prayers as a protection against finding himself in close proximity to a pagan (*arne*). However, it should be noted that quoted forms of address like *Sarkin Sarakuna* (King of Kings), *Sarkin Kasar Arewa duka wanda ya fi sarakuna duka* (Lord of all the North who is above all other kings) and *zuwa ga wanda Allah ya ba shi karama* ("to him to whom Allah has given the spirit of cordial generosity"), all calculated to flatter the receiver, are not exceptional—other than perhaps the reserved mode of address, Sarkin Musulmi—in the oratory and epistolary tradition of a society characterized by the accepted rituals of *fadanci* (institutionalized flattery) and *bangirma* (respect to those in sanctioned authority).

The charms and spells, which numbered over sixty, were designed, as is commonly the case, to secure for their possessor various benefits in the form of protection against such adversities as illness, thievery, poverty, and bullets. Others were less protective, more positive: to procure victory over one's enemies, to achieve power or gain wealth, to ensure a place in Paradise, etc. Nearly all the spells consisted of symbols to be written on wood and washed off with water which had then to be drunk. Specific formulae were to be recited at stated times. Interestingly, there was a charm for gaining the friendship of the *Nasara* (Christian, i.e. the European, almost certainly in this instance the TONA) and to incline him to go along with one's every wish or whim.[64]

In the wake of the arrest of Hamman Yaji and the sequestration of the contents of his palace in Madagali described above, a translation of the diary seized among his possessions was undertaken by the colonial authorities. What is significant is how speedily the translation of at least parts of the diary was put in hand. As the following extract from H. H. Wilkinson's special report on the Hamman Yaji aftermath, dated November 21, 1927, shows, a preliminary translation must have been available in Mubi within a matter of weeks, though, in subsequently forwarding the TONA's report to Kaduna, the Resident, G. S. Browne, was careful to say no more than that the diary "is being translated," though this was by now February 1928:

> I attach a list of one hundred persons who were being held as slaves and who have been freed by the Native Court since the removal of Hamman Yaji. There are many more names to record and cases keep coming up daily. In addition, large numbers who have asserted their right to freedom have not come before the Native Court. Cases only come to light through the claims of parents, complaints of ill treatment or in some such way.
>
> Prior to the removal of Hamman Yaji it would have been quite impossible for these unfortunate people to either complain or assert their right to freedom. Before British occupation the armed bands of the District Head openly moved among the pagans plundering, slaughtering, and capturing. The terrible sufferings of the people will be seen from the callous remarks in Hamman Yaji's diary regarding these raids. The bitterness of the pagans towards this man is inconceivable to one who has not seen it. On a visit to Sina Galli last March the pagans showed me the ruins of their village and a rock on which many had perished when the village was plundered and burnt by Hamman Yaji's armed bands just prior to British occupation. The charred guinea corn is still preserved and the village head has been sworn never to enter the town of Madagali. The spoil and captives obtained in these raids were brought to Madagali sold and distributed. Young children were separated from their mothers. Madagali was famous as a slave market.

---

64. The mention of this particular charm (other than the two references to "dreams") in the diary (March 1, 1919) was to ensure that the French *Commandant de Cercle* would not prolong his stay in Madagali!

Subsequent to British occupation slave raids were discontinued at least openly. Hamman Yaji then resorted to more subtle means of obtaining slaves, i.e., through the medium of witchcraft or holding persons to ransom. On perusal of the attached list [not included] it will be seen that a large number of children have been freed, many of whom are under ten years of age. The gratitude of parents on the restoration of their children is abundant, whereas the disappointment when their children fail to recognize them through long separation is distressing. By the removal of Hamman Yaji a great slave center has been exposed and as the people themselves say, the doors of their prison have been opened.

The Administration has won the gratitude of a very large proportion of the pagan population of the Northern Mandated Area and which I venture to say will be the main factor in bringing this long disturbed area under effective administrative control. (Resident Yola to SNP, 28 February 1928)[65]

The diary was written in Arabic, not in *ajami* (Hausa or Fulfulde in Arabic script rather than Roman). The English translation was the work of a "Capt. Reed, ADO, Yola." This is all that appears on the original typescript translation, at least two copies of which were retained among the colonial government's files of the time. We have now established that this officer was Leslie Northcott Reed MC, who had served in the Great War in India and Mesopotamia from 1914–18, during which he won a Military Cross, and then been retained in the Political Service there during its formative years. At the age of 32 he was offered a post as a cadet in the Nigerian Administrative Service, and on his arrival in Lagos in May 1925 was posted to Yola. Clearly his education (Plymouth College and St. John's College, Oxford) and his experience in India and Mesopotamia had developed his innate linguistic talent, for by 1927 he had, remarkably and uniquely for such a junior official, passed the Government examinations for Lower Standard Hausa, Fulbe, Arabic, and Shuwa and the Higher Standard Arabic examination.[66] At the time of the Hamman Yaji episode, Reed had returned from his first home leave and been reposted to Adamawa.[67] His subsequent career is obscure, and it looks as if he may have become a victim of the Colonial Service retrenchment program generated by the slump and depression of the years 1929–32. While the present location of the original Arabic diary is unknown and none of the few (probably no more than two or three, given the quality of carbon paper in the 1920s) typescript copies of the translation has yet been sighted in the Public Record Office, London, one of the typescript copies was retained in the Provincial Office, Yola. After independence, this

65. I am grateful to Professors Paul Lovejoy and Jan Hogendorn for drawing our attention to the extensive file, "Slave Dealing in Nigeria and Cameroons" (SNP 17 12577, now in the National Archives, Kaduna) and thereby filling out this part of my 1953 field notes.

66. For an account of these Examinations for District Officers see Kirk-Greene 1988.

67. He is frequently referred to in the diary between April 30 and October 26, 1926, when he was one of the rapid succession of TONAs to which the area was subjected between 1921 and 1927—in itself, arguably a contributory factor to how the District Head was able to "get away with it" for so long.

file was transferred to the Nigerian National Archives. It is this copy from which the text used in this book has been reproduced. We have, however, reconstructed and amplified the earlier index—in which the diarist was continually referred to as "Haman Yaji" as he is on the diary's first page.

Reed believed that the diary was dictated to a scribe, though there were marginalia which might have been in Hamman Yaji's own hand. He notes that some passages were omitted from the translation, and at various points in the text these exclusions are noted and parenthetically summarized. Typically, they refer to Hamman Yaji's movements, his trading, and the giving and receiving of gifts, as for example, "(The rest of this page is concerned mainly with trading matters, his own movements and the exchange of presents with various people)." There are no omissions noted after January 1924, except for a remark that two pages of the original manuscript are missing. In all there were 214 pages of manuscript with more than 1160 entries, 670 written after 1923. Reed's translation required 150 pages of typescript.[68]

The absence of the Arabic original frustrates any semantic analysis, and without it we are unable to see if the translator has "interpreted" events. On the face of it, however, the translation seems to lack pejorative bias in the selection of words, but, again, it would be useful to crosscheck. Since no resolution to these difficulties seems probable, the diary is here presented as it is. We are satisfied that, even in its present form, the diary carries an intrinsic, intellectual importance for scholars. We would not wish to see anything diminish the true value of such a rarity as the diary of a District Head in Northern Nigeria written some eighty years ago.

68. In Reed's copy there are virtually no errors beyond a few over-strikes and a few handwritten corrections. We have modified his format to produce a more concise copy.

4. Capt. L. N. Reed's Introduction [1927]

DESCRIPTION OF DIARY

This diary of Haman Yaji, ex-District Head of Madagali, is a fairly regularly-kept record of matters, which he considered worth recording, for the period from September 16, 1912, the date of the first entry, to August 25, 1927, a day or two before his arrest. While it is in a general way a document of quite considerable interest, it is disappointing in the meagerness of the information it gives on topics about which one would have liked to hear more, and very large portions of it are concerned with a monotonous recital of the writer's own movements, his trading transactions and similar matters of slight importance. Having regard to the purpose of the translation, it did not appear necessary to record all these entries in full, but at the same time it did seem desirable that some portion of the diary should be translated in detail, in order that a better idea might be given of the scope of the diary as a whole. As the later years appear to be of more particular interest from an Administrative Officer's point of view, the period January 1, 1924 onwards has been selected for translation in full, while for the earlier years only such portions have been recorded as appear to be of present-day interest.

DIFFICULTY OF SEQUENCE OF PAGES

The MS consists of 215 pages written for the most part on loose double sheets. As these had become disarranged and as there is only one reference throughout the diary to the year to which any particular sheet refers, it was a matter of no small difficulty to rearrange the sheets in their correct order. This was especially so for the earlier years, where references in the text to individuals did not assist as in the later years to fix the date. Fortunately, however, there were various indications by which the order could be ascertained, and all the pages have now been correctly arranged and numbered.

CONVERSION OF DATES

The conversion of the Muhammadan dates into the dates of the Christian calendar was done by reference to one or two known dates and calculation backwards or forwards from them. Checks were made by a conversion formula or by reference to old Muhammadan calendars where they were available.

NAMES OF THE MONTHS

The names of the Muhammadan months are given by the diarist in most cases in their Fulani form, although sometimes the Arabic form is used. The following is a list of the months and their Arabic equivalents:

Fulani	*Arabic*
Haram or Haram Awwal	Muharram
Haram Tumbindu or Tumbindu Haramji	Safar
Haram Sakitindu or Haram Petel	Rabi'a al Awwal
Banjaru Awwal	Rabi'a al Thani
Banjaru Tumbindu	Jumada al Ula
Banjaru Sakitindu	Jumada al Ukhra
Sumatendu Waube	Rajab
Wairordu Sumaye or Jaujaungel	Sha'aban
Sumaye	Ramadhan
Juldandu	Shawwal
Siutorandu	Dhu al Qa'adah
Laihaji	Dhu al Hijjah

As has been mentioned above, there is one reference to a year, namely on MS p. 171 [*Diary*, February 25, 1925]. This passage is obscure: the first of Jaujaungel is the beginning of the 8th month and the correct year is 1343. It is therefore permissible to describe the event referred to as occurring in the year 1342 plus seven months, and seven months is equal to 208 days. But the further addition: "If you subtract three months, etc." seems to have no meaning. It is possible that three months is an error for five months and that he meant to say that it is the same thing as taking away five months from the year of the Hijrah [the flight of the Prophet], namely 1343, but it is not at all obvious what the writer's intention was.

THE LANGUAGE

In general the Arabic is of a very illiterate kind and it is sometimes very difficult to discover the correct meaning. Where a passage is obscure from the linguistic point of view, it has been noted as such in the translation. Where, as frequently happens, the Arabic is quite clear but the writer's intention is obscure, a literal translation has been given, and no attempt has been made to guess at the meaning. It is, of course, also to be remarked that a diary necessarily contains references which to the diarist, writing in a telegraphic style for his own private purposes, are quite clear, but which are not apparent to one who has not been a participant in the incidents related.

In connection with the language question, it should be noted that the text is full of Fulani words, which the scribes have fallen back on, when they are at a loss for the correct Arabic.

Reference should also be made to the occurrence between entries in the diary of various scrawls, which appear to be Arabic or Fulani but which are quite unreadable. It is believed that Haman Yaji could not write very well, and it may be that these scrawls are private memoranda of his own written in his handwriting.

TRANSLITERATION OF NAMES

The transliteration of European names into Arabic distorts them until they are practically unrecognizable, and it has been impossible in the case of some French and German names to make even a guess at the correct name in the absence of other documents, e.g. office files, which might throw light on the subject. The same applies to a lesser degree in the case of pagan names and names of places, especially as the same name appears sometimes in as many as three different forms in different places in the text.

(Signed: L. N. Reed)
Assistant District Officer

EDITORS' NOTE: All remarks within parentheses are the insertions or comments of Capt. Reed. There are a few handwritten corrections and additions which may have been made by Reed or some other reader; we have placed these within braces. Our comments are within brackets. At points in the text where Hamman Yaji makes reference to "the Governor" we have inserted the name of the then-governor, however, it seems possible that in most—if not all—instances Hamman Yaji may have meant the Lieutenant-Governor. In a few instances, question marks have been substituted for illegible typescript. Finally, we changed the format for ease of reading, and we have occasionally changed Reed's capitalization, punctuation, and spelling to comply with contemporary practice.

The Diary

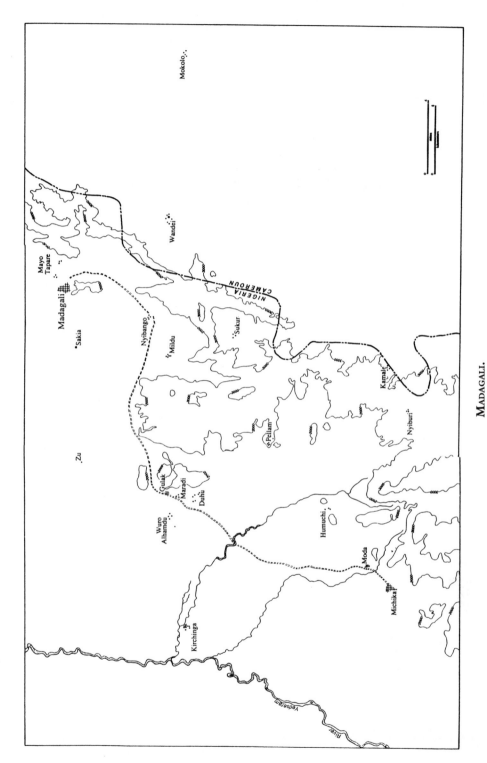

MADAGALI.

The locations of Maradi, Mayo Tapare, and Sakia are inferred from physical ruins of residences belonging to Hamman Yaji and reconstructions from the text of the diary. The locations are not known by these names today.

5. The Diary of Hamman Yaji, Ex-District Head of Madagali

1912

September 16th On Monday the 3rd of Juldandu there came to me some pagans of the Matakam tribe from Buba Magawa's village, who brought me a female slave.

September 20th On Friday the 8th of Juldandu Umar returned from his journey to Garua and informed me that a new Governor had arrived. I also received news that I had won my case against Moda.

In the morning one of the women of my household refused to give me any food.

September 22nd On Sunday the 10th of Juldandu I raided Sukur and we killed two men. Kaunga was killed.

October 1st On Tuesday the 19th of Juldandu I bought a suit of chain-armour at the price of a horse, and on the same day raided Mufuli. There we captured two calves, a cow and 14 sheep and goats, a result which displeased me.

October 3rd On Thursday the 21st of Juldandu the soldiers returned to Mufuli and found four men dead. They captured a few cattle, which, however, scattered and escaped from them.

October 7th On Monday the 25th of Juldandu I got back two rifles which were in Mufuli.

October 20th On Sunday the 9th of Siutorandu I sent some soldiers to Sukur. They found three boys and managed to reach the Arnado's house.

October 22nd On Tuesday the 10th of Siutorandu I divided my soldiers into two parties, one to go to Muduvu and the other to go to Sukur and Juyel. Alhamdu was killed.

November 1st On Friday the 20th of Siutorandu the Mandara people attacked the pagans of Kona with rifle fire.

November 18th On Monday the 8th of Laihaji Gajo returned from his journey to Ngaundere bringing 20 cartridges.

November 21st On Thursday the 11th of Laihaji I sent Atiku and Madi Kelo to Garua in regard to a complaint and I gave them a horse as a present for the Governor.

November 23rd On Saturday the 13th of Laihaji I sent to Garua to make a complaint against my Duhu people.

November 24th On Sunday the 14th of Laihaji I sent Madi Kucheb on a journey to Maifoni and I gave the Sheikh 5 dollars. On the same day I gave the Emir of Uba 15 shillings.

December 7th On Saturday the 27th of Laihaji I sent two messengers, Buba and Muhammad, to Ngaundere with two horses for the White Man; one was a present for him and the other was for sale. There was also a female slave for the interpreter.

December 10th On Tuesday the 30th [of] Laihaji the pagans called Shikawa brought me 10 slave girls. I also sent soldiers to Kamale, but they did not reach the Arnado's compound and only got a female slave whose hand had been cut off and who was as stupid as a goat. This made me very angry with them.

December 19th On Thursday the 9th of Haram Awwal Lawan 'Aji came and made his peace with me.

On the 8th day of Haram Awwal and the night of the 9th I dreamt that I rode a horse into water.

December 27th On Friday the 17th of Haram Awwal the pagans of Sukur brought me two cows as a peace offering.

1913

January 8th On Wednesday the 29th of Haram Awwal the pagans of Sina killed three of my soldiers and captured three rifles. My people killed five of the pagans.

[The dates of the following two entries are reversed.]

January 29th On Wednesday the 20th of Tumbindu Haramji the Christian sent back my horse because it was sick.

January 23rd On Thursday the 15th of Haram Wasti I started, that is to say I adopted, the practice of the Thursday and Monday fasts, while I was in Bugel.

February 4th On Tuesday the 27th of Haram Tumbindu Haramji I found that my slave girl in the absence of her fellow-slaves had said that she would not prepare my food for me. Why she would not cook my food I do not know, but anyway the result was that I got no food from her and was obliged to buy it.

February 10th On Monday the 4th of Haram Akhir I gave a friend of mine, who is a clerk in Yola, 55 shillings.

(This page [MS p. 6] is concerned mainly with entries regarding trading expeditions, gifts to him of slaves, and his own visits to his "country houses.")

March 17th On Monday the 8th of Banjaru Awwal I sent Mahawonga to hunt out slaves for me from the pagans called Dugupchi and they found 11 slave girls and one cow.

March 23rd On Sunday the 14th of Banjaru Awwal my people came back from Sinagali, and I heard that they had captured 7 pagans, 15 cattle and 30 sheep, and they returned safely.

March 30th The night of Monday the 21st of Banjaru Awwal the soldiers brought me 11 slaves.

April 3rd The night of Friday the 26th of Banjaru Awwal Atiku brought me news that the Christian wanted labourers and ordered me to get them from the pagans willingly and obediently, even though it might be by fighting them.

April 8th On Tuesday the 30th of Banjaru Awwal Ahmadu and Jauro Abba went off with my people to Mokolo and captured 23 and killed 3.

April 15th On Tuesday the 7th of Banjaru Tumbindu Becho raided in my territory from Duruk to Matakam and captured 13 slaves and 13 cattle.

May 4th On Sunday the 26th of Banjaru Sakitindu (*sic*) the Governor returned to me 410 shillings of the tax, and there remained with him 490 shillings.

May 12th On Monday the 5th of Banjaru Sakitindu I sent my soldiers to Sukur and they destroyed the house of the Arnado and took a horse and seven slave girls and burnt their houses. This was on Tuesday.

May 21st On Wednesday the 14th of Banjaru Sakitindu I sent soldiers to Hudgudur and they captured 20 slave girls.

June 3rd On Tuesday the 27th of Banjaru Sakitindu Abd Mubi arrived and with him my friend, who gave me 551 cartridges.

June 11th On Wednesday the 5th of Sumatendu Waube I sent Barde to Wula, and they captured six slave girls and ten cattle, and killed three men.

June 14th On Saturday the 8th of Sumatendu Waube Barto, Muhammadu and Buba Towo returned from their journey and brought goods which the Christian sent me—namely 32 lengths of cloth.

June 18th On Wednesday the 12th of Sumatendu Waube a Hausa-man brought me 21 cartridges.

June 19th On Thursday the 14th [*sic*] of Sumatendu Waube Musa Kufur brought me 400 cartridges.

June 21st On Saturday the 16th of Sumatendu Waube I sent Barde to Mokolo and he captured 31 slave girls and eight cattle.

June 25th On Wednesday the 20th of Sumatendu Waube I sent my people to the pagans of Midiri and Bula and they captured 48 slave girls and 26 cattle and we killed five persons.

July 6th On Sunday the 1st of Wairordu Sumaye I sent my people to Sina and they captured 30 cattle and six slave girls.

On Sunday the 3rd of Wairordu Sumaye (*sic*) the Ober-Lieutenant [*sic*] entered Mubi and met with Yunus.

July 12th On Saturday the 7th of Wairordu Sumaye (*sic*) I sent soldiers to Sina and the Sina pagans drove them off.

July 20th On Sunday the 15th of Wairordu Sumaye I sent my people to Sukur and we killed 15 and wounded very many and captured 15.

July 23rd On Wednesday the 18th of Wairordu Sumaye I returned the people of Sina six of their pagans.

August 12th On Tuesday the 9th of Ramadhan the Arnado of Tur, Tada, died, and on the same day the Arnado of Gedel also died. So I ordered them to pay three calves and 30 goats, and I ordered the people of Tur to pay two slave girls.

August 14th On Thursday the 11th of Ramadhan Madi Kachab arrived from Maifoni with 700 cartridges.

August 18th On Monday the 15th of Ramadhan the Oberleutnant "Faizi" visited the pagans of Pellam and stopped there.

August 23rd On Saturday the 20th of Ramadhan the Oberleutnant arrived in Madagali and spent five days there.

August 28th On Thursday the 25th of Ramadhan he left Madagali and went to Duhu.

In the month of Juldandu (no date) the Governor and the Oberleutnant departed and I took leave of them safely. He sent Kobawim and Rizku to Gaur, and God be praised for that.

September 28th On Sunday the 26th of Juldandu "Masa" and two White Men arrived.

September 30th On Tuesday the 28th of Juldandu I heard that the Christian "Masa" had lost his way on the road.

October 30th On Thursday the 29th of Siutorandu Muhammadu returned from his journey to Ngaundere to the Christian named "Mutamfania," who gave me 50 shillings.

(This page [MS p. 13] contains entries concerning petty trading transactions, visits of his to places in the vicinity of Madagali, and other matters of little interest.)

December 20th On Friday the 20th of Haram Awwal my son Yaya finished the Quran [Qur'an], and I gave him a slave girl and a cow.

1914

January 2nd On Thursday the 4th of Tumbindu Haramji I sent Yasin on a journey to Ngaundere and sent the Governor a black horse. I also gave them 4 horses to sell.

(The rest of this page [MS p. 14] is concerned with a bare record of his journeys during which he visited Mubi.)

(This page [MS p. 15] is only a half page and the entries are repeated with some small additions on page 16.)

February 20th On Friday the 24th of Haram Akhir Oberleutnant "Ruskis" began to build a Rest House on the top of Wurdere Hill, but whether it will be finished by nightfall I do not know.

February 23rd On Monday the 27th of Haram Akhir I left the Christian and he went on to Duhu.

February 28th On Saturday the 12th of Banjaru Awwal Yunus and Kaigamma Bakari went to see the Christian and brought back altogether from him 950 shillings.

(MS p. 15 gives the date as Banjaru Awwal 2nd, which is more likely to be correct.)

March 12th On the night of the 14th of Banjaru Awwal there was an eclipse of the moon.

(The rest of this page [MS p. 16] contains records of his movements, of a fire in one of the quarters of Madagali town, and of petty trading incidents.)

May 12th On Tuesday the 15th of Banjaru Sakitindu I heard that the Oberleutnant had arrived at Wandei, I left Nyibango and went to Mayo Tapare.

May 13th On Wednesday the 16th of Banjaru Sakitindu the Oberleutnant arrived at the Rest House at Wandei. He gave me 140 shillings.

(The rest of this page [MS p. 17] contains details concerning trading expeditions, an entry about a violent dust-storm and similar matters of little interest.)

June 2nd On Tuesday the 7th of Sumatendu Waube I appointed Takma Arnado Pellam and he gave me his daughter.

June 13th On Saturday the 18th of Sumatendu Waube I received a letter from the Christians telling me that they had taken away from me the pagans of Sirak, Mufuli and Midi?i.

July 4th On Saturday the 10th of Wairordu Sumatendu Waube (*sic*) I sent the clerk (?presumably at Marua) a horse, but I do not know whether he will accept it.

August 18th On Tuesday the 25th of Ramadhan Headman Umaru arrived with the news that there had been a battle between the English and the Germans. On the German side 500 were killed and on the English 443.

September 1st On Tuesday the 10th of Juldandu Atiku returned from Garua with news of a fight between the English and the Germans.

September 6th On Sunday the 15th of Juldandu a letter arrived from Garua to inform me that the Germans had driven back the English and scattered them. He ordered me to send him 100 carriers.

September 7th On Monday the 16th of Juldandu I sent Ardo Yaji and ten horsemen with the 100 carriers.

September 12th On Saturday the 21st of Juldandu I received news that the English had sent Ardo Michika back to Michika. On the same day a messenger arrived with the news that the Christians had fined Audu 300 shillings.

September 16th On Wednesday 25th of Juldandu an Englishman arrived in Mandara and ordered horses from me, taking 22. I accompanied them to Jenge and then returned to my house owing to the lying of the Sultan of Mandara.

September 25th On Friday the 4th of Siutorandu I sent the remaining five horses to the English at Mandara.

September 28th On Monday the 7th of Siutorandu I sent Maliki to the Emir of Yola.

October 7th On Wednesday the 16th of Siutorandu news arrived from Mubi that Musa Malam Bawa had arrived with soldiers to look at the Rest House at Mubi.

October 11th On Sunday the 20th of Siutorandu Hamma Abdullah returned from Mandara with the price of the horses—3192/6d.

October 12th On Monday the 21st of Siutorandu an Englishman named Mr. {Lyon} arrived.

October 18th On Sunday the 27th of Siutorandu Mr. {Lyon} left Madagali.

October 20th On Tuesday the 29th of Siutorandu Mr. {Lyon} left Madagali and went to Mandara.

October 26th On Monday the 5th of Laihaji I sent the Christians at Mandara a present valued at 40 shillings (? the Arabic is a little obscure)

November 6th On Friday the 17th of Laihaji I sent soldiers to Jenge and they arrested the Bulama on account of certain things, and I gave the Sergeant-Major 100 and some of them 20 and some of them ten and some of them 20 and some of them seven (the articles given are not stated).

November 7th On Saturday the 18th of Laihaji we counted the number of my horsemen who had no horses, and they came to 47. On the same day the pagans of Subala ransomed their women at 36 shillings a woman.

November 23rd On Monday the 4th of Haram Awwal the Governor sent me 500 shillings.

November 28th On Saturday the 11th of Haram Awwal I raided Gumasi and took 20 cattle.

December 3rd On Thursday the 15th of Haram Awwal I raided Tur and captured 50 cattle.

December 12th On Saturday the 24th of Muharram Awwal the French Christian arrived in Madagali and the people of Madagali all ran away. There were four White Men.

December 14th On Monday the 25th of Muharram Awwal I returned with my people to Madagali.

December 16th On Wednesday the 28th of Haram Awwal I sent the Frenchmen 77 shillings.

1915

January 16th On Saturday the 29th of Tumbindu Haramji we counted the cattle and found that in two months I acquired 379.

January 19th On Tuesday the 2nd of Haram Akhir the Christians came to Mandara.

January 22nd On Friday the 5th of Haram Akhir a Christian arrived in Madagali from Michika and ordered me to proceed to Mandara, but I refused.

January 23rd On Saturday the 6th of Haram Akhir the Christian Colour-Sergeant started off for Mandara with my son Ahmad.

February 2nd On Tuesday the 18th of Haram Akhir we raided Kurang and got 100 cattle. Governor "Diri" (?Dühring) fought with the English and killed two Whitemen of the English. This occurred on Friday the 12th (*sic*) of Haram Akhir.

(No date) I raided Humumzi and captured four slave girls and 20 cattle.

February 27th On Saturday the 11th of Banjaru Awwal in the middle of the night I heard that a Christian named Mr. "Gaya" had arrived from Duhu.

March 10th On Wednesday the 22nd of Banjaru Awwal the Christian named Mr. "Gaya" left Madagali and went to Duhu.

(The rest of this page [MS p. 23] is occupied with trading affairs, gifts to him from pagans and others, and his own movements. He also states he divided the pagans of Sukur into two separate sections.)

March 31st On Wednesday the 14th of Banjaru Tumbindu the Christian Mr. "Gaya" arrived in Madagali and stayed one night.

April 1st On Thursday the 15th of Banjaru Tumbindu the Christian Mr. "Gaya" left for Mandara.

April 28th On Wednesday the 13th of Banjaru Sakitindu 12 soldiers arrived at Mandara.

(The rest of the page [MS p. 24] is mainly concerned with his movements in the vicinity of Madagali.)

May 15th On Saturday the 30th of Banjaru Sakitindu I took on the devotional practices of the Mahdist sect under Malam Muhammad's instruction.

June 5th On Saturday the 21st of Sumatendu Waube Magaji and Sarkin Hausawa returned from their journey to the Christian at Mandara. Everything had turned out successfully and I was very pleased with them.

(The rest of this page [MS p. 25] contains entries regarding his own movements, small trading details, and the record of a heavy fall of rain.)

June 17th On Thursday the 3rd of Wairordu Sumaye I received news that the English had captured Garua.

June 24th On Thursday the 11th of Wairordu Sumaye I sent Kachella Suleiman to the Captain with 40 chickens.

June 25th On Friday the 12th of Wairordu Sumaye I raided Tufu and captured eight slave girls.

June 30th On Wednesday the 16th of Sha'aban I raided Kamale and captured 56 cattle and 40 slaves.

(These 3 pages [MS pp. 27–29] contain nothing of interest. They consist entirely of records of his own movements, details of trading expeditions with lists of articles he purchased, and records of gifts to and from his own people. He relates that the Emir of Mubi married his daughter, and he notes that his stomach first began to cause him trouble, a matter which is referred to in several later entries.)

[August 25th] On Wednesday the 13th of Juldandu I sent 200 labourers to Garua.

November 30th On Tuesday the 22nd of Haram 13 soldiers came from Garua to investigate into the lies that Bakari and Yaji had been telling.

December 3rd On Friday the 25th of Haram I set off with the soldiers on a journey to Garua.

December 17th On Friday the 9th of Tumbindu Haramji I entered Garua and stopped in the Government Station in order that I might be treated for my illness by the doctor. I remained there four days.

[December 21st] On Tuesday I had to fight cases against Rufa'u, Abdu, Jabril and Bakari Duhu, but I defeated them all. I then stayed two more days there.

December 23rd On Thursday the 14th of Tumbindu Haramji I left the Government Station and went to my own house.

December 28th On Tuesday the 19th of Tumbindu Haramji I left Garua safely.

1916

January 18th On Tuesday the 12 of Haram Akhir I sent off 370 labourers.

January 23rd On Sunday the 17th of Haram Akhir Midaina died killed by Bulama Hamad's witchcraft, so I sentenced Bulama after trying him.

January 30th On Sunday the 24th of Haram Akhir at night Salman's house was burnt down and at the same time 1000 cartridges of mine were burnt.

In the month of Banjaru Awwal I raided Kanikela and captured five slave girls, whom I let go, and 20 cattle.

February 12th On Saturday the 8th of Banjaru Awwal I arrived in Garua and saw the Captain, who told me to wait until the Colonel came back. He told me he would send labourers to put up a house for me, until the Colonel arrived. Then he said, "You are a big chief; I will not make you stay here with us, but go to your house and settle down. You know what is befitting a chief."

February 14th On Monday the 10th of Banjaru Awwal I went to see the Captain and found Jauro Kova had also come there from Yola. I then left the Captain safely.

February 15th On Tuesday the 11th of Banjaru Awwal I left Garua.

February 17th On Thursday the 13th of Banjaru Awwal I heard that Jauro Kova had also left and gone to Yola.

February 23rd On Wednesday the 19th of Banjaru Awwal I reached Mubi and the same day sent Bula Soja to the Captain with three cows.

March 15th On Wednesday the 10th of Banjaru Tumbindu I made a raid and captured cattle from Mokolo, and on Friday I captured cattle from Lamsa [Lamsha] and Dubur. The total number of cattle was 167.

[The following two entries are out of sequence.]

March 25th On Saturday the 20th of Banjaru Tumbindu I burnt the house of a pagan named Dufai.

March 21st On Tuesday the 16th of Banjaru Tumbindu I sent Jauro to the pagans of Loko and captured nine slave girls and 11 cattle.

April 1st On Saturday the 27th of Banjaru Tumbindu Kabala returned from his journey to Garua with news that the Captain had refused the calves.

April 4th On Tuesday the 30th of Banjaru Tumbindu Bakari Banel brought me a German rifle.

April 9th On Sunday the 5th of Banjaru Sakitindu I raided Hida and captured 30 cattle and 30 slave girls.

April 16th On Sunday the 12th of Banjaru Sakitindu Ardo Yaji and Bula returned from their journey to Garua with news of a quarrel between the English and the French.

April 22nd On Saturday the 18th of Banjaru Sakitindu Barde raided Mokolo and captured 40 cattle and (rest deleted).

May 7th On Sunday the 4th of Sumatendu Waube I heard that the Christians with Sheikh Sanda had arrived at Isge.

May 16th On Tuesday the 13th of Sumatendu Waube I sent my men to Kekele, but on Wednesday they made a mess of the expedition, and my slave Audu Wemgo was killed, as also were seven pagans of Humuchi together with some pagans of Pellam.

May 31st On Wednesday the 27th of Sumatendu Waube the Christians collected all the chiefs at the Government Station, and the Colonel gave me a saddle with a high pommel.

June 18th On Sunday the 16th of Wairordu Sumaye I left Mayo Tapare and met the Christian named "Sarsar" {?Sergeant} at Duhu.

June 19th On Monday the 17th of Wairordu Sumaye we marked out the boundary between me and Bakari Duhu.

(The rest of this page [MS p. 35] is occupied with a list of presents given him by various Madagali people to welcome him on his return from Garua, and with a record of visits he paid to his various houses in the neighbourhood of Madagali.)

(This page [MS p. 36] contains records of visits to his various houses in the vicinity of Madagali, details of trading transactions, an entry recording a present he sent to the Emir of Mandara, and other matters of little interest.)

July 23rd On Sunday the 22nd of Ramadhan I raided the pagans of Hindu and captured 12 slaves.

July 27th On Thursday the 26th of Ramadhan I heard that the Commandant of Garua had left and been succeeded by a Colonel. So I sent Kachella Suleiman the same day to Garua to offer my greetings.

August 7th On Monday the 7th of Juldandu we raided Mokolo and captured 30 slaves and three cows. Barde died on the Mokolo expedition.

August 18th On Friday the 18th of Juldandu I appointed as chief of my soldiers a man named Fadhl al Nar. We reckoned up the possessions of Barde which came to 40 slaves and ten horses.

August 27th On Sunday the 27th of Juldandu my son Yahya was killed by the pagans of Gaur and his slave wounded.

September 25th On Monday the 26th of Siutorandu the Christians "Itina" and "Sarsar" (? Lieutenant and Sergeant) arrived and I gave them 14 goats and three cows. He gave me six more villages—Mugil and Humuchi and others. He also gave me 60 shillings.

September 27th On Wednesday the 28th of Siutorandu the Lieutenant left for Mandara and the Sergeant with Yerima Baba went off to raid the pagans of Gaur.

September 29th On Friday the 30th of Siutorandu Yerima Baba returned from raiding Gaur. The pagans had driven off my people, wounding four men and one horse.

October 6th On Friday the 8th of Laihaji I sent my soldiers against the Sina pagans in the Daba area, and they captured 34 slaves and seven cows. They killed five people.

October 19th On Thursday the 21st of Laihaji I sent my soldiers to Sukur and they captured 18 slaves.

October 22nd On Sunday the 24th of Laihaji Mumun came and said that the Germans had gone.

   (The rest of this page [MS p. 39] is concerned mainly with trading matters, his own movements and the exchange of presents with various people.)

October 28th On Saturday the 30th of Laihaji I raided Mufuli and killed four men and ten cattle.

November 4th On Saturday the 7th of Haram Awwal I sent Sarkin Hausawa Audu to Yola to offer my condolences on the death of Bobbo Ahmadu, and I sent the Emir of Yola a horse.

November 7th On Tuesday the 10th of Haram Awwal we divided 40 shillings on all the houses. (? The tax was fixed at 40 shillings a house.)

   (The rest of the page [MS p. 40] is concerned with an account of his own movements.)

December 1st On Friday the 5th of Tumbindu Haramji I sent my people to raid the pagans named Tille and they killed five men and captured eight slaves and 18 cattle.

(The rest of the page [MS p. 41] is concerned with trading affairs and his movements.)

December 9th On Saturday the 13th of Tumbindu Haramji Muhammad Bintu and Audu Sarkin Hausawa returned from their journey to Yola, bringing a gown which the Emir of Yola gave me.

The same day I sent my son Abd al Rahman to the school of the Christians at Garua.

December 14th On Thursday the 18th of Tumbindu Haramji I raided Hindu and captured 53 slaves and seven cattle, and killed three men.

December 19th On Tuesday the 23rd of Tumbindu Haramji my uncle brought me a few cartridges.

1917

January 2nd On Tuesday the 7th of Haram Akhir I arrived at Garua and had a discussion concerning two slaves. There was also talk about rifles.

January 3rd On Wednesday the 8th of Haram Akhir I sent Jauro to Madagali regarding the rifles.

January 12th On Friday the 16th of Haram Akhir Jauro returned with the rifles.

January 14th On Sunday the 15th of Haram Akhir the Christians and all the horsemen had horse races.

January 17th On Wednesday the 22nd of Haram Akhir in the evening the Captain returned me my rifles and also my slave from Libam. He also decided the case between me and Bakari Duhu concerning our boundary, in which I won.

January 18th On Thursday the 23rd of Haram Akhir I left Garua early in the morning.

January 28th On Sunday the 4th of Banjaru Awwal I raided Gedel and captured two cows and [illegible] boys.

February 2nd On Friday the 9th of Banjaru Awwal I raided Midiri and captured four slaves and seven cattle.

February 4th On Sunday the 11th of Banjaru Awwal I received news of the death of Sheikh Sanda.

February 25th On Sunday the 2nd of Banjaru Tumbindu I received 50 shillings and two gowns for a slave girl.

March 12th On Monday the 17th of Banjaru Tumbindu I raided Hindu and captured 20 slaves.

(The rest of the page [MS p. 45] is concerned with his own movements and with trading matters. He also records that there were a number of Bororo in his area with a large number of horses.)

April 8th On Sunday the 15th of Banjaru Sakitindu I raided Mokolo and captured 30 slaves and 13 cattle.

(The rest of the page [MS p. 46] is concerned with presents to him from the Bororo Fulani, with his own movements, and similar matters. He records a thunder-storm, and mentions the death of a son of his.)

April 20th On Friday the 27th of Banjaru Sakitindu Buba Jam returned from Garua with an order for me to go to Marua.

May 7th On Monday the 15th of Sumatendu Waube Fadhl al Nar raided the Uba pagans and captured four slaves, 27 cattle, 62 goats, 11 gowns and a fez. We killed 12 men.

May 12th On Saturday the 20th of Sumatendu Waube I sent Fadhl al Nar to Libam and he captured 25 cattle.

May 21st On Monday the 29th of Sumatendu Waube I entered Marua and gave the Captain eight cows. He refused to accept them, however, and took a calf.

May 24th On Thursday the 2nd of Wairordu Sumaye I left Marua.

(The bulk of the last two pages [MS pp. 47–48] is concerned with his journey to Marua and the incidents on the way and part of his return journey.)

June 5th On Tuesday the 14th of Wairordu Sumaye my people raided Sinagali and captured ten cattle and 40 goats.

June 8th On Friday the 17th of Sairordu [*sic*] Sumaye Bajam and Harun returned from Garua and said that the Commandant instructed me that I should deal with Garua and not Marua.

June 21st On Thursday the 30th of Wairordu Sumaye I raided Hindu and captured 11 slaves.

July 4th On Wednesday the 13th of Ramadhan I went to Guzum and met the Christian named "Lisdan."

July 6th On Friday the 15th of Ramadhan "Lisdan" rode along the French border and the following day along the German border (? Arabic obscure). He told me not to have anything to do with Jauro until the Captain at Marua arrived.

The same day the pagans at Duhu marked out their boundary as passing by the other side of my house. So "Lisdan" arrested Arnado Usmanu for his offence in regard to this matter of my house.

On the same day I left him and went to Zu and he ordered me to proceed to Marua.

July 13th On Friday the 22nd of Ramadhan I had a short talk with the Captain (i.e., in Marua).

July 14th On Saturday the 23rd of Ramadhan the Captain had some horse-races.

July 15th On Sunday the 24th of Ramadhan the Christian collected the people and explained the administration of justice and the criminal law.

July 16th On Monday the 25th of Ramadhan I went to the Government Station and talked over my case against Bakari Duhu. They said they would leave the matter until after the 'Id, when the Captain would go to Gulak and Duhu. I left Bulama and Bakari Duhu to talk over the matter with the Lieutenant.

July 17th On Tuesday the 26th of Ramadhan I departed from Marua, leaving Bulama and Ardo Yaji to fight the case of Bakari Duhu. They defeated him.

July 19th On Thursday the 28th of Ramadhan I raided the pagans of Lamsha and got 50 slaves.

August 1st On Wednesday the 12th of Juldandu I sent my people to the Emir to raid the pagans called Mijilu.

August 8th On Wednesday the 29th (*sic*) of Juldandu I raided the pagans called Fakara and got 27 slaves from my own territory and 23 from Fakara together with seven cows.

August 12th On Sunday the 23rd of Juldandu two rifles arrived.

August 16th On Thursday the 27th of Juldandu I sent Fadhl al Nar with his men to raid Sukur and they captured 80 slaves, of whom I gave away 40. We killed 27 men and women and 17 children.

On the same day I sent a force to raid Dufur and they killed eight pagans. The pagans killed the leader of my force and captured one rifle.

August 26th On Sunday the 8th of Siutorandu I fixed the penalty for every slave who leaves me without cause at four slave girls and if he is a poor man 200 lashes.

September 6th On Thursday the 19th of Siutorandu I sent Fadhl al Nar to raid Hindu and we captured two women.

September 15th On Saturday the 27th of Siutorandu I sent Liman and Misau to the Christian with two horses.

September 21st On Friday the 3rd of Laihaji I raided Gedel and captured eight slaves.

September 27th On Thursday the 10th of Laihaji the Captain arrived and stopped at the Rest House without my knowing.

October 4th On Thursday the 17th of Laihaji I sent Bula with my soldiers to raid Midiri and other places. They captured three slaves.

October 9th On Tuesday the 22nd of Laihaji I sent Fadhl al Nar to raid the pagans of Wula and they captured 10 slaves and killed two men.

October 16th On Tuesday the 29th of Dhahaiya I heard news from Mubi that the Lieutenant had arrived at Mubi.

October 19th On Friday the 2nd of Muharram I raided the pagans of Hindu and captured eight slaves and killed five men.

November 1st On Thursday the 15th of Haram Awwal I raided Gumusi and captured three slaves.

November 6th On Tuesday the 20th of Haram Awwal I raided Dufur and killed two people.

November 7th On Wednesday the 21st of Haram Awwal Bula gave me a slave girl as the price of his getting the pagans of Dubulum. I do not think that they will be in his control for 12 months, for he is a mischief-maker in the land.

November 8th On Thursday the 22nd of Haram Awwal a letter arrived summoning me to Marua and God is knowing.

November 13th On Tuesday the 27th of Haram Awwal I left Madagali to go to Marua and stopped at my house at Mayo Tapare. On the same day I sent Yerima Abba to raid Garta and he captured 20 cattle and eight slaves.

November 19th On Monday the 4th of Tumbindu Haramji I went to the Government Station (in Marua) with the tax money and other things and gave them to the Lieutenant. Two Fulani had a complaint against me but I won.

November 21st On Wednesday the 5th of Tumbindu Haramji I took my leave of the Captain. He told me that the Bau pagans belonged to me.

November 24th On Saturday the 8th of Tumbindu Haramji I sent Fadhl al Nar to raid with his people and they captured eight cattle.

November 25th On Sunday the 9th of Tumbindu Haramji I went myself and raided Mokolo and captured 30 cattle but we did not count the dead.

December 1st On Saturday the 15th of Tumbindu Haramji we counted the tax of the whole land of Madagali and it came to 1803 shillings and 144 cattle.

December 11th On Tuesday the 25th of Tumbindu Haramji the Captain arrived from Wandei and said he wanted to tour my land. I gave him two oxen and he gave me 20 five-franc pieces.

December 12th On Wednesday the 26th of Tumbindu Haramji the Captain left Madagali and went to Durei.

December 25th On Tuesday the 10th of Haram Akhir the Captain returned at night and gave me 11 five-franc pieces.

December 28th On Friday the 13th of Haram Akhir I left Madagali to go to Marua.

December 30th On Sunday the 15th of Haram Akhir I reached Mokolo and sent Fadhl al Nar to raid Dufur. They captured eight cattle and killed two men.

1918

January 3rd On Thursday the 19th of Haram Akhir I went to the Government Station (in Marua) and then returned home.

January 4th On Friday the 20th of Haram Akhir I had a case with the Mokolo pagans which I won.

January 9th On Wednesday the 25th of Haram Akhir I had a case with Bakari Duhu and defeated him. He swore a false oath on the Qur'an.

On the same day the Captain returned the Mokolo pagans to me once more. I then took my leave and left Marua.

January 18th On Friday the 4th of Banjaru Awwal I sent Gora to Yola with 60 shillings.

February 19th On Tuesday the 7th of Banjaru Tumbindu I sent Fadhl al Nar to raid the Moda pagans named Dubugu. They captured 30 cattle of the humpless variety, five slaves and 44 goats.

(This page [MS p. 59] contains little of interest: he appointed one Bulama Kabarawa chief of Sukur; he received presents from various pagans; he sent his daughter to Moda to be married and he records that there were signs that rain had fallen one night.)

February 26th On Tuesday the 14th of Banjaru Tumbindu some pagans fled from English territory and entered my land. They numbered 15 houses.

March 21st On Thursday the 8th of Banjaru Sakitindu I went to Mokolo and sent my people to raid the Mokolo pagans. They captured nine slaves and ten cattle.

March 25th On the 12th of Banjaru Sakitindu at night a man named Umaru Banu came to me and I made an agreement with him either that he would kill Arnado Mokolo or that he would ruin him.

March 26th On Tuesday the 23rd (*sic*) of Banjaru Sakitindu I went in person and raided Mokolo. I captured 120 persons and had three of my men wounded. We killed a large number of them.

April 4th On Thursday the 22nd of Banjaru Sakitindu I received information that the tax was to be four shillings a man and if English money was paid three shillings and three pence.

April 11th On Thursday the 28th [*sic*] of Banjaru Sakitindu my people raided the pagans of Dinlim and captured 14 slaves, 33 cattle, 68 sheep and 45 goats, the total of the livestock being 118.

April 27th On Saturday the 15th of Sumatendu Waube I sent my horsemen and Fadhl al Nar's people to raid Bau. They captured 28 cattle.

April 29th On Monday the 17th of Sumatendu Waube my people returned to Bau and captured 40 cattle.

May 18th On Saturday the 7th of Wairordu Sumaye Umaru Shamaki re-turned from selling my cattle in Mubi. He got 370 shillings for them, 99 shillings being English money.

(The rest of this page [MS p. 62] is concerned practically entirely with a record of his movements in the vicinity of Madagali.)

May 23rd On Thursday the 12th of Wairordu Sumaye the pagans of Wakka fought with the pagans of Ngenge and they killed two Wakka men and burnt the Ngenge houses.

(The rest of the page [MS p. 63] is concerned with his own move-ments, some trading incidents, and the exchange of presents with his followers.)

July 3rd On Wednesday the 23rd of Ramadhan I fixed the price of Yerima Baba's horse at three slave girls.

July 11th On Thursday the 2nd of Juldandu I sent my people to raid Midiri and they captured 31 cattle and three slaves.

(The rest of the page [MS p. 64] contains records of his movements, details of presents he gave his followers and a note that he received orders about the tax.)

July 15th On Monday the 6th of Juldandu I entered Marua and met Captain "Duru." I gave him a horse and five calves.

July 16th On Tuesday the 7th of Juldandu I went to the Government Station and had a dispute with Bakari Duhu in which I defeated him. I found there a pagan named Badima. On the same day I left Marua.

July 19th On Friday the 10th of Juldandu I sent Fadhl al Nar off at night to raid the pagans of Ramdere. They captured 33 cattle and 17 slaves and 65 sheep.

July 24th On Wednesday the 15th of Juldandu the pagans of Mugudi raided Ardo Harun and wounded him.

July 25th On Thursday the 16th of Juldandu I raided the pagans of Wulunku, capturing 15 slaves and 60 livestock. The son of Joda was killed.

(Here a line at the bottom of the MS has been cut off.)

August 20th On Tuesday the 12th of Siutorandu Jauro and Wanga raided Arnado Muduvu, named Suvu, and killed him and his son and captured 13 of the people of his house.

(The rest of the page [MS p. 66] is concerned with his own movements, visits of various persons to him, and presents to him from pagans whom he had raided.)

August 31st On Saturday the 23rd of Siutorandu Bajam and Maliki returned from their journey to Marua and said they had fought the case against Bakari Duhu and had defeated him and had got back for me the pagan girl. So I gave them a slave girl.

September 5th On Thursday the 28th of Siutorandu the Lieutenant marked out the boundary at Ghania and they took away from me some land in Mandara territory. The same day they arrived in Madagali and spent three days and collected the tax.

September 8th On Sunday the 1st of Laihaji I went out with the Christian and I stopped at my house in Wuro Alhamdu while the Christian stopped at Gulak.

September 9th On Monday the 2nd of Laihaji the Christian started off and marked the boundary. We got possession of the whole of Duhu "bush," and as a result Bakari Duhu ran away and crossed over the river.

September 11th On Wednesday the 5th of Laihaji the Lieutenant went off to Moda.

September 15th On Sunday the 7th of Laihaji Jauro raided the pagans named Wudila [Wudala?] and captured 21 slaves.

September 29th On Sunday the 22nd of Laihaji Fadhl al Nar raided Futu in the morning and captured 23 cattle, 22 gowns, three red fezzes and 15 goats.

October 4th On Friday the 27th of Laihaji I heard that the people of Michika had sent to Marua to complain about the Futu affair.

October 16th On Wednesday the 9th of Haram Bakr Guldum brought me the stocks (?) of two rifles and I gave him ten shillings. I decided I would give him a slave girl.

October 19th On Saturday the 12th of Haram Mishan returned from his journey to Marua with a letter from the Lieutenant in which he ordered me to arrest Bakari Duhu. He also told me to collect the tax from the pagans of Isge. This I will do willingly and obediently.

On the same day the pagans of Midiri brought me a calf. The pagans of Bau, after running away from fear, also brought me a calf.

October 28th On Monday the 21st of Haram Awwal Bello and Gora came to me from their journey to Fort Lamy. The daughter of Rabeh sent me a rifle, which I bought for 50 five-franc pieces.

November 1st On Friday the 25th of Haram Awwal at night news about the tax arrived from the Lieutenant. In the morning I sent off Muhammad Kobo and Buba to Marua regarding the lying news of a fight between the French and the Germans.

November 5th On Tuesday the 29th of Haram Awwal we heard that Moda and Michika had had a fight in which one man was wounded.

November 10th On Sunday the 5th of Tumbindu Haramji we raided Zakura and captured 18 cattle and three slaves.

November 18th On Monday the 14th of Tumbindu Haramji I sent Bula and Wanga to raid the Isge pagans and they captured 22 cattle, 18 slaves and ten goats.

November 23rd On Saturday the 18th of Tumbindu Haramji a letter arrived from the Captain in which he told us that our news regarding the French and the Germans was incorrect.

December 6th On Friday the last day of Haram Tumbindu I sent some honey and 50 shillings to the Captain.

(The rest of the page [MS p. 71] contains records of his own movements, details of presents given him by various pagans and others, and an entry regarding a trading expedition to Kano.)

December 25th On Wednesday the 20th of Haram Akhir I raided Bau and captured 52 cattle, 29 slaves and 63 goats.

December 26th On Thursday the 21st of Haram Akhir I sent Muhammad Bindiga to Marua with 30 cattle and 40 goats representing the Bau tax.

December 28th On Saturday the 23rd of Haram Akhir I sent mounted men and footmen to Sugel [Bugel] and they captured 21 cattle and 4 persons and killed one horse.

December 31st On Tuesday the 26th of Haram Akhir I received a horse from Hayatu of Mubi.

1919

January 27th On Monday the 24th of Banjaru Awwal on my arrival in Madagali I heard that while I was in Tongo the pagans of Lamsha killed

Abbo and his horse and his slave. Then I sent Fadhl al Nar with his people to raid the Dufur pagans. They spent three nights there on the hill and on Friday came down again. The same day Yerima Baba returned from his journey to Marua regarding the tax. There remained 2020 German shillings outstanding. They captured 19 of the Dufur pagans.

February 5th On Wednesday the 3rd of Banjaru Tumbindu I sent Fadhl al Nar with his people to the area of the Tekem people and they captured 120 and killed one man.

February 14th On Friday the 12th of Banjaru Tumbindu I received a letter from the Captain demanding soldiers from me.

February 20th On Thursday the 18th of Banjaru Tumbindu my people and Moda's people raided Tur and captured 70 slaves, 14 cows and 90 sheep and goats.

February 21st On Friday the 19th of Banjaru Tumbindu I gave the Emir of Moda three slaves and his soldiers two cows and ten goats.

February 22nd On Saturday the 20th of Banjaru Tumbindu I sold one of my slaves for 260 shillings in Mubi.

February 25th On Tuesday the 23rd of Banjaru Tumbindu Gora brought me 50 cartridges.

February 26th On Wednesday the 24th of Banjaru Tumbindu Bello brought me 20 cartridges.

March 1st On Saturday the 27th of Banjaru Tumbindu Jarma Bajam arrived with news that the Commandant had spent the night at Disa. So the same day I sent off Jarma and Barade to the Commandant regarding my pagans in Gwoza and others. I promised them that if they got what I wanted from him I would give them a slave-girl each. I told Malam Muhammad something so that Kaigamma Bakr may hanker after something (?).

   The same day I made arrangement with my scribe Amin by which if I do a certain thing the Christian will not stop at Madagali. I gave him a slave for this, and if God does prevent him from staying here I will give him two slaves (?probably refers to a charm).

March 2nd On Sunday the 28th of Tumbindu Haramji (*sic*) the Commandant arrived at Madagali and stayed for two nights. He paid 50 shillings.

March 4th On Tuesday the 1st of Banjaru Sakitindu the Commandant left Madagali.

March 12th On Wednesday the 9th of Banjaru Sakitindu I sent Dakare to Garua to buy cartridges from Hama Yadam. I gave him 30 shillings.

March 13th On Thursday the 10th of Banjaru Sakitindu I raided in the Uba hills and captured 31 slaves and gave the Emir of Uba 20 of them. I also got 17 cows and gave the Emir of Uba eight, and 160 sheep, giving the Emir of Uba 80. I also captured 34 articles of various kinds.

March 20th On Thursday the 17th of Banjaru Sakitindu Moda's people were badly defeated in a raid on their pagans. There were 24 of them, their leaders being Waziri Kadiri, Durtu and Kachella Abdu.

March 21st On the 18th of Banjaru Sakitindu I went down to my house in the direction of Mugudi and sent my soldiers to the pagans of Moda in order to bury their dead.

(The rest of the page [MS p. 76] is concerned with his own movements, some trading transactions, including the selling of a horse to Hayatu of Mubi, and a visit of Ardo Michika to him.)

April 13th On Saturday the 10th of Sumatendu Waube Hamman Dakare brought me 25 cartridges.

April 14th On Sunday the 11th of Sumatendu Waube the Emir of Mubi sent me ten cartridges.

April 17th On Thursday the 15th of Sumatendu Waube I heard that the Emir of Kano had died, may God pardon him. The same day Madi Kuchab sent me 22 cartridges from Fort Lamy.

April 21st On Monday the 20th of Sumatendu Waube my uncle arrived from Dikwa with 16 cartridges.

April 26th On Saturday the 24th of Sumatendu Waube I took over the Beit al Mal, and there will be a fine for every one who leaves the Mahdist sect; and I started with Bakari Hamarwabe. (The Arabic is a little obscure, but there seems little doubt that this is the meaning.)

April 29th On Tuesday the 27th of Sumatendu Waube I raided the pagans of Rowa and captured 50 cattle and 33 slaves. We calculated my fifth share as 17 slaves and 25 cattle. Fadhl al Nar broke his rifle.

May 7th On Wednesday the 6th of Wairordu Sumaye I raided Sir with Lawan Aji of Gaur and we captured 8 slaves, 144 cattle and 200 sheep. We divided them as follows: I got 72 cattle, five slaves and 100 sheep and Gaur the same.

(The rest of the page [MS p. 78] is concerned with his own movements.)

May 17th On Saturday the 16th of Wairordu Sumaye I sent Burza and Ardhunga on a long journey with 1500 shillings to buy me rifles and cartridges. I gave them a slave so that they might sell him to buy themselves food.

June 6th On Friday the 7th of Ramadhan news arrived that the Christians had arrested Emir Garga of Michika.

(Other entries on this page [MS p. 79] are: his own movements, the marriage of his son, a gift of honey to the Captain, the visit of a Hausa trader from whom he bought some goods, and gifts from various persons from among his followers.)

June 19th On Thursday the 20th of Ramadhan Audu Hausa came from Kano with 600 cartridges, seven rifles and three red fezzes. He also stole 200 shillings.

July 1st On Tuesday the 2nd of Juldandu Madi Kusab brought a rifle which fired nine cartridges, which he had bought for 170 shillings.

July 8th On Tuesday the 7th of Juldandu the Lieutenant arrived at Madagali to mark the boundary between me and Isge and I gave him a horse.

July 9th On Wednesday the 10th of Juldandu I went off with the Lieutenant and climbed Wandei hill. I stopped at my house in Tongo and the Lieutenant stopped in Mugudi on the other side of the boundary between me and the Emir of Marua.

July 10th On Thursday the 11th of Juldandu I left Tongo and stopped at my land named Koshehi, while the Lieutenant left Mugudi and met me in Koshehi.

That night a letter arrived from the Captain calling me in to the celebration of the Christians.

July 11th On Friday the 12th of Juldandu I sent Yerima Abba to Marua to see the celebrations of the Captain.

July 12th On Saturday the 13th of Juldandu I received news that the pagans of Mugudi had robbed a caravan of Zira Bugel and had killed one man and captured his people and two horses.

July 15th On Tuesday the 16th of Juldandu I raided Sinagali capturing 40 cattle and 40 sheep and goats. Fadhl al Nar's rifle got broken.

July 16th On Wednesday the 17th of Juldandu Captain "Shukuga" arrived in Madagali.

July 18th On Friday the 19th of Juldandu Yerima Abba returned from the Captain's celebrations. He brought two horses belonging to the pagans of Mugudi, which he had captured from them.

July 24th On Thursday the 25th of Juldandu I sent Fadhl al Nar to raid Kamale and he captured 34 slaves, 26 cows and 130 goats.

July 27th On Sunday the 28th of Juldandu I caused the name of my land to be changed and gave away two slave girls on the occasion of changing the name, and I fixed a fine of 5s. for anyone who made a mistake in this name.

August 12th On Tuesday the 15th of Siutorandu I bought two female slaves for 160 shillings. On the same day Babel arrived with 70 cartridges

August 21st On Thursday the 23rd of Siutorandu I sentenced Wurduru to 12 months' imprisonment for killing a man of the Sina pagans.

August 26th On Tuesday the 29th of Siutorandu I sent off Juaro Bazza with 150 shillings for my own requirements and 30 shillings as a present for a clerk in Bornu.

August 28th On Thursday the 1st of Laihaji a Christian of the English came and put up in the town. So I left Mayo Tapare and went to meet him.

August 29th On Friday the 2nd of Laihaji I paid Sabel Surmatali a slave for 60 cartridges. In the future I shall buy them with cash.

September 13th On Saturday the 17th of Laihaji I left Wuro Alhamdu in order to meet the Captain at Duhu.

September 14th On Sunday the 18th of Laihaji I left Guram and the Captain left Duhu and we went to Madagali. I gave him three well-bred horses and the same day he went off to the Wandei hill and spent the night at Tongo.

September 16th On Tuesday the 20th of Laihaji I raided the pagans of Kara, who are between me and the Mandara people named Dhunfa, and we captured four slaves, of whom I returned two and kept two. We got a cow and killed four men.

October 1st On Wednesday the 5th of Haram the soldiers returned from raiding Bau and brought 25 slaves and 27 cattle. They killed four men. Sheep and goats came to 124.

October 5th On Sunday the 9th of Haram I received a letter from the Captain telling me about the tax. Each Muslim and pagan, man and woman, have to pay three francs.

October 30th On Thursday the 5th of Tumbindu Haramji I raided the Mokolo area and captured 14 people. Jauro was wounded.

November 5th On Wednesday the 11th of Tumbindu Haramji the Captain ordered me to go to Marua.

November 12th On Wednesday the 18th of Tumbindu Haramji (after arriving in Marua the previous day) I went to the Government Station and met the Commandant and the Captain. The same day I left Marua.

I bought a horse from Lawan Ania for 900 shillings English plus 100 shillings which I gave him as a present.

November 17th On Monday the 23rd of Tumbindu Haramji I sent Jauro to Bau and they captured 15 slaves.

November 26th On Wednesday the 2nd of Haram Akhir the Emir of Rei sent me seven gowns.

November 30th On Sunday the 6th of Haram Akhir at night I raided Waru and we captured 23 slaves and killed 17 men.

December 2nd On Tuesday the 8th of Haram Akhir I gave the Emir of Rei a horse, two six-year-old cows and a female slave.

December 30th On Tuesday the 7th of Banjaru Awwal I raided Wula and we captured 20 slaves.

1920

January 6th On Tuesday the 13th of Banjaru Awwal I sent Fadhl al Nar off at night to raid the area of Zira Kumbura.

January 14th In the month of Banjaru Awwal I sent Musa off with three slave girls to sell them and bring me back cash. This was on Wednesday.

February 15th On Sunday the 24th of Banjaru Tumbindu I raided the pagans of Gulak and captured 22 cattle, and from Mildu we took 13 cattle.

February 28th On Saturday the 7th of Banjaru Sakitindu I received a letter from the Captain saying he had raided the pagans of Kuhum and had captured a large quantity of cattle and sheep and had also taken 70 prisoners and killed ten.

March 11th On Thursday the 17th of Banjaru Sakitindu I sent Fadhl al Nar to raid the Gaur pagans. They captured two slaves, one of whom died, and 30 goats.

March 16th On Tuesday the 24th of Banjaru Sakitindu the Captain arrived in Madagali and at once sent soldiers to round up the Bororo cattle in Duhu. They captured 100 cattle.

March 28th On Sunday the 7th of Sumatendu Waube I sent Fadhl al Nar to raid Zugun and they captured 25 slaves. They also captured eight slaves from the Mandara pagans and killed four men. In addition they got eight cattle and 22 sheep.

March 29th On Monday the 8th of Sumatendu Waube the pagans of Mugudi raided the Kamale pagans and killed one man and wounded two. Then the Kamale pagans fought them and killed two and wounded two.

April 6th On Tuesday the 15th of Sumatendu Waube I sent Fadhl al Nar to raid the Futu pagans. They captured four slaves and 30 cattle, and killed one man.

On the same day one of my rifles was damaged while in the charge of Jauro. It was an all-round rifle.

April 10th On Saturday the 20th of Sumatendu Waube I sent Fashakha and Kalifa to raid the pagans of Lamsha and they captured eight slaves. I left them their livestock.

April 13th On Tuesday the 23rd of Sumatendu Waube I sent Fadhl al Nar against the Kalo pagans and they captured one slave and 44 cattle, and killed 25 men.

April 14th On Wednesday the 24th of Sumatendu Waube I sent Jauro and Bula against the Isge pagans and they captured 16 slaves, two horses, two donkeys and 20 goats.

April 20th On Tuesday the 30th of Sumatendu Waube I sent Fadhl al Nar to raid the pagans of Gumusi and they captured 40 cattle.

May 1st On Saturday the 11th of Wairordu Sumaye I sent Jauro Soji to the Sergeant and the soldiers of the Captain collected together and raided Gaur Habe and Shir. He gave me three cows. Because of him I found that many of my pagans ran away.

I gave Malam Muhammad two slaves as a deposit.

(This page [MS p. 92] contains only two lines; in them he says he sent a messenger to buy him a tent.)

May 8th On Saturday the 18th of Wairordu Sumaye I sent Fadhl al Nar with his people to raid the Gusdo pagans. They captured 69 slaves, 50 cattle and 160 goats.

May 12th On Wednesday the 22nd of Wairordu Sumaye I sent Jauro Soji against the Fatawi pagans. They raided them and captured 37 slaves, 100 goats and 17 cattle.

May 15th On Saturday the 25th of Wairordu Sumaye I sent Jauro Soji to raid the pagans of Gumasi. They took from them 70 slaves, 48 cattle and 90 goats.

May 19th On Wednesday the last day of Wairordu Sumaye I sent Fadhl al Nar to raid the Muktu pagans. They captured 11 slaves and 13 cattle. They killed nine of the pagans and two Michika men. One of our men was wounded.

May 28th On Friday the 9th of Sumaye a letter arrived from the Captain telling me to return the property of Isge. He added that I do not own all of the Isge land.

June 2nd On Wednesday the 14th of Sumaye I sent Fadhl al Nar against the Kiria pagans. They raided them and captured 50 slaves, 88 cattle and 50 gowns.

June 3rd On Thursday the 18th of Sumaye I sent Jauro Soji against the Gatahurki pagans. They raided them and captured 77 slaves and 40 cattle.

June 18th On Friday the last day of Sumaye on the Id al Fitr I gave my scribe Amin ibn Nakashiri a gown on my appointing him Alkali.

July 2nd On the night of the 16th of Shawwal I sent an expedition under the command of Jauro against Bau.

July 3rd On Saturday the 16th the expedition under Jauro returned with 12 prisoners and eight cows.

July 7th On Wednesday the 20th of Shawwal I raided Wula Digel and took 75 prisoners and ten cows.

July 23rd On Friday the 6th of Siutorandu I heard that the pagans of Bau had sent a deputation to me and that the party was waylaid on the road by pagans of Wusfu, who killed one of them.

July 24th On Saturday the 8th of Siutorandu I heard news that Abangu's pagans had raided his brother, the pagans of Wangila, and had had two men killed and wounded. Three of Wangila's men were killed. When I heard this I sent an expedition under Fadhl al Nar to capture Abangu and his people, and they captured him and everyone with him.

July 30th On Friday the 13th of Siutorandu my messenger Gora returned from his journey with 130 cartridges, some good and some bad.

August 2nd On Monday the 16th of Siutorandu a letter arrived from the Captain saying that the English were coming: this is what he wrote (?4 words of the Arabic being half obliterated). Then on Wednesday another letter arrived saying that my land has been transferred from the French to the English. Let us hope that the French are telling lies. There are three days between the two letters.

August 7th On Saturday the 21st of Siutorandu Dangadi returned from Marua with a letter from the Captain saying that he now had no authority in my land.

August 16th On Monday the last day of Siutorandu I sent Jauro Soji with my men to raid between Sina and Mala. They captured 23 slaves, 100 goats and killed 4 men. We had one wounded and one killed.

August 23rd On Monday the 8th of Laihaji I sent Bula Soji to raid the pagans of Wudala [Wudila?] and they captured 30 slaves and goats.

September 4th On Saturday the 20th of Laihaji I received a letter from the Captain in which was a complaint made by the pagans of Gaur and the people of Mandara against me.

September 10th On Friday the 26th of Laihaji between the two hours of prayer of the evening and the sunset I received two letters, one from the Emir of Yola and the other from the Captain. They concerned the coming of the English, and said that an Englishman from Yerwa and the Captain of Marua were to meet in my land between Waha and Habada in order to fix the boundary of my land.

September 14th On Tuesday the last day of Dhu al Hijjah the Emir of Bornu returned me three of my slaves.

September 15th On Wednesday the 1st of Muharram I sent Fadhl al Nar with my horsemen to Mandara in order to fix the boundary.

September 22nd On Wednesday the 8th of Muharram the Captain arrived.

September 26th On Sunday the 14th of Muharram we heard of the coming of the English and their carriers and labourers. Then Ajia gave me a horse and 100 shillings, Wakalta 100 shillings, Yerima Abba 100 shillings, Sarkin Arewa eight shillings, Wambai the same, Mayau Shamaki and Kofa 90 shillings, Lamido Chudde a horse, Sarkin Fada, Sarkin Shanu, Bulama Abba, Hamman Fedo, Baraya, Ardo Wula, Yerima Karim and Sa'id eight cows.

September 27th On Monday the 14th of Muharram I started off and met the English Judge, who had some of the chiefs with him. The Captain then left and stopped at Humuchi for a few days and then went off. I bought from Interpreter Adamu an extraordinary fine gown and he gave me 15/– for a cow and 6/– for chickens.

(He then journeyed down the Yola road.)

October 10th On Sunday the 27th of Muharram I left Holma and stopped at my house in Zummu, where I met the Emir of Yola and gave him two horses. I stayed three nights there.

(He then returned back to Nyibango.)

October 23rd On Saturday the 10th of Tumbindu Haramji while I was at Nyibango I heard that the pagans named Diskin had raided Wappara,[69] so I made arrangements and sent Fadhl al Nar with his men to raid the pagans of Sukur. They captured from them 39 slaves and 24 goats and killed five men.

October 26th On Tuesday the 13th of Tumbindu Haramji I gave the Emir of Yola two horses and his messenger, Maliki, a woman and a gown.

November 6th On Saturday the 24th of Tumbindu Haramji my son Abd al Rahman returned from the school of the French Christians and I told him: "There are three things for you to look after—the mosque, your dress and your food."

---

69. Dr. Nicholas David has pointed out that this is probably a typographical error and should read, "I heard that the *pagan* named Diskin had raided Wappara, . . ." The District Note Book reports Diskin as the name of the ruler of Sukur at approximately this time.

I gave the messenger Samaki Yola 90s/–.

At the same time I bought a chestnut horse from Yerima Audu Marua for eight cattle and 300s/–. I bought it to seal the compact between us.

(The rest of the page [MS p. 100] is concerned mainly with his own movements.)

December 17th On Friday the 5th of Banjaru Awwal I heard that the Judge with the spectacles was coming (Mai Madubi).

December 19th On Sunday the 7th of Banjaru Awwal I welcomed the Judge Mai Madubi. He spent the night and then on Monday I met him and he told me what he had to say.

December 25th On Saturday the 13th of Banjaru Awwal the Judge Mai Madubi ordered me to go with him to look at the boundary of my land. I refused, so he went and came back and told me that he had cut the boundary through my land and given my land back to Bornu.

December 27th On Monday the 15th of Banjaru Awwal I left the Judge Mai Madubi in view of his evil words and conversation and his mischief-making in cutting off my land.

December 31st On Friday the 19th of Banjaru Awwal my messenger Magaji returned and according to what he said the Judge Mai Madubi ordered that there should be a decision made in the case between my pagans and my chieftainship over the Duhu land, that is to say the chief of Duhu.

1921

January 20th On Thursday the 10th of Banjaru Tumbindu I met the Emir of Yola and the Judge Mai Madubi. He gave me the Duhu land and then I took my leave of them.

(The rest of the page [MS p. 102] is concerned with his own movements.)

February 26th On Saturday the 17th of Jumadi Akhir I appointed my son Da'ud chief of Bugel.

March 12th On Saturday the 1st of Sumatendu Waube I heard that the Christian had gone in the direction of Kova.

(The rest of the page [MS p. 103] is concerned with his own movements, gifts of slaves to his sons, and gifts to him from various pagans.)

March 15th On Tuesday the 4th of Sumatendu Waube I had three of my female slaves flogged with 15 lashes each for adultery.

March 19th On Saturday the 8th of Sumatendu Waube I heard that the pagans of Mugudi had stolen a cow of mine from my house at Nyiburi.

Previously I had heard of the arrest of Malam Ali, and so I wrote a letter to the Emir of Nafada and my man came back with the truth, which was that the Emir of Nafada said he had not written a letter and had not heard about their imprisonment.

April 11th On Monday the 1st of Jaujaungel I heard that my son Musa is suspected of having killed his son.

April 13th On Wednesday the 3rd of Wairordu Sumaye I remembered that I started the new ceremonial ablution last Friday.

April 24th On Sunday the 15th of Wairordu Sumaye a man of the Pellam pagans asked me for the headship of those pagans and he gave me two slaves in order that I might appoint him.

April 30th On Saturday the 21st of Wairordu Sumaye I found that my son Bello's female slave had run away from him to Mai Abba's village. So I sent my man Hamman Gulak with a letter to the Emir al Yemen and he returned with her to me.

May 10th On Tuesday the 1st of Ramadhan some dogarai arrived from the Emir al Yemen with 800s/– English, and they paid me 10/– to be allowed to stay with me.

(The rest of the page [MS p. 106] contains details of his own movements, a domestic incident, a remark that fish is a lawful food, and entries regarding trading incidents.)

June 11th On Saturday the 4th of Juldandu I gave Adamu—the one with two sons—two gowns, and I have decided to try to get him to enter the great sect from Saturday the 4th day of the month of Juldandu.

June 16th On Thursday the 10th of Juldandu two Christians went out to mark out the boundary of my land, and they cut off a very large part of it on the Bornu side. They returned on Tuesday the 15th of Juldandu.

On Thursday the 10th of Juldandu a messenger arrived from the Emir al Yemen bringing me a considerable quantity of goods—24 veils for women, two ordinary gowns, a large gown, a black turban and trousers.

June 16th On Thursday the 10th of Shawwal some Christians went out with Sa'id and Magaji to mark out the boundary between me and the Emir of Bornu. They started the boundary from below the village of Birni on the river bank and took it to a wild fig tree and from there to the head of the Mayo Yenango. Thence they followed the river bank to a baobab tree, and thence they followed the Zu road, then the bottom of the hill, then the Isge road, then the Disa road, then the river Julaiwa, then the Sakawa road, then the river Gori and the hill Wangolori, then the river Lammukara, then the hill Ganta, and thence to the side of Tuvu from below it. Then on the Tuesday the Christians returned to Madagali.

July 2nd On Saturday night the 25th of Shawwal I sent my daughter to the Emir al Yemen to be his bride, and I sent with her large quantities of goods and horses, so that they could not be counted for their large numbers.

July 3rd On Sunday the 26th of Shawwal Mr. Carlyle left with the Emir al Yemen's son and their party. My men accompanied them to Duhu. He scolded Yaji of Duhu and turned away his brother.

July 5th On Tuesday the 28th of Shawwal I left my house in Madagali and went to see the Christian Mr. Vereker at the Rest House, and after taking my leave of him I went to my house in Zu.

July 9th On Saturday the 3rd of Siutorandu two messengers arrived from Mr. Carlyle to arrest Kabasa in connection with the matter of his wife running away. So I handed him over to them and sent my man Sa'id with them.

[August 21st] On Saturday the 15th of Dhu al Hijjah I left Mubi.

(No date given) I arrived in Yola and met the Christian and the Emir of Yola.

August 28th On Sunday the 22nd of Dhu al Hijjah I took my leave of the Emir al Yemen and the Christian.

> (The rest of the page [MS p. 109] is mainly concerned with his return journey to Madagali.)

> (This page [MS p. 110] contains an account of his movements, a long list of goods brought to Madagali by two Hausa traders, notes of gifts to his son and other people, and details of gifts made to him.)

October 26th On Wednesday the 23rd of Tumbindu Haramji Malam Yero returned from his journey to Yola. He informed me that the Emir of Yola and the Christian ordered me to appoint a Kadi, so I gave Malam Muhammad the power in Madagali.

October 28th On Friday the 25th of Tumbindu Haramji I sent for Arnado Muduvu, Fashakha, and took from him 3 cows and a man of his, and I returned to him one cow, his wife and all his goods.

November 4th On Friday the 3rd of Haram Petel I gave the Emir al Yemen a fine horse that had not been used on trek: this was a present to him.

November 12th On Saturday the 11th of Haram Petel I heard that the Christians had arrived at Duhu, so I left my house in Madagali and went to my house in Zu, where I stayed the night. Then I met the Christian and welcomed him. On Sunday I returned to my house in Madagali.

November 14th On Monday the 13th of Haram Petel the Christian arrived in Madagali.

November 23rd On Wednesday the 22nd of Haram Petel I left my house at Mayo Tapare and went to the Rest House to salute Mr. Vereker and then returned to Mayo Tapare.

November 24th On Thursday the 23rd of Haram Petel the Christian left my town and I accompanied him to Zu, where I took my leave of him and spent the night with them at Zu. The following day they went to Duhu and I started after them and stopped at my house in Wuro Alhamdu. I heard that the Christian separated Jauro Duhu from his pagans. The total time they spent in my town was ten days.

December 9th On Friday the 9th of Banjaru Awwal Kabala brought me news that the Christian of Bornu had come to Tukubare {Tukuadu} [written above], and on hearing this I determined to send a messenger, named Sa'id, to him to see him about the boundary above the Mayo Yenango and find out how it went.

December 18th On Sunday the 18th of Banjaru Awwal I stopped at Kirshingu and made a house there and built a mosque. On Tuesday Ardo Moda came to me with news from the French.

December 28th On Wednesday the 28th of Rabi'a al Akhir I gave Sarkin Arewa a slave girl as a present.

1922

January 6th On Friday the 7th of Rajab (*sic*) I had pains in my legs so that I was unable to pray in the mosque for two days.

The same day I made Hamman Tukur chief of Nyibango and I also fined Ajia goods to the value of 200s/–.

January 27th On Friday the 27th of Rajab Mr. Vereker returned. So I rode to meet him and he took some tax.

January 29th On Sunday the 29th of Rajab at night I gave Bello Nakula [Nakola?] 100s/– in connection with the matter of Jauro Duhu, and the following day the Christian left.

January 31st On Tuesday the 2nd of Banjaru Sakitindu I heard that the Christian had deposed Arnado Duhu and appointed another man. This pleased me very much.

February 12th On Sunday the 14th of Jumadi al Akhir I appointed Hamman Siwada chief of the guests and he gave me two rams and 40s/–.

February 26th On Sunday the 27th of Jumadi al Akhir I gave Ardo Michika 20/– on his coming to Maradi and my son-in-law Yerima Moda, Baba, 8s/–.

March 5th On Sunday the 5th of Sumatendu Waube I sent my messenger Jauro to the Shehu of Bornu to offer my condolences on the death of his brother.

March 17th On Friday the 17th of Sumatendu Waube Jauro returned from his journey to Bornu, bringing a white gown and a short sleeveless gown.

March 23rd On Thursday the 23rd of Sumatendu Waube my son Da'ud sent as a present to me 370s/– and God is knowing.

March 24th On Friday the 25th of Sumatendu Waube I gave my son Abd al Rahman the chieftainship of Kova.

The same day I bought a horse from some Beri-Beri for 275s.

April 10th On Monday the 12th of Sha'aban I took away the pagans of Webengo from the possession of my son Bello on account of his tyrannous behavior towards them in flogging the son of Umar Ardo Tur, Hamman Noh.

The same day I heard of the death of the Emir of Rei and I sent messengers to offer my condolences.

April 20th On Thursday the 21st of Sha'aban my slave Risku the Ardo of Wula raided the pagans of Kurang and they brought me news of what had happened in the matter of the burning of their houses.

May 7th On Sunday the 8th of Ramadhan the slave Buba killed a pagan of Garta, who had come to steal their cattle.

The same day I started the reading of Ta Ha (the twentieth chapter of the Koran).

May 15th On Monday the 17th of Ramadhan Dadandi returned from his journey with the news that the Christian Mr. Vereker had taken my land Bugel and had given it to Jauro Demsa Salih, so that my Bugel land has been taken away from me. But God knows whether this is true or not.

June 1st On Thursday the 5th of Juldandu I gave my son Baba a slave. At the same time I heard that a slave had brought a complaint against me before Mr. Vereker. His name is Barka, his father's name is Khairu and his mother's Nahwu. A female slave also ran away from my house in Nyibango.

June 5th On Monday the 9th of Juldandu Hamman Gulak returned from his journey to Mubi to see Mr. Vereker. According to him, Ardo Michika complained against me in regard to Kova, but he got nothing out of it and I defeated him.

June 10th On Saturday the 14th of Juldandu I arrested three men of the pagans of Sukur and Damai on a charge of fighting with each other. I also had a talk with Arnado Mildu, Banera, and I fined him 10s. for his evil talk.

June 14th On Wednesday the 18th of Shawwal I left my house at Humuchi and went to the Rest House at Moda and met the Christian Mr. Vereker. I had a case to fight with Ardo Duhu Yaji and defeated him, at which I was very pleased. Then I returned to Humuchi, having obtained possession of Duhu. In the course of the discussion Mr. Vereker gave an order for Yaji's removal from his chieftainship.

June 25th On Sunday the 29th of Shawwal I heard that Jauro Duhu, Yaji, had returned to his original quarrelsome habits. The same day I gave my carriers 100s. and a calf. God knows what they expected in the way of wages.

June 26th On Monday the last day of Shawwal my man returned from his journey to Rei bringing three slaves and a considerable quantity of cloth and other goods. (The various articles are enumerated in full.)

June 28th On Wednesday the 1st of Siutorandu the Christian Mr. Vereker sent me a lad who made an accusation against my people. What he said was that Fajia bought him from us, so that she might live in my village. (? The Arabic is rather clumsy.)

July 12th On Wednesday the 16th of Siutorandu Hamman Kobo returned with a letter from Mr. Vereker regarding the dispute about Jauro Duhu's chieftainship. Jauro Duhu complained to Mr. Vereker and the latter ordered me to appoint whomsoever I liked from among my own people. I at once sent some horsemen to sit down at Guram and find out what the news is.

July 14th On Friday the 17th of Siutorandu I gave my son Hammawa the pagans of Pellam from among the districts of Waida.

July 17th On Monday the 20th of Siutorandu I heard news that the French and the English had quarrelled in regard to the boundary, the French saying that they had a right to land in Bornu and the English saying "No."

July 24th On Monday the 27th of Siutorandu I heard from Bugel that my son Da'ud had gone to meet the Christian Mr. Vereker to complain that Jauro Demsa had seized his horse. However, he got nothing out of it.

The same day Jauro returned from his journey to Mr. Vereker at Mubi and he gave him the land which I had promised him. The people of Duhu have made their excuses now that there is no use for excuses.

July 26th On Wednesday the 1st of Dhu al Hijjah I left my house at Zu and on the way received a letter from Mr. Vereker saying that the Jauro's status of slavery displeased the people of Duhu. However, I am satisfied with him. I gave Mr. Vereker's messenger Othman 100s.

July 30th On Sunday the 4th of Dhu al Hijjah my messengers Barade Umaru and Jauro returned with the joyful news that the Christian Mr. Vereker had returned to me my Duhu people for me to appoint a chief of Duhu.

August 4th On Friday the 10th of Dhu al Hijjah my illness returned to me with great violence.

August 8th On Tuesday the 14th of Dhu al Hijjah I renounced the practice of praying to God for things of this world, and adopted the practice of praying for things of the world to come.

August 13th On Sunday the 19th of Dhu al Hijjah I arrested my man Yaji and imprisoned him for his offence in going to my brother Abd in order to cause mischief. His action made me angry and I ordered my men to take him to Nyibango. They reached Diga, where Ardo Yaji fled to the house of Ardo Belel, and there my men broke his head.

August 18th On Friday the 24th of Dhu al Hijjah I treated some of the Madagali people roughly, the chief of them being Ardo Suyudi and Ardo Garga, for these two men refused to eat my food.

August 19th On Saturday the 25th of Dhu al Hijjah the people of Ardo Yaji promised me on oath not to disobey my commands.

August 25th On Friday the 1st of Muharram my wife Umm Asta Belel said that in respect of her being a Muslim she was tired of it, and in respect of her being a pagan it would be better for her.

September 15th On Friday the 22nd of Muharram my slave Azmada bought Mildu for 10s.

September 16th On Saturday the 23rd of Muharram I rewarded Malam Gaji for all his work by giving him a small slave. That is in full settlement of his work.

September 19th On Tuesday the 26th of Muharram two men, one from the pagans of Mildu, and one from the pagans of Kirshinga, belonging to

Jadko, came to me for me to try a case between them. They were accused of fighting over a question of their wife. One of them I arrested for highway robbery and the other for wounding a man. I also arrested the wife's daughter for causing the mischief between the two of them.

September 26th On Tuesday the 4th of Tumbindu Haramji I gave my man Sa'id a female slave.

October 1st On Sunday the 8th of Tumbindu Haramji my son Abd al Karim returned from a journey to Mr. Davies, but the latter was not pleased with him.

October 15th On Sunday the 23rd of Tumbindu Haramji I exchanged female slaves with my man Ajia, I receiving Kutara and he Fanta.

November 2nd On Thursday the 12th of Haram Petel I fined the pagans of Wengo 28s. for allowing the birds to eat my crops.

November 7th On Tuesday the 17th of Haram Petel the pagans of Sina brought a woman of theirs to me, who they said stole from people.

On the same day I arrested three men of the Kamale pagans for attacking the Christian.

November 18th On Saturday the 28th of Haram Petel two of the Christian's interpreters, Sambo and Othman, came to me and I gave them 20s. out of the profit I made in Yola.

November 24th On Friday the 5th of Banjaru Awwal I exchanged a female slave with my son Yusuf by giving him a young one and taking Suikado. But he said he did not want a girl, he wanted a boy slave.

November 28th On Tuesday the 9th of Banjaru Awwal I sent the Emir of Malabu a horse, when he sent his brother to me.

December 1st On Friday the 12th of Banjaru Awwal I sent my man Fadhl al Nar to the village of Kachella Aji to look at my farm, for a man of the pagans of his village had given me some information about it. However, the man's tale was proved false and Kachella Aji was right, so I fined the liar two goats.

December 8th On Friday the 19th of Banjaru Awwal I received a letter from the Christian of Dikwa.

December 15th On Friday the 25th of Banjaru Awwal we discussed the matter of the Tur pagans during our evening conversation. We agreed that we would not forget the matter but that we would not mention it for two months.

December 24th On Sunday the 5th of Banjaru Tumbindu I heard a rumor that Mr. Vereker was coming but I do not know whether it is true or not.

1923

January 7th On Sunday the 20th of Banjaru Tumbindu Hamman Gulak returned from his journey bringing a letter from Mr. Davies, asking for the tax to be sent to him.

January 20th On Saturday the 2nd of Banjaru Sakitindu I gave Malam Bakari, the doctor who cures madness (literally, the physician of the demons), a horse.

February 5th On Monday the 17th of Banjaru Sakitindu Arnado Sukur gave me two small slaves, one a boy and the other a girl.

February 12th On Monday the 25th of Banjaru Sakitindu I sent the Emir of Yola a stallion in return for the present I received from him.

February 16th On Friday the 29th of Banjaru Sakitindu I sent the Emir of Garua a horse as a present from me to him.

February 26th On Monday the 9th of Sumatendu Waube I left my house in Zu and stopped at my house in Madagali and the following day, Tuesday, the Christian Mr. Davies arrived.

March 5th On Monday the 16th of Sumatendu Waube the Christian Mr. Davies ordered me to go out with him on a tour of Duhu. So I went and we passed by Zu and spent the middle of the day there. Then I went to the Rest House at Duhu and returned to my house.

March 6th On Tuesday the 17th of Sumatendu Waube I started from my house at Wuro Alhamdu and went to Duhu to see the Christian and took my leave of him. I completed for him the tax of my land, the amount being £8103 (*sic*) and 810s.

March 9th On Friday the 20th of Sumatendu Waube I received a letter from the Christian Mr. Davies ordering me to go to Mubi to meet the Resident.

March 18th On Sunday the 29th of Sumatendu Waube I went to the Rest House in Mubi and joined all of the other chiefs who were collected there and I was the first one to be called in. So I went and talked with the two of them and then took my leave.

April 10th On Tuesday the 23rd of Sha'aban Mr. Davies sent for me. God grant me good fortune in my journey. He sent for me to come to Moda on a matter of advantage to me. So I left Madagali on Tuesday and we met on Wednesday the 24th of Sha'aban.

(This interview is not mentioned any further: the rest of the page [MS p. 129] is concerned mainly with trading matters.)

May 18th On Friday the 30th of Ramadhan I gave Hamma Sule a gown on his appointment as a chief and he gave me 100 in German money.

(The rest of the page [MS p. 130] is concerned with his own movements, a record that he divorced his wife, the repayment of a loan and similar matters of little interest.)

May 28th On Monday the 11th of Siutorandu [? Juldandu] I summoned Samaki and Sarkin Shanu before me and they had a dispute. Sarkin Shanu had told me what had happened between them both as to words and actions, and I came to the conclusion that Samaki was a bad man and it seemed to me that Sarkin Shanu was better than him as far as badness went and mischievous talk. The cause of the trouble was that I had ordered them to bring me some slave girls but Samaki refused as did also his brother. However, they now asked pardon.

June 3rd On Sunday the 17th of Siutorandu [? Juldandu] I sent my man Jauro with Hama Sinu and another man of mine to bring me Atiku, but when he got him he did not send him to me but returned to Gulak. Then the pagans sent for him and took one of them away from him, and the two sons Hamawa and Abbas were in Gulak at the time. Then when they returned they made for Madagali but the pagans of Gulak waylaid them. So when I heard this I took away these pagan districts of mine from Hamawa.

June 8th On the following day, Friday, I received a letter from the Christian Mr. Davies asking why I had imprisoned Fur.

June 13th On Wednesday the 28th of Juldandu I heard that Arnado Gulak had fled across the river and had gone to the Lamsu pagans.

June 14th On Thursday the 29th of Juldandu I received a letter from the Christian Mr. Davies asking why I had not arrested Arnado Gulak.

June 15th On Friday the last day of Juldandu two pagans came to me from Duhu and asked me to admit them to Islam.

June 22nd On Friday the 7th of Siutorandu I received news from Ardo Wula that he promised to return me my slave Dira'. I had sent him a letter about Hama Siwu's men.

July 2nd On Monday the 17th of Siutorandu the pagans of Gulak came to me and said that they had agreed upon Sudi, so I appointed him chief of Gulak and he gave me a horse and a cow.

July 4th On Wednesday the 19th of Siutorandu a man came from Ardo Garga of Michika with a letter asking me to give my daughter in marriage to his son, but I would not agree.

July 8th On Sunday the 23rd of Siutorandu I received a letter from the Christian Mr. Davies ordering me to count the Fulani cattle.

The same day I heard that the Kadi Muhammad had sentenced Bulama Galadima and his relatives and that they had fled. So I ordered them to be brought back to me. Then I had them brought in front of me and I had a talk with them, and then they returned to their homes.

July 27th Lawan Isa the husband of Adda brought a complaint against the Kadi Muhammad accusing him of misappropriating part of a deposit he had placed with him. The Kadi denied this and gave his oath, but Lawan Isa said that he had the better right to take the oath and I left it to him.

July 29th On Sunday the 14th of Laihaji I forgave Sarkin Shanu his offence and he gave me four cows.

Mr. Davies arrived and I rode out to meet him. He ordered me to fetch my labourers.

July 31st On Tuesday the 16th of Laihaji I went to the Rest House with my labourers and Arnado Kuffari and he [Mr. Davies, presumably] distributed our pay to us. He gave Sarkin Shanu 120s. and for the work on the Rest House he gave 40s. To me he gave 108s.

August 1st On Wednesday the 17th of Laihaji Mr. Davies came to the entrance of my house and arranged for a prison. Then he returned to the Rest House.

August 2nd On Thursday the 18th of Laihaji I left the Christian safely and took my leave. He ordered me to clear the road and count the cattle.

August 3rd On Friday the 19th of Laihaji the case of Arnado Afango, who was accused of selling a slave, was heard but it was not proved against him.

August 4th On Saturday the 20th of Laihaji I started on the clearing of the road.

August 13th On Monday the 29th of Laihaji I sent Atiku to Mubi to welcome Mr. Oakley.

August 15th On Wednesday the 2nd of Muharram I received a letter from Mr. Davies saying he did not agree to the cattle count and he ordered me to count them again.

August 17th On Friday the 4th of Muharram Baba Dagashi gave me a black gown.

August 21st On Tuesday the 8th of Muharram I gave messenger Othman a horse, and on the same day I received a letter from Mr. Oakley saying that he was coming to visit me.

August 24th On Friday the 11th of Muharram Sarkin Shanu and Malam Mukhtar returned from their journey to the Judge Mr. Davies at Mubi, bringing a letter from the Judge Mr. Oakley in which he ordered me to collect the Jangali in my land. The same day I heard that the Christian Mr. Oakley had arrested seven of the followers of the Mahdist sect in the village of Michika, who had arrived there.

August 30th On Thursday the 17th of Muharram I received a letter from the Christian Captain Oakley asking me for the number of orphans who have no father or mother, and I was to send this to him with two men named Yaya and Hussein.

September 4th On Tuesday the 23rd of Muharram the son of Gariwa returned with a letter from the Christian saying that he was a madman.

September 7th On Friday the 25th of Muharram I received a letter from the Christian Judge Oakley ordering me to count my people and also to hunt down Lawan Aji and seize his cattle.

September 9th On Sunday the 27th of Muharram I gave Baba Dagashi a horse.

September 15th On Saturday the 3rd of Tumbindu Haramji I sent a letter to the Judge Captain Oakley.

September 23rd On Sunday the 11th of Tumbindu Haramji I received a letter from Captain Oakley telling me that when I have finished the collection of the Jangali tax, I am to go to him with it.

September 27th On Thursday the 15th of Tumbindu Haramji Eliasa returned from his journey to the Emir of Laro with 78s. English, the price at which he had sold my horse. The price was a very poor one, much too little. So I had Turi and Eliasa up in front of me and they quarrelled among themselves about it. However, it was clear that Eliasa was the culprit who had sold my horse so cheaply, and I was very displeased with this bad work of his.

September 28th On Friday the 16th of Tumbindu Haramji I deposed Kabarawa the chief of the Mildu pagans.

October 1st On Monday the 19th of Tumbindu Haramji I sent Abd al Karim and Malam Mukhtar to Mubi with the Jangali money.

October 4th On Thursday the 22nd of Tumbindu Haramji Abd al Karim and Malam Mukhtar returned from Mubi and said the Christian Judge Oakley ordered me to go to Mubi to see him.

October 7th On Sunday the 25th of Tumbindu Haramji Mai Bornu went to the pagans of Duhu and he and Ardo Duhu went along the boundary between me and Duhu. They saw what mischief the pagans had done, so Mai Bornu returned to Duhu and arrested three of the pagans of Duhu together with Jauro Hamajam of Duhu. He brought them before me and tried to make peace between me and Hamajam.

October 8th On Monday I said goodbye to him and gave him 40s. English.

October 12th On Friday the 1st of Haram Petel the pagans of Lamsha killed my slave Ardo Wula, and I received the news at Humuchi on Saturday. Their reason for this is that the Christian ordered him to do it (*sic*).

October 14th On Sunday the 3rd of Haram Petel I received a letter from Captain Price brought to me by Kachakama in which he ordered me to send my man to him with the Kadi to meet him at Mubi. So I have got off the journey to Mubi.

October 27th On Saturday the 16th of Muharram Petel [*sic*] I sent a letter to Ahmad with a dark grey turban and a blanket. I also told him my age and his. My age is 56 and his is 38.

   On the same day I gave Madu a gown on his appointment as chief of Mildu, and he gave me four cows.

October 28th On Sunday the 17th of Haram Petel I heard that my men had taken my horse and given it to the Ma'aji of Yola.

October 29th On Monday the 18th of Haram Petel I said that I had not given the Ma'aji of Yola a thing until I had got from him 1000 shillings.

October 30th On Tuesday the 19th of Haram Petel I received a letter from Captain Price ordering me to send Abd al Karim to the Kadi Muhammad together with the Fulani, as he did not accept his decision originally.

November 8th On Thursday the 28th of Haram Petel my female slave who had run away returned, and the same day I fined the pagans of Chuka 1s. each, with the exception of one man whom I fined a black gown. The reason for fining them was that I had ordered them to be told that my slave had run away and they were to capture her. This they refused to do, and said they had never heard about it and that Suleiman had not told them. The man I fined a gown, however, actually caught my slave and sent her to her home.

November 9th On Friday the 29th of Haram Petel Hamman Kobo returned from Mubi with the news that the Christian had brought my son Al Karim back to Mubi for the beginning of his trial and had ordered the Kadi to go and see him.

November 13th On Tuesday the 4th of Banjaru Awwal I sent Hamman Kobo to the Christian Captain Price at Mubi with the Kadi for the trial of the case between Abd al Karim and the Kadi.

November 14th On Wednesday the 5th of Banjaru Awwal I fined Iyawa 20s. German for accusing his wife of adultery.

November 21st On Wednesday the 12th of Banjaru Awwal Hamman Kobo returned from Mubi with the joyful news that my son Abd al Karim escaped the imprisonment which the Kadi had awarded him.

November 23rd On Friday the 14th of Banjaru Awwal Abd al Karim returned from Mubi. The Kadi had wanted to imprison him for six months, but the case was not proved against him.

November 26th On Monday the 17th of Banjaru Awwal the pagans of Wengo brought me three gowns, two black ones and the other a white upper garment. I gave one to Fukul's son and allowed Malam Umar to have one.

December 1st On Saturday the 22nd of Banjaru Awwal I had a talk with the Kadi Muhammad. He said: "Why are you angry with me?" and I said: "I am not angry, but if my people are to be brought before the Court, you should let me know and let me hear the witnesses."

December 1st On Saturday the 22nd of Banjaru Awwal I sent a pagan from Gusi to Captain Price on a charge of stealing 12s. and three cows.

December 10th On Monday the 1st of Banjaru Tumbindu I received a letter from Captain Price saying he was coming to visit me.

December 11th On Tuesday the 3rd of Banjaru Tumbindu I met the Christian and returned with him to Madagali. He had my brother Rufa'u with him.

December 12th On Wednesday the 3rd of Banjaru Tumbindu I went to the Rest House, where Captain Price asked me about cartridges. He said: "You have bought cartridges." I said: "No; I have not heard of such a thing," and he believed me. Then he asked Yerima Abba and said to him: "I have heard that he has left off the business of [*sic*] that thing in which there is no harm." The reason for this remark is that Mr. Palmer started this business.

December 14th On Friday the 5th of Banjaru Tumbindu the Christian Captain Price came to the entrance to my house in Madagali and gave me 20s. He made Hamman Gulak pagan assessor, and gave Sarkin Pawa the market with my permission. I then gave him a letter showing forth the misdeeds of Sarkin Yaki of Gwoza. Then I took my leave of him.

[December 15th] The following day the Christian Captain Price left, and I sent one of my boys named Isiaku to him for him to teach him how to cook my food.

December 17th On Monday the 8th of Banjaru Tumbindu Yerima Abba returned from his journey to Duhu, having accompanied the Christian Captain Price. The latter collected all the pagans of Duhu and ordered them to obey the Emir of Madagali. They said they would not do so, so he arrested Arnado Duhu and two men of the place and sent them to me. He also burnt Arnado Lumado's house and treated them harshly. Then he wrote a letter, which he sent to me.

December 23rd On Sunday the 14th of Banjaru Tumbindu Arnado Duhu appeared before me and brought me a pot of honey.

December 27th On Thursday the 18th of Banjaru Tumbindu the interpreter Katimbera left and I gave him a white gown.

December 30th On Sunday the 21st of Banjaru Tumbindu I sent a letter to the Emir al Yemen regarding the visit of Mr. Palmer and the Shehu to me.

1924

January 1st On Tuesday the 23rd Banjaru Tumbindu I left my house at Maradi and went to my house at Humuchi.

On the same day I sent my man Sa'id to Gulak, since they had come to an agreement with Abd al Kerim to make peace among themselves. So they made peace.

On the same day I heard that Ardo Suyudi, Lawan Mana and Mai Bornu had gone to Baba Dagashi. I was doubtful about this, so I at once sent Malam Hamman to Baba Dagashi to bring me the truth of the matter.

January 3rd On Thursday the 25th of Banjaru Tumbindu I left my house at Humuchi and stopped at my house at Nyiburi.

On the same day I heard that the pagans of Sina had quarrelled with Arnado Bakai.

January 8th On Tuesday the 1st Banjaru Sakitindu at night my son Abd al Rahman came to me and told me that the pagans of Kova had gone to the pagans of Michika and seized their property. The Michika pagans killed one of the Kova men, while the latter wounded a Michika man. I at once sent my men off on horseback.

January 9th On Wednesday the 2nd of Banjaru Sakitindu Jauro Othman brought me a black gown, which Ajia had sent him previously, when he quarrelled with the Kadi Hammad.

January 11th On Friday the 4th of Banjaru Sakitindu I gave the Galadima of Marua two gowns, since he had come to visit me and had given me a saddle.

On the same day Dadandi returned from his journey to the Christian Mr. Rosedale, who sent to say he was coming to visit me.

January 12th On Saturday the 5th of Banjaru Sakitindu I left my house at Nyiburi and stopped at my house in Nyibango.

January 13th On Sunday the 6th of Banjaru Sakitindu I sent Jaman Umaru and a carrier on a journey to Yola, as the Christian of the Quarter had ordered me to send him in.

January 13th On Sunday the 6th of Banjaru Sakitindu I left my house at Nyibango and stopped at my house at Mayo Tapare, and then I returned to my house at Madagali.

(There are two marginal notes. The first is opposite the date January 3, 1924 and is as follows: "And he gave me two cows and a gown," and the other can be referred to no particular date and runs: "The same day the Fulani came down.")

On the same day I fined Ardo Garga, Lawan Mana and Mai Bornu 60s., a gown and a cow.

January 14th On Monday the 7th of Banjaru Sakitindu I left my house in Madagali in order to meet the Christian Mr. Rosedale, as he had ordered me in his letter to proceed to Kova. Then I stopped in my house in Zu.

January 15th On Tuesday I left there and stopped at my house in Wuro Alhamdu, where I spent one night.

January 16th On Wednesday I went from there to my house in Maradi.

January 17th On Thursday I left there and stopped at Kova, where I met the Christian Mr. Rosedale. He marked out the boundary between Kova and Michika and Moda. Then I returned to Wuro Alhamdu.

When I took my leave of the Christian I ordered (*sic*) him to go to the Kamale pagans. So he went with Yerima Abba and ordered them to pay up their tax. This they refused to do, the whole lot of them, except for two people. Then he went off to Moda, while Yerima Abba returned.

January 22nd On Tuesday the 15th of Banjaru Sakitindu a letter arrived from the Christian Mr. Rosedale ordering me to send my son Abd al Rahman to them.

January 24th On Thursday the 17th of Banjaru Sakitindu I sent Abd al Rahman to Yola, and the same day I departed myself from Wuro al Hamdu [Alhamdu, elsewhere] and put up in my house in Zu.

January 25th On Friday the 18th of Banjaru Sakitindu I started off in the morning from Zu and stopped at my house in Madagali.

January 26th On Saturday the 19th of Banjaru Sakitindu we heard thunder and saw clouds, and it became somewhat dark.

January 27th On Sunday the 20th of Banjaru Sakitindu God was gracious to his servants and gave them rain.

On the same day my man Baraya gave me a cow, which had not calved; it was pure white in colour.

At the same time I sent off Sarkin Shanu to Adamayel telling him to pay the zakah on his cattle, namely five cows, and I sanctioned the giving of one of them to Malam Bobore.

January 29th On Tuesday the 22nd of Banjaru Sakitindu I received news that the pagans of Mugudi had raided my house at Nyiburi and had wounded my horse and a man of the Kamale pagans. On their side two Mugudi men were killed.

January 30th On Wednesday the 23rd of Banjaru Sakitindu I received a letter from the Christian Mr. Rosedale telling me to stop people robbing travelers on the main road.

On the same day I received news that the pagans of Michika had raided the people of the Emir of Mubi and had killed five men. (This sentence is half deleted in the text.)

February 1st On Friday the 25th of Banjaru Sakitindu a letter arrived from the Christian Mr. Rosedale ordering me to repair the road, the prison and the Court House.

On the same day I bought a donkey from Sarkin Shanu for a cow.

On the same day I left my house in Madagali and stopped at my house in Mayo Tapare.

February 3rd On Sunday the 27th of Banjaru Sakitindu Dada ran away.

February 5th On Tuesday the 29th of Banjaru Sakitindu I left my house in Mayo Tapare and stopped in my house in Madagali.

On the same day I bought a horse from Bulama Abba for three cows.

February 6th On Wednesday the last day of Banjaru Sakitindu Sarkin Hausawa Audu returned from his journey to Kano bringing three turbans with him.

On the same day Malam Umaru returned from his journey to Bornu. He brought three black gowns.

February 8th On Friday the 2nd of Rajab I received a letter from Captain Coste saying he would stop the pagans of Mugudi entering my land.

At the same time I heard that Ahmad had raided the pagans of Wula.

February 9th On Saturday the 3rd of Rajab I received a letter from the Christian Mr. Rosedale ordering me to go to meet him at Sina. So I at once left my house in Madagali and stopped during the heat of the day at my house in Nyibango. I then went on from my house in Nyibango to my house in Nyiburi, where I spent one night. Then I started off for Sina and met the Christian and spent the night with him there. I arrested a man of the Sina pagans and imprisoned him and the following morning sent him off.

February 11th On Monday I left there and stopped at my house in Nyiburi. There I heard that the Christian Mr. Rosedale wanted to give Sinagali to Lawan Aji. I spent one night there.

Then I left my house in Nyiburi and stopped at Kamale with the Christian.

February 12th On the 6th of Rajab at Kamale the Christian Mr. Rosedale imprisoned Arnado Kamale together with Koji and they spent the night in prison.

Jauro Hamman Bintu lost 7/6d of the tax of the Sina pagans.

February 15th On Friday the 10th of Rajab Kachagama and Salim returned from Pellam with the tax, which was 10d short.

February 17th On Sunday the 12th of Rajab I left my house at Nyiburi and stopped at my house in Humuchi.

February 18th On Monday I left there and stopped at my house in Wuro Alhamdu.

February 20th On Wednesday the 15th of Rajab I left my house at Wuro Alhamdu and stopped at Zu. Then I left there on hearing that the Christian Mr. Davies had arrived in Madagali. I at once sent my man Sa'id with Umar Gulak to welcome him. Then I arrived at my house in Madagali.

February 22nd On Friday the 16th of Rajab I went to the Rest House and met the Christian Mr. Davies.

February 23rd On Saturday the 17th of Rajab I received a letter from the Christian Mr. Rosedale saying that a pagan of Madagali named Mele had brought a complaint against me for taking his money from him by force.

February 24th On Sunday the 18th of Rajab I sent Jidr and Malam Ibrahim on a journey to Bornu with 100s. to buy me goods.

On the same day a letter arrived from the Christian Mr. Rosedale saying that a soldier had run away with his rifle and 100 cartridges. He told me that if I heard news of him I was to capture him.

February 25th On Monday the 19th of Rajab the Christian Mr. Davies left.

February 26th On Tuesday the 20th of Rajab Dadandi returned from his journey to the Christian Mr. Rosedale. The news he brought was that the Christian ordered Jauro Duhu to send him their General Tax.

February 29th On Friday the 23rd of Rajab at night Ajia quarrelled with Tayau because he was slow in carrying out an order of mine, so I fined Ajia 4s. English.

March 1st On Saturday the 24th of Rajab I left my house at Madagali and stopped at my house at Mayo Tapare. The same night I gave Sarkin Hausawa a cow.

March 3rd On Tuesday night the 27th of Rajab after breaking my fast I left my house at Mayo Tapare and stopped at my house at Nyibango.

March 4th On Wednesday the 28th of Rajab I received a letter from Mr. Davies to the French Christian.

The same night a female slave of mine, named Awwa, refused to cook me my food, and gave as her excuse that she had no water. This made me a little angry.

March 4th On Wednesday the 28th of Rajab I heard of the death of Jauro Hamman, Umaru Jabo and Umaru Dija, so I at once left my house at Nyibango and went to Jauro Hamman's house to offer my condolences to his son.

March 8th On the 1st of Jaujaungel I sent off the whole of the General Tax of my land, £330-12-5.

On the same day I gave Iya, Jauro Hamman's son, his father's position, and he gave me 2 cows. I said to him: "If you do bad work, even though it may be once only, I shall punish you."

March 9th On Sunday the 2nd of Jaujaungel Malam Mukhtar returned at noon from his journey to the Christian Mr. Rosedale bringing me a letter. I immediately decided to go to my house at Mayo Tapare.

March 12th On Wednesday the 5th of Jaujaungel I sent my mounted men to the Fulani of Nyibango, since they had disobeyed my summons. On their arrival I talked to them and then sent them with a letter to the Christian. My man Sarkin Tafarki went with him.

On the same day I left my house at Mayo Tapare and stopped at Madagali. On arrival I received a letter from the Christian asking me if I heard of the people who rob and extort under my protection. (? This appears to be the meaning, but the Arabic is that of an illiterate person.) I replied the following day that they did not rob and extort under my protection.

March 13th On Thursday the 6th of Jaujaungel Ardo Garga died at noon.

March 17th On Monday the 10th of Jaujaungel Sarkin Tafarki returned from his journey to the Christian with a letter, in which I was ordered to collect the Jangali of the Fulani, who had refused to pay.

On the same day I left my house at Madagali and went to my house at Nyibango.

[March 18th] The following day I seized their cattle at a place named Mazawa.

March 21st On Friday the 14th of Jaujaungel I sent Malam Umaru to Mubi to buy (? sell) the cattle which I had taken from the Fulani.

On the same day I left my house at Nyibango, after the Kadi Muhammad had returned from his journey to Mubi and informed me that the Christian was coming. I stopped at Mayo Tapare, where I spent the night. Then I left there and stopped at my house in Madagali.

On the same day Malam Mukhtar returned with the Village Head's share of the General Tax.

March 24th On Monday the 17th of Jaujaungel I decided to institute the prayer of the Mahdist sect on the following Friday. It may be that God will answer our prayer, and I pray God to grant us that which will gladden my heart.

On the same day the Emir of Uba sent his agents to me, and Dadandi returned from his journey to Mubi.

March 25th On Tuesday the 18th of Jaujaungel I sent off the Emir of Uba's man, named Kaigamma Abbas, and gave him 5s. English. To the Emir I gave a horse.

March 27th On Thursday the 20th of Jaujaungel I left my house at Madagali to go to Zu, as the Christian Mr. Rosedale had ordered me to meet the Resident at the Michika Rest House.

Then I left my house at Zu, and spent the night on the road near Moda by the bank of the river Galbije. Then I left there and went to the Michika Rest House. Then the Resident arrived in a motor-car, and I went to welcome him.

When he had alighted he said what he had to say, and I then spent the day in the shade, leaving after the midday prayer for Wuro Gayadi.

March 29th On Saturday the 22nd of Wairordu Sumaye I left my house at Wuro Gayadi and stopped at Maradi.

(Marginal note: On the same day Malam Umaru returned from selling the cattle of the Fulani for 542s.)

March 30th On Sunday the 23rd of Wairordu Sumaye I sent my man Barade Umaru to Yola to offer his condolences on a death. I gave him 100s. and for his food for the journey 6s.

April 1st On Tuesday the 25th of Wairordu Sumaye Bobbo Inna returned from his journey to Mubi, as the Christian Mr. Rosedale had asked me for details of my ancestors from the beginning.

On the same day I bought a horse from the people of Kova for a cow, a calf and cash to the value of a small calf.

I gave my son Abd al Rahman a small slave and I said to him: "Listen; I am not going to clothe you any more."

April 3rd On Thursday the 27th of Wairordu Sumaye my son, Malam Ibrahim, Abu Bakr and others, returned from their journey to Bornu. They brought a black gown, and a roll of coloured cloth. They told me that there was no sale for the cattle which they took with them, and they left these cattle in Bornu as also the amount of money which they had taken with them, namely 210s. The gown which they brought I gave to my man Sa'id in payment of my debt to him, and I at once decided not to send any cattle to Bornu again for sale.

April 9th On Wednesday the 4th of Ramadhan Malam Mukhtar was sent off with the Fulani tax, which amounted to 1282s. and I gave him 2s. for his food.

April 13th On Sunday the 8th of Ramadhan Malam Mukhtar returned from his journey to Mubi, bringing back the money which he had taken with him. The Christian Mr. Rosedale said that he had taken 600s. and given it to the Kadi Muhammad to write up in his register and send to Yola himself. As for the rest, I was to keep it until I wished and to divide it up among the cattle owners.

April 14th On Monday the 9th of Ramadhan Sarkin Hausawa returned from Bornu, bringing goods, namely saddle cloths, two turbans, kolas, 76s., four writing pads, a sash and a gown. The latter, however, he did not buy.

At the same time Dadandi returned from his journey to the Christian Mr. Rosedale with Dhumair, whom he had taken with him. The latter was found not guilty of the murder and of the other things he was accused of, and the Christian explained his order to me.

April 15th On Tuesday the 10th of Ramadhan I left my house at Maradi and stopped at my house at Wuro Alhamdu.

April 16th On Wednesday the 11th of Ramadhan I heard of the death of my horse, which was with Mana.

April 18th On Friday the 11th (*sic*) of Ramadhan Barade returned from Yola from paying my condolences [to] the Emir al Yemen. He bought me there a sword belt and four rugs.

April 19th On Saturday night the 14th of Ramadhan my slave Jauro ran away to Gwoza. So I sent Malam Garga to bring him back, but Jauro refused to come. So Malam Garga returned and told me that Jauro said he would only come back if Hamman Bindu went to fetch him. However, I refused to send Hamman to him, but ordered Fadhl al Nar to go.

April 23rd On Wednesday the 18th of Ramadhan Jauro Soja returned from Gwoza after Fadhl al Nar had got to him. I was at Wuro Alhamdu at the time.

April 26th On Saturday the 21st of Ramadhan Lawan Aji came to me with his people who live with him. Their wish was that I should give them the pagans of Sina, so that they might make Sina their home and establish a village there. I was in Wuro Alhamdu at the time.

May 1st On Thursday the 26th of Ramadhan I left my house at Wuro Alhamdu and met the Christian Mr. Rosedale at the back of Duhu. He told me he would put the pagans of Duhu under me, if they would obey me. I then returned to Wuro Alhamdu.

On the same day I left there after the evening meal and got caught in the rain on the road. I stopped at Zu for the night.

Then I left there and stopped at my house in Madagali after the evening meal.

This journey lasted 36 days.

May 4th On Sunday the 28th of Ramadhan the Christian Mr. Rosedale entered Madagali. I met him and he handed over to me the pagans of Duhu. They came to me and I spoke with them.

On the same day I gave my man Sa'id a gown.

May 6th On Tuesday the 1st of Shawwal we celebrated the Salat al Fitr. After we had finished I passed on to the Christian Mr. Rosedale, and gave Sarkin Katsina a coloured turban. The Christian gave me some kolas and he also have [gave ?] me money in payment for four rams which he had ordered from me. When I returned from the entrance to Madagali I gave the Fulani of Bebel 10s. and some kolas.

May 7th On Wednesday the 2nd of Shawwal the Christian Mr. Rosedale ordered e [me ?] to send the boys to school.

May 9th On Friday the 4th of Shawwal the Christian Mr. Rosedale left.

May 14th On Wednesday the 9th of Shawwal I sent the boys off to school in charge of Wuku.

May 15th On Thursday the 10th of Shawwal Dadar ran away to Gwoza after I had sent him on a journey.

May 18th On Sunday the 13th of Shawwal I sent my wife, the daughter of Bulama Zangura, to her father and I gave her a cow and a calf and fixed the time for her being away at 20 days. I gave her father a dark grey turban and her mother a mat and 100 kolas.

The same day I paid my debt of 29s. to the doctor Barrasi.

May 21st On Wednesday the 16th of Shawwal a letter arrived from the Emir of Uba saying that Hamman Joda and Buba Joda had stolen a horse belonging to my man, Ardo Hamman Abba, and that the Christian Mr. Rosedale had arrested them.

May 26th On Monday the 21st of Shawwal I sent Sarkin Hausawa Audu on a journey to Bornu with 96s. to buy a roll of cloth and kolas.

May 27th On Wednesday night the 23rd of Shawwal my young slave Samaki and Jauro quarrelled in front of me. Samaki shouted at me and made me angry. So I took some things away from him, namely my horses and my pagans and gave them to Jauro Bamgel. Then I sent him before the Court, but nothing was proved against him.

May 28th The following day Sarkin Arewa ran away with his family of 13 persons. Ali Dada and Kolo also ran off to Gwoza.

May 29th On Thursday the 24th of Shawwal, while I was sitting with my female slave Kujji talking to her, she said: "Poverty has oppressed him," as though she said: "His property is destroyed." So the same day I returned to Samaki his property.

May 30th On Friday the 25th of Shawwal I left my house in Madagali and went to my house in Mayo Tapare.

On the same day I gave the people of Madagali cash to the amount of 68 shillings.

June 1st On Sunday the 27th of Shawwal Mahmud returned from his journey to Mubi with the scribe Zakariah who is a native of Mubi.

On the same day the son of the Emir of Mandara, Hamid, arrived to see about his female slave.

At the same time Haba came down from the Mokolo hill with his family consisting of 19 people.

June 2nd On Monday the 28th of Shawwal I gave the people of Madagali 100 shillings.

June 3rd On Tuesday the 29th of Shawwal Sarkin Hausawa returned from his journey to Bornu, bringing 100 kolas and three rolls of cloth and a few other things.

June 4th On Wednesday the 1st of Siutorandu I left my house at Mayo Tapare and stopped at my house at Nyibango.

June 5th The following day I sent Abu Kar to Yola to bring back my share (? of the inheritance). I ordered him to give the Emir al Yemen 100s.

(Marginal note: The same day I returned Bula his property and gave Sulama [Bulama] Zanfura's son 20s. and other things for what they sent me by my wife.)

June 9th On the 6th of Siutorandu some concubines from my house in Nyibango left and were met by Pella in the morning on the road. They did not reach Zu until late in the morning.

June 11th On Wednesday the 8th of Siutorandu I left my house at Zu and stopped at my house at Wuro Alhamdu.

June 13th On Friday the 10th of Siutorandu I left my house at Wuro Alhamdu in the middle of the morning and passing by the pagans of

Pellam stopped at Arnado Wainda's and I gave him Bumbum. Then I put up in my house in Nyiburi in the evening.

June 15th On Sunday the 12th of Siutorandu I remembered that I had been free from stomach trouble for some days, and I therefore ate a meal such as I had not eaten for some time.

On the same day a man named Humbusa from the village of Uba brought his horse to me. However, it was too dear and I refused it. So he returned with the horse on Monday.

June 17th On Tuesday the 14th of Siutorandu I left my house at Nyiburi and put up at my house at Humuchi.

June 18th On Wednesday the 15th of Siutorandu a rock from the top of the Humuchi hill rolled down and fell on Arnado Humuchi, who died the same day.

June 19th Thursday the 16th of Siutorandu I left my house in Humuchi and stopped at my house in Maradi.

June 20th On Friday the 17th of Siutorandu a letter arrived from the Christian Mr. Rosedale with Bobbo's complaint about his female slave.

June 21st On Saturday the 18th of Siutorandu a letter arrived from the Christian Mr. Rosedale containing a reply about my handmaiden in Mugudi.

On the same day Malam Mansur sent me his horse for me to buy it at whatever price I wished.

On the same day the Emir of Uba sent me a letter by hand of his man Ardo Abba for me to decide a case between him and his wife, and when Ardo Abba had arrived and I had asked him about the case, I sent him to the Kadi Madagali.

On the same day I went to my farm, following along the Garua boundary at first. Then I returned to my house in Maradi.

June 22nd On Sunday the 19th of Siutorandu the Christian Mr. Rosedale sent a reply about Bobbo's complaint. He said that Bobbo was at fault, as he had stolen Saiyurandu the female slave whom they had seized.

June 24th On Tuesday the 21st of Siutorandu two letters arrived from the Christian Mr. Rosedale saying that the people of Mai Kadiri had complained against Jadko for seizing on goods in the market. The second matter was that he asked why I had not returned Bobbo's female slave. So I at once ordered Yakub and Abd al Rahman to go to see him about it.

On the same day I left my house in Maradi and stopped at my house in Wuro Alhamdu.

On the same day Maliki returned from his journey to Yola bringing 207s. I gave my man Sa'id 5s., leaving a similar {amount} still due from me.

June 25th On Wednesday the 22nd of Siutorandu I left my house in Wuro Alhamdu and stopped at my house in Zu.

On the same day I sent Sarkin Hausawa Audu to Yola with 186s. to buy me some goods.

June 26th On Thursday the 23rd of Siutorandu I left my house at Zu and returned to my house in Madagali.

I spent 23 days on this journey.

June 27th On the following day, Friday, I gave Tayau a black gown.

June 29th On Sunday the 26th of Siutorandu I sent Atiku to Yola with money for Audu.

On the same day I sent Buba Dija to the Christian Mr. Rosedale with a letter about the news brought by my messenger from the pagans of Tur.

July 1st On Tuesday the 28th of Siutorandu I dismissed my scribe Zakariah and we reckoned the period he had worked with me as eight months.

July 3rd On Thursday the 29th of Siutorandu two men from Michika complained against Dawaka for taking their donkey. They also said he took 26s. from them. The Kadi said that Dawaka had paid up.

July 4th On Friday the 1st of Dhu al Hijjah Buba Dija returned from his journey to the Christian Mr. Rosedale with a letter which he ordered me to send to Dikwa.

July 6th On Sunday in the month of Dhu al Hijjah I left my house in Madagali and went to my house at Mayo Tapare.

July 6th [7th] On Monday night I sent Ture to Dikwa with the letter of the Christian Mr. Rosedale. The letter was about the Tur question.

July 10th On Thursday the 7th of Dhu al Hijjah I left my house at Mayo Tapare and stopped at my house in Madagali. On the same day Sarkin Hausawa Audu returned from his journey to Yola, bringing 6 black gowns and two coloured turbans.

On the same day Abd Nasadah sent in two rams as usual.

July 11th On Friday the 8th of Dhu al Hijjah I gave Jijiwa a gown on his appointment as chief in place of his father. He gave me a horse and two cows. I warned him not to do any mischief.

On the same day a letter arrived from Yola, telling me I should have to go on a journey.

July 12th On Saturday night, the 9th, I married my daughter.

July 13th On Sunday the 10th of Dhu al Hijjah we celebrated the Id.

On the same day I left my house in Madagali and stopped at Wuro Alhamdu, as the Christian had summoned me to go into Yola.

July 14th On Monday the 11th of Dhu al Hijjah I left my house in Wuro Alhamdu and met with a man named Bakr who had a letter from the Christian containing a complaint against Yerima Abba to the effect that Yerima Abba had taken some money unlawfully.

July 15th On Tuesday the 12th of Dhu al Hijjah I left my house in Humuchi and stopped at my house at Kuzum.

July 16th Then I left there and stopped at my house at Mubi on Wednesday, staying there for two nights. The Emir of Mubi gave me a calf, and I gave him a horse.

July 18th On Friday I left there and stopped at my house in Kwagol.

Then I left there and stopped in my house in Zummu. Zummu gave me a calf, but I refused to accept it.

July 20th On Sunday I left there and stopped at my house at Woderimo and the Emir of Malabu sent me a lot of corn.

Then I left there and stopped at my house in Malabu, where Malabu gave me some corn.

Then I left there and stopped at my house in Giri.

July 23rd On Wednesday the 20th of Dhu al Hijjah I left my house in Giri and crossing the river in a boat stopped at my house in the Quarter (Jimeta).

[July 24th] I spent a night there and then in the morning went to the Station where I met Mr. Rosedale, who told me to return and come back tomorrow. So I returned and

July 25th came back the next day, Friday, to see the two of them. They told me that which God ordered that they should say, and then I took my leave and went to Yola to meet the Emir al Yemen. I then took my leave of him and returned to my house in the Quarter.

I gave the Emir al Yemen two rams and he gave me a calf.

July 26th On Saturday the 23rd of Dhu al Hijjah I bought from Baba Badam a lot of goods, namely five gowns, two striped upper garments made of wool, one woollen mat (the mat I sent to the wife of the Emir of Yola), some writing paper, tea and two packets of red nose ornaments. This all cost me 940s.

I gave Jauro a gown as also Magaji.

July 27th On Sunday the 24th of Dhu al Hijjah I left my house in the Quarter and passed by Baba Badam sitting in front of his house. So I sat down with him and gave him a horse, as he gave me a roll of cloth, some rice and some kolas. Then I got into the boat and crossed the river by the grace of God, and I stopped in my house in Giri.

Then I went on to Malabu, where the Emir of Malabu gave me a ram and some corn.

Then I left there and stopped at my house at Woderimo.

Then I left there and stopped in my house at Zummu, and I gave the Emir of Zummu a horse.

July 31st On Thursday I left there and stopped at my house in Kwagol, who [*sic*] gave me a calf, which I refused to accept.

August 1st On Friday I left there and stopped at my house in Mubi. The Emir of Mubi gave me a calf and two loads of corn.

August 2nd On the last day of Dhu al Hijjah I got two turbans for 54s., the money to be paid on the completion of the General Tax.

August 3rd On Sunday the 1st of Haram Awwal I left my house at Mubi, but found the river was full and too much for some of my carriers. So I could not manage it and returned to Mubi.

August 4th On the following day I started off and got across the river and reached Uba, and I stopped in my house at Kuzum. The Emir of Uba gave me a calf, a ram and a calabash of food. In return I gave him a good horse.

August 5th On Tuesday the 3rd of Muharram I left my house at Kuzum and stopped at my house in Humuchi.

On the same day I gave Baraya a striped upper garment of wool, as he had given me a horse.

August 6th On Wednesday the 4th of Muharram I left my house at Humuchi and stopped at my house at Maradi.

August 8th On Friday the 6th of Muharram I heard that the son of Jauro Hamma, Iya, had been drowned in the river at Mubi, as also a man from Gulak.

On the same day I left my house at Maradi and stopped at Wuro Alhamdu.

August 9th On Saturday the 7th of Muharram I left there and stopped at my house at Zu.

August 10th On Sunday the 8th of Muharram I left my house at Zu and returned to my house at Madagali.

This journey took 28 days.

At the time of my return the grain of the guinea-corn had begun to form.

On the same day the Kadi Muhammad gave me 3 black woollen mats and Yerima Abba gave me a ram.

August 11th On Monday the 9th of Muharram Yerima Nana gave me a roll of cloth, Sarkin Shanu gave me a mat and Baraya also gave me a mat. This was to welcome me.

On the same day Umaru Shamaki returned from his journey to Bornu, bringing 200 kolas, a roll of cloth and some beads.

August 12th On Tuesday the 10th of Muharram Sarkin Fawa gave me three head ornaments.

On the same day the pagans of Tur came to see me.

August 13th On Wednesday night, the 11th of Muharram I gave my carriers a calf.

August 15th On Friday the 13th of Muharram I left my house in Madagali and went to my house in Mayo Tapare.

On the same day Ture returned from his journey to Yola, after his return from Bornu. I gave him a gown and a turban.

August 17th On Sunday the 15th of Muharram I left my house at Mayo Tapare and went to my house at Nyibango.

August 19th On Tuesday the 17th of Muharram I left my house in Nyibango in the middle of the morning and met Hamma Kobo. He brought me some Gwoza news, namely that the pagans of Guduf had raided the Gwoza people and speared their chief, Sarkin Yawi, and his horse, and had killed one man.

Then I stopped at my house at Mayo Tapare, having spent two nights in Nyibango.

August 20th On Wednesday the 18th of Muharram I left my house in Mayo Tapare and went to my house in Madagali.

August 23rd On Saturday the 21st of Muharram Ardo Yaya of Duhu came to me and asked me to mark off for him a place where he might settle. He said that this was in accordance with the order of the Christian and the Emir al Yemen. I gave him no reply.

August 25th On Monday the 23rd of Muharram Lawan Dani sent me two shoes, that is shoes to fit two feet, and also a hide dyed red.

August 26th On Tuesday the 24th of Muharram I started the religious ablution, but I wonder whether it will last beyond this month or not.

On the same day I gave my son Idris a horse as a pledge for a debt he asked me to pay him, until I can get a cow and a calf.

On the same day Atiku came back from his journey to Mubi, bringing a letter from the Christian Mr. Rosedale. The same day I sent him the news about the people of Sarkin Yawi and the action of the latter in seizing their young women.

From what the Christian said, I cleared myself over the matter about which I journeyed to Yola.

August 27th On Wednesday the 25th of Muharram my female slave, the wife of Disinda, died.

On the same day Kova and Dile brought me a case against Musa, but it was not proved against him. I imprisoned Sadia over this matter, for it all originated with her.

August 28th On Thursday the 26th of Muharram my horse died.

At night Kova and Dile took their leave of me and I told him [*sic*] to wait until I gave him a gown to wear and then he could go where he liked.

On the same day I sent Kamanda with a dogari to Yola to get me {my pay.}

At the same time I fined Musa 10s. for taking a woollen mat from a woman without the Kadi's permission.

August 29th On Friday the 27th of Muharram Tayau and Asta slaughtered a ram of mine without my permission and they said they would give me the price of it.

On the same day I gave Kova a gown.

August 30th On Saturday the 28th of Muharram I saw in a dream a book named Wata'a (? but note that Imam Malik's collection of Hadiths is called Muwatta).

On the same day I sent Aidi with the Duhu pagans to the Christian at Yola. I also gave him a letter to the Emir of Zummu. With this party I also sent Mai Bornu 50s., the Ma'aji 15s. and the boys at the school 20s.

(Marginal note: The following day, Monday, I sent Yerima Abba to Yola.)

September 1st On Monday the 1st of Tumbindu Haramji I heard that the Christian Mr. Rosedale had sent me a letter to tell me that the Emir of Yola had died.

September 5th On Friday the 5th of Tumbindu Haramji I left my house in Madagali and stopped at my house in Mayo Tapare.

September 8th On Monday the 8th of Tumbindu Haramji I left my house in Mayo Tapare and stopped at my house in Madagali.

September 9th On Tuesday the 9th of Tumbindu Haramji I heard that some slaves of Mokolo had gone to Tur, so I sent my slaves to them to recover them, but they found they had scattered, so they returned to me without doing anything.

September 10th On Wednesday the 10th of Tumbindu Haramji Ahmad sent me a letter and asked why I had sent my slaves to Tur, as it was his land, he said.

September 12th On Friday the 12th of Tumbindu Haramji a French soldier came in to me.

September 13th On Saturday the 13th of Tumbindu Haramji I heard that Ahmad had sent his slaves to Tur and told them that if they saw any people of the Emir of Madagali they were to kill them. So I therefore sent off my people to Tur, as perhaps they may do what they said.

The same day I sent a letter to the Christian Mr. Rosedale to inform him about it.

September 14th On Sunday the 14th of Tumbindu Haramji Jailani and Elias returned from their journey to Tur. When they reached there they found Ahmad's slaves. They fired guns at them, but they refused to run away, and they captured two of my men, Irdu and Galwa.

September 17th On Wednesday the 17th of Tumbindu Haramji the Emir of Mandara, Adam, sent me a large hat and I gave him the present of a gown. The hat I gave to Buba Mabas.

September 19th On Friday the 19th of Tumbindu Haramji Ardo Nyibango, Tukur, told the pagans of Muduvu something he ought not to have said, so I fined him 50 shillings.

September 20th On Saturday the 20th of Tumbindu Haramji at night I asked Sarkin Fada if the people of my villages committed {? word unknown}, and he said; "No: we do not do it."

On Saturday the 20th of Tumbindu Haramji I left my house at Madagali and stopped at my house in Zu.

September 21st On Sunday I left there and went to my house at Wuro Alhamdu.

On the same day I heard of the return of the Emir of Uba.

September 22nd On Monday the 22nd of Tumbindu Haramji Yerima Abba returned with Kamanda from their journey to Yola.

September 23rd On Tuesday the 23rd of Tumbindu Haramji I left my house at Wuro Alhamdu and stopped at my house at Maradi.

On the same day I fined Ardo Yayawa 10s. English for his offence in refusing and declining to perform the mourning ceremonies on the death of the Emir al Yemen Muhammad. I gave some of the money to my people.

September 24th On Wednesday the 24th of Tumbindu Haramji the female slave of Abdu Nasadah, named Maimuna, fled to me.

September 24th On Wednesday the 24th of Tumbindu Haramji Wuddal brought 3s. in cash after I had given him a woollen mat to go to Sawadi.

On the same day I sent Hamman Kobo on a journey to Yola to fetch the inheritance of my daughter.

September 26th On Friday the 26th of Tumbindu Haramji a man from my village of Bebel came to me and said that a robber, after stealing some goats, met with a woman named Ummu Jailani and killed her. It is not known who he is.

October 3rd On Friday the 4th of Haram Petel I sent Malam Mukhtar with Maliki on a journey to Mubi to the Christian Mr. Rosedale.

(Marginal note: On this day Interpreter Salih arrived.)

October 4th On Saturday the 5th of Haram Petel I left my house at Maradi and went to my house at Wuro Alhamdu, where I spent one night.

October 5th On Sunday I left there and stopped at Zu.

October 6th On Monday the 7th of Haram Petel I left my house at Zu and stopped at my house at Madagali.

I spent 17 days on this journey.

The reason for my return was that Hamman Pedu had fallen ill.

October 7th On Tuesday the 8th of Haram Petel I gave the Kadi Muhammad a cow.

October 8th On Wednesday the 9th of Haram Petel I sent Umaru Shamaki on a journey to Bornu with 120s/3d in order to buy kolas and goods.

October 8th On Wednesday the 9th of Haram Petel Hamman Kobo returned from his journey to Yola and on the same day Malam Mukhtar and Maliki returned from their journey to Mubi. They brought with them a man sent by the Christian Mr. Rosedale to count my land. He therefore sent his man to count the whole of my land.

October 10th On Friday the 11th of Haram Petel Umaru who was accused of the murder of a man ran away. Jailani Bebel had brought the complaint about him to me.

October 11th On Saturday the 12th of Haram Petel I sent Atiku with Headman Umaru to Yola with the whole of the Jangali of my land amounting to £424-16-0. I gave them 10s. for their food.

On the same day I imprisoned the son of Mai Bornu, Hamma, and fined him two woollen mats and 4s.

October 14th On Tuesday the 15th of Haram Petel Dogari Hamman returned from his journey to the Christian. Jailani also returned with a complaint against me.

October 15th On Wednesday the 16th of Haram Petel Malam Umaru returned from his journey to Bornu bringing kolas and white cloth.

On the same day I sent Othman on a journey to the Christian with the papers and witnesses in the case of {the} murdered woman.

October 16th On Thursday the 17th of Haram Petel Sarkin Tafarki and Dadandi returned from their journey to the Christian Mr. Rosedale. A man also arrived from Giara demanding the return of his wife.

October 17th On Friday the 18th of Haram Petel Othman returned from his journey to the Christian, who sent a reply to say he was coming to visit me.

On the same day I gave the scribe Buba the duty of looking after Sule.

October 20th On Monday the 21st of Haram Petel I heard that the Christian Mr. Rosedale had stopped at the village of Duhu.

October 22nd On Wednesday the 23rd of Haram Petel the Christian Mr. Rosedale entered Madagali. I met him and he told me that the clearing of the road had been badly done. I replied that it was well done. However, he told me to put labourers on to it.

October 24th On Friday the 25th of Haram Petel I gave Mai Gari the duty of looking after Duhu, that is to say as "chimajo," and he gave me a red woollen mat. He said to me: "If the pagans come with any complaint they may have, do not let them go to Hamman Gulak." I replied: "No, but if they come to you, you can send them to Hamman Gulak if you like."

October 25th On the following day the Christian Mr. Rosedale went to Tur.

October 27th On Monday the 27th of Haram Petel (I received) from Allah Kyauta 35s., which he gave me on account of the market.

October 29th On Wednesday the last day of Haram Petel we had heavy rain.

October 30th On the following day, Thursday, the 1st of Banjaru Awwal, the Christian Mr. Rosedale went to the hill of Wandei to mark out the boundary. He made it so that the pagans of Tur came into French territory and I get no portion except some farm land. But Bukata was previously in my land.

November 1st On Saturday the Christian returned and spent one night and then moved off. So I parted from him, praise be to God.

The complaint made by Jailani, however, did not do him any good, but a case was proved against Kaji, and I sent him to the Mubi prison the same day.

On the same day I fined Arnado Muduvu three cows and 100 shillings. One cow I gave to Hamman Jarma and Sa'id for their wages.

November 5th On Wednesday the 8th of Banjaru Awwal Dadandi returned from his journey with the Christian. He informed me that a pagan had brought a complaint against Kachella Aji regarding his wife, and he ordered me to settle the matter at 50s. He gave a time limit of 20 days.

November 6th On Thursday the 9th of Banjaru Awwal I heard that Gumlam had returned from his journey to Rei, bringing 15 cattle and a striped gown. So I sent Maliki to Bugel to meet him. Maliki took seven cows to buy them from me and I gave Dauda two, a cow and a calf.

On the same day I dismissed the men of Baba Badam, who had come to receive his money.

[November 7th] On the following day I received a letter from the Christian Mr. Rosedale about the road.

November 8th On Saturday the 11th of Banjaru Awwal I returned to Ahmadu Kuja his female slave by the hand of his brother Bukhari.

November 11th On Tuesday the 13th of Banjaru Awwal my daughter returned from Yola with six horses and her female slaves.

November 12th On Wednesday the 14th of Banjaru Awwal I gave my son Isa all the pagans and told him that if he arrested them without their committing an offence, I would strip him of his possessions.

November 13th On Thursday the 15th of Banjaru Awwal a letter arrived from the Christian Mr. Rosedale containing a complaint made by Jailani that I had taken Kuja's wife and his son and his property.

November 14th On Friday the 16th of Banjaru Awwal I left my house in Madagali and stopped at Mayo Tapare.

November 15th On Saturday the 17th of Banjaru Awwal Gamlam [Gumlam] returned from his journey to Rei. He brought an elephant's tusk and presents, namely a gown and an ornamental cloak.

On the same day I gave Hirsu [Hursu] two horses to sell.

On the same day I left my house at Mayo Tapare and stopped at my house in Madagali.

November 17th On Monday the 19th of Banjaru Awwal the pagans of Tur, who had settled down at Wamga, brought me two female slaves, one of whom had been ransomed by the exchange of a boy. The reason for their being seized was that they were {witches}.

On the same day Hamman Pedo died between noon and evening.

On the same day Isiaku and others ran away.

November 19th On Wednesday the 21st of Banjaru Awwal I sent Sarkin Hausawa on a journey to Bornu to buy me kolas.

November 22nd On Saturday the 24th of Banjaru Awwal I left my house in Madagali and went to Zu.

(Marginal note: On the same day a letter came about outstanding tax and telling me to send the tax to them.)

November 23rd On Sunday the 25th of Banjaru Awwal I left my house at Zu and went to my house in Wuro Alhamdu.

On the same day the pagans of Duhu came to me with two slaves, who were {witches}.

On the same day one of my teeth was pulled out while we were on the road.

November 24th On Monday the 26th of Banjaru Awwal I fined Suleiman 8s.

November 25th On Tuesday the 27th of Banjaru Awwal I left my house at Wuro Alhamdu and went to my house in Maradi.

November 26th On Wednesday the 28th of Banjaru Awwal Jabbule returned from Sarkin Yawi.

On the same day I heard that Sarkin Yawi of Gwoza had died.

November 26th On Wednesday the 29th of Banjaru Awwal I gave Yakuda a place and separated him off from Madhadu, and he gave me a horse.

On the same day I gave Dadandi Mulpul.

November 28th On Friday the 1st of Banjaru Tumbindu Sarkin Hausawa returned from his journey to Bornu bringing among other things kolas and a coloured turban.

November 29th On Saturday the 2nd of Banjaru Tumbindu I sent Dadandi to the Christian Mr. Rosedale and with them the two robbers of the Duhu pagans.

On the same day Malam Abu Bakr came to me.

December 1st On Monday the 4th of Banjaru Tumbindu I heard that Kachakam[a] had run off with my horse and breast-plate.

On the same day I gave Babel 2s.

December 2nd On Tuesday the 5th of Banjaru Tumbindu Dadandi returned from his journey to the Christian Mr. Rosedale, and told me to try the two slaves from the Duhu pagans and to put them wherever I wanted them.

Then I sent Barade Umaru with a letter of welcome and a horse to the Emir of Yola.

On the same day Dadandi informed me of the coming of the Emir of Yola, and so I left my house at Maradi and went to my house at Wuro Alhamdu, where I stayed one night.

Then I left there and went to my house in Zu, where I stayed one night.

December 4th Then on Thursday I left there and entered my house in Madagali.

On the same day the Emir of Yola sent me a letter telling me of his visit, and I at once sent Yerima Abba to him.

December 5th On Friday the 8th of Banjaru Tumbindu the Emir al Yemen arrived in a motor car and passed on to the boundary between myself and Bornu. He then returned and met me at the Rest House. I had a talk with him.

My people were looking at the wheels of the motor car, both the Fulani and the pagans. So I made the Fulani go away, but I allowed the pagans to behave in their accustomed fashion.

Then the Emir of Yola left without staying the night, while I sent Yerima Abba with two horses to him, one as a present to him and one for sale.

December 6th On Saturday the 9th of Banjaru Tumbindu I sent Budalel to the Christian Mr. Rosedale with a letter telling him that the Fulani from French territory had moved over the border to my land. I also returned a woman of the Duhu pagans.

I also gave Mai Bornu 20s., Hayatu a gown and his messenger 1s.

December 7th On Sunday the 10th of Banjaru Tumbindu I left my house in Madagali and went to look at the road, and then returned to my house in Mayo Tapare.

December 10th On Wednesday the 13th of Banjaru Tumbindu I left my house in Mayo Tapare and went to Nyibango.

On the same day Yerima Abba returned from his journey to the Emir of Yola, Maigari, who said he would buy Hamman's horse and asked if he should pay in cows or in something else. I told Yerima Abba I would fine him a small amount for his offence in sleeping on the road and for delaying in the matter of clearing the road.

On the same day Bukhari came to me with a horse for me to buy.

On the same day I wrote a letter to Maliki telling him to return, and I told him of the misfortune which had befallen my friend Umaru.

December 12th On Friday the 15th of Banjaru Tumbindu I paid my debt to Madikunchi with a horse which we valued at 140s. In return I received a ram. There remains due to him 72s.

On the same day Yerima Abba sent me a letter telling me that the Governor [Sir Hugh Clifford] was coming. So for this reason I cancelled my proposed visit to my house in Nyiburi. I sent two horsemen, Sarkin Hausawa and Sa'adu, to Baza to find out the truth for me, and I sent Dadandi to the Christian Mr. Rosedale to ask him about it.

On the same day there arrived the son of my friend Umaru with a letter.

On the same day I gave Hamman three woollen mats as a consolation for the loss of his cow.

December 13th On Saturday the 16th of Banjaru Tumbindu at night Sarkin Hausawa and Sa'adu returned and told me that the Governor's visit had been delayed.

On the same day I left my house at Nyibango and went to Nyiburi.

December 17th On the 20th of Banjaru Tumbindu I imprisoned Buba for misappropriating the price of a female slave of mine. I also seized on his cow, until such time as he pays back what he took. He confessed and returned it to me.

On the same day Waisu arrived with a letter from Yerima Abba saying the Governor [Clifford] had arrived in Yerwa and that the Shehu of Yerwa had gone out to repair the road.

December 18th So I left my house at Nyiburi on Thursday and stopped at my house in Humuchi, where I spent the night. Then I went to Wuro Alhamdu.

On the same day I received a letter from Yerima Abba the contents of which were that the Governor had entered Yerwa with a white man. But at the same time Elias came back with a different story, so I delayed doing anything.

On the same day I sent Umaru to Bornu to buy me kolas. I gave him 15s. and 2s. for his food. He was also to find out for me news about the Governor's visit.

December 21st On Sunday the 24th of Banjaru Tumbindu I left my house in Wuro Alhamdu and went to Maradi.

December 22nd On Monday the 25th of Banjaru Tumbindu Malaki [Maliki] came back at night from his journey to Bugel. Among other things he brought 132/6d.

On the same day Salman brought me news that the Governor was delayed, and it was said he would not arrive for 22 days.

December 23rd On Tuesday the 26th of Banjaru Tumbindu Musa returned from his journey to Yola. The reason for his journey was that Tayau had stolen some money and run off with it. When he heard about it he captured him and took him to the Christian, who imprisoned him. Then they asked for witness from me.

December 24th On Wednesday the 27th of Banjaru Tumbindu Buba Koda returned. I heard that my slave Burti had said that he would run away, and then I found that he had run away. As to the shillings I gave Buba, Atiku took them from him and gave them to the Kadi Mubi.

December 25th On Thursday the 28th of Banjaru Tumbindu I left my house at Maradi and went to Nyibango.

On the same day Umaru Samaki returned from Bornu with 100 kolas.

December 26th On the next day I counted the fish I had got, and they came to 215, apart from those I had sent to Madagali.

And when I stood on the river bank and looked upon it with the look of a tired man,

I found multitudes of fishes in great quantities both South and North in all directions:

And the sight caused us amazement and fear, and I knew by this that there was no such pond anywhere to be found.

(Marginal notes, dates being uncertain:

(a) On this day I began to perform the devotional exercise of the prayer of the Fatihah.

(b) On this day I began to perform the devotional exercises of the prayer of the Prophet Moses.)

December 28th On Sunday the 1st of Banjaru Sakitindu I left Nyibango and returned to my house at Maradi. Then I sent off Malaki [Maliki], Sarkin Hausawa and Abdu, and I gave him 125 in money (presumably shillings). Malaki, however, was to collect the money which the Emir al Yemen was to buy my horse for. I gave Malaki a white gown to wear.

On the same day Abu Bakr returned from his journey to Mindif, and he told me that the Frenchman had imprisoned Kachakama and had taken the goods he had.

December 29th On Monday the 2nd of Banjaru Sakitindu I sent Dali Garba to Mubi as a witness in Tayau's case. I also sent a letter by him regarding the goods which Kachakama had. I sent Allah Kyauta 5s.

On the same day some Bororo came to me and gave me two calves and I gave one of them a horse of mine.

December 31st On Wednesday the 4th of Banjaru Sakitindu I left my house at Maradi and stopped at my house at Wuro Alhamdu.

On the same day my wife gave birth to a male child and I have given him the name of Hamman Wabe. If God will, when his age is seven days, his mother will come out again.

1925

January 2nd On Friday the 6th of Banjaru Sakitindu I left my house at Wuro Alhamdu and stopped at my house at Humuchi.

On the same day Ardo Humsi and Dali Garba returned from their journey to Mubi with Tayau. The Christian said he had sent Tayau to the Court. He also sent a letter about Kachakama.

January 3rd On Saturday the 7th of Banjaru Sakitindu I received a letter from Yerima Abba saying that my brother Abdu had received the headship of Gwoza and asking whether he had any right to it or not.

January 4th On Sunday the 8th of Banjaru Sakitindu I left my house at Humuchi and stopped at my house at Nyiburi.

On the same day Mai Bornu's son came to me from his visit to Moda.

January 7th On Wednesday the 11th of Banjaru Sakitindu I sent Ardo Humsi to Mubi.

January 8th On Thursday the 12th of Banjaru Sakitindu I heard that the Christian from Bornu had come to Bula and I sent my man to welcome him.

January 9th On Friday the 13th of Banjaru Sakitindu I left my house at Nyiburi and stopped at my house at Nyibango.

January 10th On Saturday the 14th of Banjaru Sakitindu I left my house at Nyibango and went to my house in Madagali.

I met the Christian from Bornu and he bought my horse for £8 from Yerima Abba without my permission. He went off the same day and said he intended to return.

(Marginal note: On the same day I sent Dadandi to Mubi and gave Allah Kyauta a horse.)

January 13th On Tuesday the 17th of Banjaru Sakitindu I sent Malam Umaru on a journey to Bornu with 20s. and seven ox hides.

On the same day Dadandi returned from his journey to Mubi as also Biba Adama.

January 14th On Wednesday the 18th of Banjaru Sakitindu Alhaji returned from his journey to Rei, bringing a letter from the Emir of Rei.

On the same day Headman Umaru returned from his journey to Mubi. He said the Christian Mr. Rosedale informed him that what the Christian of Bornu said was said in haste.

January 15th On Thursday the 19th of Banjaru Sakitindu Disinda returned from his journey to Gwoza, but he had not recovered his wife. They told him that he should have her only if he came to them. Similarly Hamajam only recovered 5s.

On the same day there came to me a man named Abu Sabil from the Wadai country. He brought a letter from his Emir and a present of a sword belt from him.

On the same day I named a slave girl Tada after I had freed her.

January 16th On Friday the 20th of Banjaru Sakitindu I investigated the question of my village which the mischief-makers talk about. They say the Christian of Bornu said that unless the Emir of Madagali returns from his journey in 3 days we will prevent him from entering his house. The chief of them are Amin Bajam, Ardo Suyudo, Sule and others.

On the same day I gave Yerima Abba full power and jurisdiction, if I went out into the "bush."

January 20th On Tuesday the 14th of Banjaru Sakitindu Baba Dagashi came to me with the road money amounting to £11.

January 21st On Wednesday the 25th of Banjaru Sakitindu I sent the Emir of Wadai a striped upper garment and I gave his man Abu Sabil two packets of salt and sugar for coming to me with the sword-belt.

On the same day I gave Malam Madugu 10s.

January 22nd On Thursday the 26th of Banjaru Sakitindu Dadandi returned from his journey to Mubi with my letter.

On this day a letter came to me from the Emir of Gaur Bello asking for protection.

January 23rd On Friday the 27th of Banjaru Sakitindu Malam Umaru returned from his journey to Bornu bringing kolas and a letter.

On this date I left my house at Madagali and went to Mayo Tapare.

January 26th On Monday the last day of Banjaru Sakitindu the people of the Nyibango river came to me with the money to buy the fishing rights: this was 43 shillings, but I do not know what the rest amounts to. I gave my people 6s.

[January 27th] On Tuesday the 1st of Sumatendu Waube I changed Dogari Kobaumi for Aguram with the pagans of Muduvu.

January 30th On Friday the 4th of Sumatendu Waube I left my house at Mayo Tapare and went to Madagali.

On this day I journeyed to the bush at Wuro Lainde

February 1st On Sunday the 6th of Sumatendu Waube Adamayel paid up his "zakah" on his cattle: this was four cows.

On the same day I heard that his man said he would settle down and he wanted to know if he was right in doing so or not.

February 4th On Wednesday the 9th of Sumatendu Waube Gedel ran away.

February 6th On Friday the 12th of Sumatendu Waube Sayir returned from his journey to Marua without a horse. He had a letter from the Emir of Marua, as I had sent him a letter to make peace between us.

On the same day a letter came to me from Captain Price concerning Buba's cow and about his coming to see me.

February 7th On Saturday the 13th of Sumatendu Waube I sent Dadandi on a journey to Mubi to the Christian Captain Price and I gave him a horse to give to Allah Kyauta.

On the same day I paid Yerima Abba his debt of 100s. and a cow on account of his horse.

(Marginal note: On Monday there was an eclipse of the moon and on the same day I paid off my debt of 15 shillings to Malam Abu Bakr.)

February 11th On Wednesday the 18th of Sumatendu Waube I again had pains in my stomach.

February 12th On Thursday the 18th of Sumatendu Waube Buba Diji returned from his journey to Yola.

February 16th On Monday the 21st of Sumatendu Waube Sarkin Hausawa returned from his journey to Yola with three white gowns and two lengths of silk, two rolls of white cloth, a length of coloured cloth, some writing paper, ten sashes and some scent. However, the whole lot of it did not please me.

[February 17th] On the following day I sent Mai Bornu's son on a journey to Bornu with a horse to give to the Shehu of Bornu and 15s for my son Musa. I gave them 5s. for their food.

February 19th On Thursday the 24th of Sumatendu Waube Baba Dagashi came to me with £6 road money.

February 20th On Friday the 26th of Sumatendu Waube I left my house in Madagali and stopped at my house in Mayo Tapare, where I spent one night.

February 21st On Saturday the 27th of Sumatendu Waube I left my house in Mayo Tapare and went to Nyibango.

On the same day Maliki Wa'aindi returned from his journey to Yola with 180s.

On the same day I sent Sarkin Hausawa's son to Bornu to buy kolas.

February 24th On Tuesday the last day of Sumatendu Waube I left my house at Nyibango between the two times of the noon and evening prayers and stopped at Zu, where I spent one night.

February 25th On Wednesday the 1st of Jaujaungel I left my house in Zu and went to Wuro Alhamdu. I found that Ajia had ruined part of my house, a thing which made me angry. This occurred on Wednesday the 1st of the month of God Sha'aban in the year 1342 and seven months, that is 208 days, if you subtract three months from them and reckon by the date of the Flight of our Prophet, may the blessing and peace of God be upon Him (see note in Introduction).

February 26th On Thursday the 2nd of Sha'aban I gave the Kadi's son, Biyeri, a horse, and he promised me that when he returned home he would send me a spell.

On the same day I sent Dadandi to the Christian regarding the tax.

February 28th On Saturday the 4th of Sha'aban Mai Bornu's son returned from his journey to Bornu. He brought a gown and a red woollen mat.

On the same day the Kadi Muhammad sent me a letter in which he refused to obey an order. I would not accept this, and wrote another letter and sent Hamman Gulak to Captain Price.

March 1st On Sunday the 5th of Sha'aban I left my house at Wuro Alhamdu and went to Maradi. I bought from a Shuwa two saddle cloths for 105s.

On the same day I sent Othman to Yola with a horse.

March 3rd On Tuesday the 7th of Sha'aban I bought a horse from a Bororo for four cows.

March 7th On Saturday the 11th of Sha'aban I left my house at Maradi and went to my house at Nyibango, where I spent one night.

March 8th On the following day, Sunday, I left there and went to Maradi, where I stayed two nights.

March 10th On Tuesday the 14th of Sha'aban I left my house in Maradi, and stopped at my house in Humuchi.

March 11th On Wednesday the 15th of Sha'aban the Emir of Holma's man arrived bringing me a white gown.

On the same day I bought his horse for 80s. and I also gave him a white gown worth 40s.

On the same day I bought Malam Mansur's horse for 90s. and two cows.

March 16th On Monday the 20th of Sha'aban Othman and Hamman Gulak returned from their journey to Yola. Hamman Gulak brought two rolls of cloth.

March 18th On Wednesday the 22nd of Sha'aban my horse died after Munyal had ridden it.

(Marginal note: On the same day God gave us rain.)

March 21st On Saturday the 25th of Sha'aban I left my house at Nyiburi and stopped at Nyibango, where I spent one night.

March 22nd On Sunday I left there and returned to my house in Madagali. I spent 29 days on this journey.

March 24th On Tuesday the 28th of Sha'aban I sent Malam Umaru to Bornu with 95s. to buy a gown, some writing paper, a sash and a turban.

March 25th On Wednesday the 29th of Sha'aban the Kadi Muhammad refused to hear a case, so I wrote to the Christian Captain Price about it.

March 26th On Thursday the 30th of Sha'aban the Ramadhan new moon appeared.

March 30th On Monday the 4th of Ramadhan I made a solemn agreement on the Koran with Lawan Aji regarding his chieftainship to the effect that he would not contravene my boundary. He then gave me a horse and undertook not to do anything without telling me about it, and similarly in other matters.

March 31st On Tuesday the 5th of Ramadhan Malam Umaru returned from his journey to Bornu bringing kolas, a gown and writing paper.

April 3rd On Friday the 9th of Ramadhan Musa returned from his journey to Yola bringing a tin of kerosene.

On the same day I left my house in Madagali and stopped in my house in Mayo Tapare.

(A scrap of paper inside pages 169–172 of the MS reads: from his journey to Bornu with 100 kolas, two rolls of cloth and scent which my friend Mai Dawa sent me. On the same day I sent Mahmud to the Christian at Mubi, Captain Price, with a letter.)

April 7th On Tuesday the 13th of Ramadhan I left my house at Mayo Tapare and stopped at my house in Nyibango.

April 8th On Wednesday the 14th of Ramadhan I sent Atiku on a journey to Yola with £327 of General Tax.

April 10th On Friday the 16th of Ramadhan I sent Dadandi to the Christian Captain Price.

April 13th On Monday the 21st of Ramadhan I left my house at Nyibango after the evening meal and stopped at my house in Mayo Tapare.

I spent eight days on this journey.

April 16th On Thursday I left Mayo Tapare and stopped at my house in Madagali.

April 17th On Friday the 23rd of Ramadhan Dadandi returned from his journey to Mubi.

On the same day the people of Gwoza came with a letter looking for Zirashima. They said that he had run away with their property.

April 24th On Friday the 29th of Ramadhan my man Sa'id son of Kaigamma Abu Bakr gave me his slave Mai Korgai by name, as he was afraid after some of his slaves had run away.

April 24th On Friday the last day of Ramadhan I paid my debt of 10/9d to Ardo Bulama.

April 25th On Saturday the last day of Ramadhan we celebrated the Id al Fitr.

On the same day I asked the pagans of Kaboro about the land between Magar and Madagali. They said that that land belonged to Magar and by no means to Madagali or any one else. This was all because Lawan Mana and Sa'id son of Kaigamma Bakr had a quarrel.

April 26th On Sunday the 2nd of Juldandu Dadandi and Umaru returned from their journey to Mubi, bringing a letter from Captain Price, in which he gave me permission to allow my scribe Amin to try cases. So I made a solemn agreement with him as follows. He said: "Do not listen to the words of slanderers and mischief-makers, but judge me only in a matter in which I have personally disobeyed you." And I said: "Similarly, I undertake not to hear them but only to judge what I know. I also order you to go to the house which has been built for the Court every Friday and Monday, and I am allowed to hear the case of every one of the disputants who brings a case in the Court."

April 27th On Monday the 3rd of Juldandu Sarkin Hausawa said that the female slave I lent him to prepare his food for him on a journey was now owned by him, because of the loan, so I sent him to the Kadi Amin, who said, "This slave belongs to a slave of the Sarkin Hausawa. Am I therefore to return her to him or not?" and God is knowing in this matter.

On the same day Alhaji Abba said that he was dissatisfied with the Imam Ahmadu in the mosque, because they were saying the morning prayers at night.

April 28th On Tuesday the 4th of Juldandu Headman Umaru returned from his journey to Yola with 68s.

April 29th On Wednesday the 5th of Juldandu Jauro Soji ran away with 8 of his family.

(Marginal note: On Friday the 7th I sent Hamman Kobo to Yola.)

May 2nd On Saturday the 8th of Juldandu I sent Malam Umaru on a journey to Bornu with 193s. to buy me some goods.

On the same day I left my house in Madagali and went to Mayo Tapare.

May 3rd On Sunday the 9th of Juldandu Ardo Humuchi Yaji bought the slaughtering fees from me for a calf and three sheep.

May 5th On Tuesday the 11th of Juldandu I received news of what had happened to Lawan Aji. Pagans named Kila had killed his man Mahabasi.

May 8th On Friday the 14th of Shawwal I left my house in Mayo Tapare and went to Madagali.

May 10th On Sunday the 16th of Juldandu Malam Umaru returned from his journey to Bornu bringing 100 kolas, ten rolls of cloth, two turbans, two head garments and beads.

May 13th On Wednesday the 19th of Juldandu I sent Othman to Yola with a horse for the Emir al Yemen. I also sent the boys to school.

May 15th On Friday the 21st of Juldandu I heard that the Fulani of Mayo Wandu had moved camp on account of the Jangali tax. So I sent Abd al Kerim, Sarkin Shanu, Sa'id, Malam Mukhtar and Dogari Kobauma [Kobaumi] to find out the reason for their moving, for it was proved that this was the correct amount due from the Fulani.

May 20th On Wednesday the 26th of Juldandu my man Audu met Amin ibn Yukuda [Yakuda] by the side of the road. He tells me that Amin ran off and outstripped him, but left behind a bag of papers and his turban. So Audu came back and told me about this. The cause of this is that Amin went to Hamajam Geddo's house and entered it to commit a theft, but did not get anything. Then afterwards some property of Sarkin Zongo's daughter came to light, namely a woollen mat, five sashes and other things.

May 21st On Thursday the 27th of Juldandu I gave my boy some clothes after I had had him circumcised.

On the same day I gave Hursu presents on his marriage.

May 23rd On Saturday the 29th of Juldandu I left my house in Madagali and went to my house in Mayo Tapare.

May 26th On Tuesday the 2nd of Siutorandu I left my house in Mayo Tapare and went to Madagali, where I stayed one night.

May 27th On Wednesday the 3rd of Siutorandu I left there and stopped at my house in Zu.

On the same day Ture came back from his journey to the Christian Captain Price, bringing a letter from Captain Price summoning Lawan Aji.

May 29th On Friday the 5th of Siutorandu I left my house at Zu and stopped at my house at Wuro Alhamdu.

May 31st On Sunday the 7th of Siutorandu Abd Jamare arrived from Wadai.

June 2nd On Tuesday the 9th of Siutorandu I left my house at Wuro Alhamdu and stopped at my house at Maradi.

On the same day the Christian Captain Price sent me a letter and I sent him a list of people from French country, who are in my land.

June 6th On Saturday the 14th of Siutorandu Othman returned from his journey to Yola bringing a large gown with him and 224s.

[June 7th] On the following day I gave my people 20s.

June 8th On Monday the 16th of Siutorandu a letter arrived from Captain Price ordering me to go to see him.

June 9th On Tuesday the 17th of Siutorandu I left my house at Maradi and following the boundary between me and Duhu arrived at Humuchi. Then after the evening meal I left there on hearing that the Emir al Yemen had arrived at Mubi, and I did not rest even for an hour nor enjoy any sleep, until I reached Mubi on Wednesday.

There I met with the Resident of Yola and the Emir of Yola, who put me into his car and took me to his house. But he did not give me the car to take me back to my house. Then I paid my men.

June 11th On the following day, Thursday, I went to the Rest House, where I met the Emir al Yemen. He again put me into his car, but this time told me to return with it to my house.

I gave the Emir a horse and the District Head of Mubi a horse.

June 12th On Friday the 20th of Siutorandu I took my leave of the Emir al Yemen and the Resident Yola and Captain Price, and he praised me very much for completing my General Tax and for other things. Then I took my leave of the Emir of Yola, who said to me: "I will give you a motor car."

June 14th On Sunday the 22nd of Siutorandu I left Mubi and stopped at Kuzum, where I spent one night.

June 15th On the 23rd of the month I left Kuzum and stopped at my house in Humuchi, where I stayed one night.

June 16th On Tuesday the 24th of Siutorandu I left my house in Humuchi and stopped at my house in Nyiburi, where I spent one night.

(Marginal note: I left there and went to my house in Wuro Alhamdu.)

June 17th On Wednesday I left there and went to my house in Humuchi and then I left there and went to my house at Maradi, where I stayed one night.

June 19th On Friday the 27th of Siutorandu I sent Othman to Yola and I gave the Emir al Yemen 100s., a bed covering and 50 kolas. I also gave Mukaddas 50s.

June 21st On Sunday the 29th of Siutorandu I left my house at Wuro Alhamdu and went to Zu. Then I left there and returned to my house in Madagali.

June 23rd On Tuesday the 1st of Laihaji I sent my men to the Sarkin Fada Bukr to arrest Buba Linga.

June 29th On Monday the 7th of Laihaji I left my house in Madagali and stopped at my house in Mayo Tapare.

On the same day Asabu and Tayau returned from their journey to Bornu, bringing two rolls of cloth.

July 2nd On Thursday the 10th of Laihaji we celebrated the Id al Adhdha. On the same day I returned to my house in Madagali.

July 6th On Monday the 14th of Laihaji Mamma Dunga died.

On the same day Galadima arrested people who dance wanton dances.

July 10th On Friday the 18th of Laihaji the marriage case between Barade Umar and his wife Sadiya was finished in the Court. I told Barade that I acquitted him.

On the same day a great deal of rain fell.

July 14th On Tuesday the 22nd of Laihaji Othman returned from his journey to Yola.

On the same day Dadandi returned from his journey to Mubi.

July 15th On Wednesday the 23rd of Laihaji a messenger from the Christian at Gwoza arrived. His name was Gerima Kolo. He said that the son of Umaru Fodo had stolen some cartridges.

July 18th On Saturday the 26th of Laihaji I left my house in Madagali and went to Zu.

July 19th On Sunday I left there and went to my house at Wuro Alhamdu.

July 20th On Monday the 28th of Laihaji I received news that Malam Hamidu had fled with his family.

On the same day Hammadu returned from his journey to Bornu bringing 100 kolas, two rolls of cloth and some scent, which my friend Mai Dawa sent me.

On the same day I sent Mahmud to the Christian Captain Price with a letter.

July 24th On the 2nd of Muharram I settled the dispute between Hasan and Wolamasu at two cows and 40s. The affair concerned a murdered man.

On the same day I sent Malaki to Yola with a horse as a present to the Emir al Yemen, and with 45s. to buy me a gown.

On Friday the 2nd of Muharram I finally dismissed the Imam of Nyiburi. I had kept him 45 days and his pay was three cows. I gave him 4s. and will give him the whole amount if God in His power grants us the fulfilment of our desire.

July 27th On Monday the 6th of Muharram I sent Hamman Kobo to Rei with three horses, one a present to him from me and the other two for sale. I also gave him a striped upper garment.

July 31st On Friday the 10th of Muharram Gora went to Yola.

On the same day I arrested Galwa and Buba Maradi for their offence in not obeying my summons and I had them flogged and imprisoned. Galwa, however, I will free from slavery when he comes out of prison in three days' time, if there is a reason for his being freed.

On the same day Hamman Gulak gave me 10s., so I paid off the debt of my man Sa'id.

August 1st On Saturday the 11th of Muharram a letter came to me from Abdu Mubi, in which it was said that my man Sa'id sent to his female slave to tell her not to stay with him. So I sent a letter to him and told him my people would not harm the girl Wairata.

August 7th On Friday the 17th of Muharram I drank some cold milk and when I had finished it, I had a vomiting fit, and from that time on I had a bad cold.

On the same day a man of the Duhu pagans, Dumure, gave me a strip of cloth.

On the same day I gave some of my people a horse, namely Yerima Abd al Kerim and Barade Umaru, while others I gave gowns on their visiting me to congratulate me on my regaining strength.

August 11th On Tuesday the 21st of Muharram Jidiri returned from his journey to Yola, bringing with him some plantains. I asked Galadima about them, and he said that if they were planted they would produce fruit in about 12 months. I told him I thought not, but God is knowing.

On the same day Yerima Bello sent me 12s. of which I gave my scribe Amin 8s. and returned Yerima Bello 4s. He also sent me a white gown and a woollen mat. The gown I gave to Daltilka and returned Yerima Bello the mat.

August 16th On Sunday the 25th of Muharram Hamman Gulak, Yerima Yakub, Yerima Abd al Kerim and Barade Umaru complained about the money for my horse which I had given them. So I returned 15s. to the complainants.

August 18th On Tuesday the 27th of Muharram I left my house in Maradi and went to Humuchi.

August 20th On Thursday the 29th of Muharram I received news that a man of the Mildu pagans named Bisikiri had killed Arnado Madu and that Arnado Madu's brother had killed the murderer. The cause of the murder was the murder of his guest. Anyway, the result was three men killed.

August 21st On Friday the last day of Muharram I bought a horse from Ayub for 70s.

August 22nd On Saturday the 1st of Tumbindu Haramji I left my house in Humuchi and went to Nyiburi.

August 25th On Tuesday the 4th of Tumbindu Haramji I left my house in Nyiburi and stopped at my house in Nyibango. On the road between Nyiburi and Nyibango I was caught by a heavy downpour of rain.

August 26th On Wednesday the 5th of Tumbindu Haramji Dadandi returned from his visit to the Christian Mr. Leonard. He told me that the Christian ordered me to go to meet him on the road between my house and Moda.

August 27th On Thursday the 6th of Tumbindu Haramji I left my house at Nyibango and went to my house at Zu. After the evening meal I started off again and reached my house at Wuro Alhamdu in the middle of the night.

August 28th On the following day, Friday, I started off and met the Christian Mr. Leonard by the river Talwarchira. I was on one bank and he was on the other, and when he was about to cross the river, I told him to wait, so that my carriers might carry him across on my hammock. However, he refused and his carriers carried him.

August 30th On Sunday the 9th of Tumbindu Haramji I went to the Rest House at Duhu and saw the Christian Mr. Leonard. I entered and talked to him at great length. He told me that if the pagans of Duhu brought me their General Tax, he would hand them over to me. So I went off to Guram and in a little while Jauro Duhu and his pagans brought me their tax amounting to 855s.

September 1st On Tuesday the 11th of Tumbindu Haramji I left my house at Wuro Alhamdu, on hearing that the Christian had reached Madagali. His first intention when he left Duhu was to go to Mildu only. However, we went to Madagali.

On this journey I spent a month and a half.

September 2nd On Wednesday the 12th of Tumbindu Haramji I sent Musa to Yola with the tax of the Duhu pagans, which was £42-15-0.

On the same day my man Sa'id gave me a ram.

September 3rd On Thursday the 13th of Tumbindu Haramji the Christian came to me and I went with him to my house, that of Suleiman. Then we went to the house of Abba Dottiwa, and then to the market, where we stayed a little while. He then described to us the advantages of villages with mountain castles, and we then went and stood by the gate of Ardo Bulama. Here I took my leave of him, but returned to him again after the noon-day prayer. He then ordered me to produce the people who were in chains and asked me about them. I told him about this matter, and he then went in person to Sarkin Shanu's house, but found no prisoners, as he had said.

September 4th On Friday the 14th of Tumbindu Haramji the Christian went off to Duhu with the people who were in chains, and I followed along after him and stopped at Zu.

September 5th On Saturday the 15th of Tumbindu Haramji I left my house at Zu and went to the Rest House at Duhu, where I met the Christian. He ordered me to release the people in chains, if I wished, and I did so.

September 6th On Sunday the 16th of Tumbindu Haramji I took my leave of the Christian Mr. Leonard. I also talked to him about the boundary between me and Duhu, and he ordered Jauro Duhu to go along the boundary every month and inform me by letter that he had done so.

September 8th On the 18th of Tumbindu Haramji I ordered Sarkin Shanu and my son Abd al Kerim and others and Jauro Duhu to go along the boundary and mark it out from near the house of a man named Derebi on to a "bobori" tree, then on to a "golombi" tree and then on to a wild fig tree.

September 9th On Wednesday the 19th of Tumbindu Haramji I left my house at Wuro Alhamdu and went to Zu, where I spent one night.

September 10th On Thursday I left there and entered Madagali, where I stayed six days.

September 11th On Friday the 21st of Tumbindu Haramji I gave Awa Marghi 6s. and Ni'ma 2s.

September 12th On Saturday the 22nd of Tumbindu Haramji I left my house in Madagali and went to Mayo Tapare.

September 14th On Monday the 25th of Tumbindu Haramji Galadima's horse died.

September 17th On Thursday the 27th of Tumbindu Haramji I left Mayo Tapare and went to Madagali.

> On the same day I gave Abbas the Fulani of Karchinga.
>
> (Marginal note: On this day Dadandi returned with my letter which I had sent to Mubi regarding the Duhu boundary.)
>
> On Friday night there was heavy rain.

September 18th On Friday the 29th of Tumbindu Haramji, on Saturday the last day of the month (*sic*) I sent Buba to Yola to buy me some goods, namely two tins of kerosene, a lamp and a tent. I gave Malaki 8s.

September 22nd On Tuesday the 2nd of Haram Petel the Christian Mr. Leonard sent me two letters ordering me to write up the whole of my land and in the other asking me the reason for the decrease in the cattle count, which did not reach what he would agree to.

September 23rd On the following day, Wednesday, I sent Malam Mukhtar and Atiku to Mubi, so that he might see the register.

September 26th On Saturday in the month of Tumbindu Haramji Petel (*sic*) Musa returned from his journey to Yola bringing £19-19-4, the money of the Madagali Village Heads. He also brought my pay, £17.

September 27th On Sunday the 7th of Tumbindu Haramji Petel I sent Headman Umaru and Dadandi to Yola with £432. I also sent by the hand of Dadandi a letter of welcome to the new Governor. [This would seem to refer to Sir Graeme Thompson, but, in fact, he did not arrive in Nigeria until 1926.]

On this day I sowed onions.

September 28th On Monday the 8th of Haram Petel I paid my debt of 90s. to Malam Mansur: 40s. of this was the cost of "aflas" (?) and the rest I had borrowed from him.

September 30th On Wednesday the 11th of Haram Petel Maliki returned from his journey. He brought the news that the Emir al Yemen promised to sell me a motor car.

October 2nd On Friday the 13th of Haram Petel Malam Mukhtar and Atiku returned from their journey to the Christian Mr. Leonard and had got him to agree to the cattle-count.

October 6th On Tuesday the 17th of Haram Petel I sent Kachella Umaru to the Christian Mr. Leonard in regard to the pagans who were raiding each other.

October 11th On Sunday the 22nd of Haram Petel the pagans of Mildu came to me and asked for a chief to be appointed to them. The chief man, Dhubagawa by name, gave me 180s: this is what I received, if they agreed to him, and there is still due from him 120s. more.

October 12th On Monday the 23rd of Haram Petel Kachella Umaru returned from his journey to Mubi.

October 13th On the following day, Tuesday, Interpreter Allah Kyauta came to me with a letter from the Christian Mr. Leonard about the chief of Mildu and about the people whom I had appointed, who were oppressing the pagans.

On Tuesday the 24th of Haram Petel I sent Hamadu Aji to Bornu to buy me kolas and cloth.

October 15th On Thursday the 25th of Haram Petel Allah Kyauta went off. I gave him 30s. and a saddle-cloth.

On the same day Sarkin Tafarki left.

October 16th On Friday the 27th of Haram Petel I asked my scribe Amin to forgive me for speaking a little harshly to him regarding Arnado Sukur.

(Marginal note: On the same day Dadandi and Headman Umaru and Eliasa returned from their journey to Yola.)

October 17th On Saturday the 28th of Haram Petel I left my house in Madagali and went to my farms and then returned to Mayo Tapare.

October 20th On Tuesday the 2nd of Banjaru Awwal Hamadu Aji returned from his journey to Bornu. He brought 100 kolas and one roll of cloth.

On this day God sent us very much rain.

October 22nd On Friday the 5th of Banjaru Awwal at night I left my house at Mayo Tapare at sunset and went to my house at Nyibango, reaching it before the moon set. I did not feel weak from the journey.

Gora and Malam Abu Bukr [*sic*] returned from their journey to Yola and the record-book was returned to Gora. Mukaddas sent me some salt.

October 25th On Sunday the 7th of Banjaru Awwal Atiku returned from his journey to Mubi.

October 26th On Monday the 8th of Banjaru Awwal I made Dhubagawa chief of Mildu and gave him a gown.

In the morning Atiku quarrelled with Barade Umaru.

October 30th On Friday the 12th of Banjaru Awwal I left my house in Nyibango and visited Bebel. Then I returned to my house in Madagali.

I spent eight days on this journey.

(Marginal note: On this day I was seized with great pain which lasted until Banjaru Tumbindu, when I obtained relief on a Friday.)

November 2nd On Monday the 15th of Banjaru Awwal I handed my horse to Hursu for him to sell it even though for only 400s. I told him to buy me a reed mat, a turban, a gown and a woollen mat.

November 11th On Wednesday the 24th of Banjaru Awwal Shakari returned after having been arrested by the Christian Mr. Leonard on a charge brought by the pagans of Mildu that he had killed Arnado Madu.

November 13th On Friday the 25th of Banjaru Awwal I gave Malam Umaru 200s. to trade with. I told him to spend it where he wished, and said I had no use for anything except hard cash.

November 14th On Saturday the 26th of Banjaru Awwal I ordered the pagans of Wamga to pay 100s. all of them, whereas only some of them have been paying.

November 17th On Tuesday the last day of Banjaru Awwal my slave asked me for the donkey road, for which he gave me a striped upper garment, a gown, a donkey and 37s. The agreement was that the people of Madagali should take their donkeys at an appointed place and pay to him only.

On the same day Malam Abu Bakr finished paying his debt of 14s., of which I gave 8s. to my people.

I received 11s. and a donkey and gave it to my son Ahmadu.

November 18th On Wednesday the 1st day of Banjaru Tumbindu Kachella Madi gave me a woollen mat with the request that I would leave him in his village for the future so that he might make his people repair the well.

November 23rd On Monday the 7th of Banjaru Tumbindu Malam Umaru returned from his journey to Bornu. Among the things he brought back were two calves, five rolls of cloth, 26 kolas and a tin of scent, three packets of scent and two bottles.

November 24th On Tuesday the 8th of Banjaru Tumbindu the pagans of Kamale accused one of their men of being a "witch" and they caught him and brought him to me. They wanted too to reap his corn, so I sent horsemen to them.

November 27th On Friday the 11th of Banjaru Tumbindu I sent my wife to her family at Marua and returned her to her people. I gave her 15s. and two woollen mats.

I am writing this to record that I was attacked by an illness—a cold—on Sunday the 7th of the month of Banjaru Awwal, and I have been troubled by it until now, Friday the 11th of Banjaru Tumbindu, when my head has got some relief from it.

November 28th On Saturday the 12th of Banjaru Tumbindu I went to my farm after having ordered the people of Madagali to help me in the harvesting. On my return I gave them a horse.

November 29th On Sunday the 13th of Banjaru Tumbindu Barkindu returned from his journey to Kano. He brought back 200s. and 58 pieces of iron valued at 20s: ten of them had been spent on food for the two of them. I ordered him to buy me a gown, kolas, two turbans, some silk, a scarf and some wide cloth.

December 1st On Tuesday the 15th of Banjaru Tumbindu I sent Sarkin Tafarki to Bornu to buy me kola nuts.

December 3rd On Thursday the 17th of Banjaru Tumbindu Yerima Nana and his men returned from their journey to Nyiburi. They said that the pagans of Sina are better than the pagans of Kamale and other pagans.

December 6th On Sunday the 20th of Banjaru Tumbindu Malam Umaru went to Michika to sell two calves of his.

December 7th On Monday night the 21st of Banjaru Tumbindu Sarkin Tafarki returned from his journey to Bornu and among the things he brought with him were 63 kolas and 28s.

December 9th On Wednesday the 24th of Banjaru Tumbindu I sent Buba Kudeji to Yola with a letter.

December 10th On Thursday the 24th of Banjaru Tumbindu Malam Buba died. O God, forgive him and have mercy on him, and visit us not with calamity now he has gone.

December 11th On Friday the 26th of Banjaru Tumbindu my house at Nyibango was burnt to the ground.

December 14th On Monday the 27th of Banjaru Tumbindu I sent Buba Kudeji with a letter to Yola to get my pay.

On the same day Malam Umaru returned from his journey to Michika. According to him he lost 8s. over his sale.

December 15th On Tuesday the 28th of Banjaru Tumbindu Jauro Adamayel gave me a one-year-old cow, which had never calved, while Ardo Hamman of Mayo Wandu gave me a calf.

December 17th On Thursday the last day of Banjaru Tumbindu I heard that the pagans of Duhu had stolen my cow, so I sent my horsemen to follow their tracks.

December 19th On Saturday the 2nd of Banjaru Sakitindu I left my house at Nyibango and stopped at my house at Zu.

On the same day Bello Nakola [Nakula?] and Baba Dagashi came to me to examine the road, but they refused to stay with me because of my disagreement with them. While I was at Nyibango I sent to Bello and told him to wait until I met him at Zu, but he refused to wait for me at Zu and passed on to my village, where he spent two nights. He then left Madagali and met me on the road to Zu at the end of the Chabbula

[Chambula, Hymbula] hill. So I sat down with the two of them in the middle of the road and talked to them for a while, and then I said goodbye to them. They went on to Duhu with my son Abd al Kerim. Then I rested halfway along the road and then started after the evening prayer and stopped at Wuro Alhamdu.

December 22nd On Tuesday the 6th of Banjaru Sakitindu Malam Mukhtar returned from his journey to Yola bringing a letter from the Christian Mr. Leonard ordering me to collect the tax quickly this month.

December 25th On Friday in the month of Banjaru Sakitindu I left my house at Wuro Alhamdu and stopped at my village of Maradi.

On the same day Yerima Baba of Moda came to see me.

December 29th On Tuesday the 12th of Banjaru Sakitindu I left my house at Maradi and went to Nyibango.

December 30th On Wednesday the 13th of Banjaru Sakitindu Malam Umaru returned from his journey to Bornu. Among the things he brought back with him were a black gown, 5 rolls of cloth and much goods.

On the same day Atiku returned from his journey to Yola together with Buba. They brought with them 99s.

1926

January 1st On Friday the 15th of Banjaru Sakitindu I sent Koka on a journey to Bugel with 17s., 5s. for himself and the rest for Dauda.

On the same day I sent Hamman Kobo a horse and 6s. as his own horse had died.

On the same day I arrested a pagan of Nyibango together with his father on a charge of wounding a man, and I imprisoned him for this.

January 2nd On Saturday the 16th of Banjaru Sakitindu I left my house at Nyibango and returned to my house at Maradi.

January 3rd On Sunday the 17th of Banjaru Sakitindu I heard that someone from Bornu had come to look at the road and had then returned. He did not, however, reach me.

January 5th On Tuesday the 19th of Banjaru Sakitindu my brother, Waziri Sabara, gave me 4s.

(Slip attached to p. 184 of MS:

"In the name of God; Praise be to God the One, and the blessing of God be upon Him after whom there is no Prophet.

"Let him who pauses to regard this writing know that the Emir of Madagali, Muhammad Yaji, may God lengthen his age, ordered Malam Abu Bakr to mark out the site of the mosque in Gubla, and he desired that his village should build it. So I set out for this purpose after sunset on the 24th day of Jumadi al Ukhra, and journeyed to the place, Gubla, and waited for the appearance of the Eastern stars. Then I took exceeding care and marked out the line, and with the help of God (be He exalted) I laid out a line straight in the direction of the Kiblah on to the place of the Ka'abah. Peace.

"Dated the 12th of November 13: the 24th of Jumadi al Ukhra 1345."

Note that the 24th of Jumadi al Ukhra is equivalent to January 10, 1926; also the figure 13 after November in the text appears to have no meaning.)

January 6th On Wednesday the 20th of Banjaru Sakitindu I returned to my house at Gubla and the mosque.

January 8th On Friday the 22nd of Banjaru Sakitindu I left my house at Wuro Alhamdu and went to my house at Zu.

January 9th On Saturday the 23rd of Banjaru Sakitindu I left my house at Zu and returned to my house in Madagali

I spent 30 days on this journey.

January 10th On Sunday the 24th of Banjaru Sakitindu I sent Buba Kudehi [Kudeji] to Yola and ordered him to take 40 dollars and give them to Mai Bornu.

January 11th On Monday the 25th of Banjaru Sakitindu I sent Hamadu to Bornu.

January 16th On Saturday the 1st of Sumatendu Waube I gave the Emir al Yemen's man 15s.

January 17th On Sunday the 3rd of Sumatendu Waube Barkindu returned from Kano with 15 rolls of cloth, 300 kolas, a black gown, two turbans and a roll of silk.

January 19th On Tuesday the 5th of Sumatendu Waube Hamadu returned from his journey to Bornu and among the things he brought were a roll of cloth, two woollen mats and 26 kolas.

January 22nd On Friday the 7th of Sumatendu Waube my women slaves, Ni'ma Dadiya and Koita, came shrieking out against me and saying that they did not get enough to eat and that they could not give birth to any children.

January 23rd On Saturday the 8th of Sumatendu Waube I left my house in Madagali and met the Christian Mr. Leonard at Duhu. I stayed at my house at Wuro Alhamdu, where I spent two nights.

On Monday I took my leave of him.

January 25th On Monday the 10th of Sumatendu Waube my wife Siyuma died, may God (be He exalted) have mercy on her and the Prophet (be He glorified).

On the same day Jerju complained against me before Mr. Leonard, and the latter returned to him one cow, two calves and 40s. to be in charge of him as wakil.

January 28th On Thursday the 13th of Sumatendu Waube I left my house in Wuro Alhamdu and went to my village of Humuchi, where I spent two nights. I bought a horse from Ardo Hamman Abba for four cows and a calf.

January 30th On Saturday in the month of Sumatendu Waube I left my house at Humuchi and went to my village of Nyiburi, where I bought a horse from Malam Hamman Nuar for four cows and a calf.

On the same day I sent Ture off to Bugel to offer my condolences on the death of a man named Hamma Adda.

January 31st On Sunday the 16th of Sumatendu Waube I sent Dagadi to Mubi with a letter.

February 3rd On Wednesday the 29th (*sic*) of Sumatendu Waube Hamman Kobo returned from his journey to Rei, bringing 400 five-franc pieces.

On the same day Dagadi returned from his journey to Mubi and informed me that the Christian Mr. Leonard praised and thanked me extremely and boundlessly.

On the 19th of Sumatendu Waube I ordered Malam Umaru Shamaki to go off on a journey to Kano taking with him 14 cows. I also ordered Malam Umaru to sell (? buy) me a gown, a striped upper garment and four turbans.

On the same day I gave Bello Nakura the horse on account of the matter between a man named Bajam and the Kaigamma. Bajam had started off with Bello Nakura and had gone to Moda, so I sent my man to bring him back. I gave Bajam 30s. as compensation for his compound which the Kaigamma had destroyed, pulling down the houses in it. So the tale-bearer told Bello Nakura about it and Bello told him to go to Mubi to the Christian Mr. Leonard. However, God prevented him with His power and majesty.

February 5th On Friday the 21st of Sumatendu Waube I left my house at Nyiburi and went to Humuchi, where I spent one night.

February 6th On Saturday I left there and went to my house at Maradi, where I spent two nights.

February 8th On Monday the 24th of Sumatendu Waube I left my house at Maradi and went to Wuro Alhamdu, where I spent one night.

February 9th On Tuesday I left there and went to Zu.

February 10th On Wednesday the 26th of Sumatendu Waube I left my house at Zu and returned to Madagali.

On the road I received a letter from Bukhari that Ahmadu, Jamari and Gagana had been imprisoned for selling two persons entrusted to their care. This is hearsay.

February 11th On Thursday the 27th of Sumatendu Waube Hamadu returned from his journey to Bornu. Among the things he brought with him were 100 kolas and beads.

February 17th On Wednesday the 3rd of Jaujaungel I ordered Buba Malabu to move to his village or I would take it away from him. This was because he talked mischievously in saying, "When the Christian sent for you to come to Government Station, who was it who got the place ready for him except us?" Anyway, all of the people of Madagali heard this mischievous talk.

On the same day I sent Muhammadu to the Christian Mr. Leonard, as he had ordered me to do. The reason was that Kariba went to him with a complaint about his slave girl, and came back to me with two letters saying I had a man named Muhammadu, who is in possession of a rifle and ammunition.

February 18th On Thursday the 4th of Wairordu Sumaye I sent Madi and Buba to meet Malam Umaru on the road from Kano. I gave them 11s. as their hire, and I also gave them two old turbans.

(Marginal note: On the same day I gave my daughter to Sa'id in marriage.)

February 19th On Friday the 5th of Wairordu Sumaye I left my house in Madagali and went to Mayo Tapare.

February 20th On Saturday the 6th of Wairordu Sumaye I bought three horses from Bororo people for ten cows.

February 19th On Friday the 7th of Wairordu Sumaye I went to my house in Mayo Tapare, where I stayed two nights.

Then I left my house at Mayo Tapare and stopped at my house in Madagali.

February 21st On Sunday the 9th day of Sumaye (*sic*) a letter arrived from the Emir al Yemen summoning me in to him urgently without delay.

February 22nd On the 8th of Wairordu Sumaye I left Madagali on my journey to Yola, and stayed in my house at Zu for one night.

February 23rd On the 10th of Wairordu Sumaye I left my house at Zu and stopped at my village of Wuro Alhamdu for one night.

February 24th On the 11th of Wairordu Sumaye I left my house at Wuro Alhamdu and stopped at my village of Humuchi for one night.

February 25th On Thursday in the month of Wairordu Sumaye I left my village of Humuchi and stopped at Kuzum for one night.

February 26th On Friday the 13th of Wairordu Sumaye I left Kuzum and stopped at Mubi.

February 27th On Saturday the 14th of Wairordu Sumaye I left Mubi and stopped at Kwagol for one night.

February 28th On Sunday the 15th of Wairordu Sumaye I left Kwagol and stopped at Zummu, where the Emir of Zummu gave me a large calf. In returned I gave him a horse.

March 1st On Monday the 16th of Wairordu Sumaye I left Zummu and stopped at Woderimo for one night.

March 2nd On the 17th of Wairordu Sumaye I left Woderimo and stopped at Malabu.

March 3rd On the 8th (*sic*) of Wairordu Sumaye I left Malabu and stopped at Giri. This was on Thursday the 18th of Wairordu Sumaye, and I spent one night there.

March 4th Then on Friday the 19th of Wairordu Sumaye I arrived in Yola.

March 12th On Friday the 27th of Wairordu Sumaye I went to Yola and met the Emir al Yemen the 1st. Then I returned to my house.

March 16th On Tuesday the 2nd of Ramadhan I went to the Government station and met the Resident and the Emir al Yemen, and then I took my leave of him. After returning, I left after sunset for Yola and took my leave of the Emir al Yemen.

I had stayed there 12 days.

On Tuesday the 2nd of Ramadhan a letter came to me from Ajia, saying he had quarrelled with the Kadi Amin over a question of two slaves who had been bought in Mokolo. I had ordered him to take them from him and then I heard that he had made a complaint to the Christian.

On the same day I left Yola and stopped at Giri.

March 17th On Wednesday I left there and went to Mayo Kulengi.

March 18th On Thursday I left there and went to Marwau and on Friday I went to Bugel, where I gave Dauda a calf and trousers.

March 22nd On Monday I left there and went to Mayo Koyel and on that day I gave the Emir of Bebel a horse.

(Marginal note: On the same day I heard that my son had passed through.)

March 23rd On Tuesday I left there and went to . . .

[March 24th] Gelle, and on Wednesday I reached Mubi.

March 25th On the following day I went to the Government Station and took my leave of the Christian Mr. Leonard.

March 26th On Friday the 12th of Ramadhan I left my house at Mubi and went to Kuzum.

March 27th On Saturday the 13th of Ramadhan I left my house at Kuzum and went to Humuchi. On the same day Malam Umaru returned to me from his journey to Kano, and brought with him 800s. and goods to the value of 200s.

On the same day Yakub returned from his journey to buy me horses and I gave him a shirt, 20s. and a roll of cloth.

March 28th On Sunday the 14th of Ramadhan I left my house in Humuchi and went to Maradi.

March 29th On Monday I left there and went to Wuro Alhamdu.

March 30th On Tuesday I left there and went to Zu, and

March 31st then on Wednesday I left there and went to Madagali.

I spent on this journey 37 days.

April 1st On Thursday the 18th of Ramadhan I heard that the Christian Mr. Leonard had sent for the Kadi Amin. So I sent Atiku to Mubi with 100s. to give Allah Kyauta.

April 5th On Monday the 12th (*sic*) of Ramadhan I gave Hafidu al Sheikh a horse as an alms offering.

April 6th On Tuesday the 13th of Ramadhan I received two letters from the Christian Mr. Leonard. In one he asked me whether I had repaired my market previously, and in the second he wrote about witnesses in the case of Ardo Bawuru's son and the murder among the Duhu pagans.

April 7th On Wednesday the 23rd of Ramadhan I left my house in Madagali and went to Mayo Tapare.

April 8th On Thursday the 24th of Ramadhan I left my house at Mayo Tapare and went to Nyibango, where I stayed 4 days.

April 10th On Saturday the 26th of Ramadhan the people of Duhu brought me a man who had committed a murder.

On the same day Sa'idu returned from Gulak with a man who had committed a murder. I had sent him to arrest this man. So I then sent Dadandi with both of them to the Christian Mr. Leonard.

On the same day I left Nyibango and returned to Mayo Tapare.

April 12th On the 28th of Ramadhan I left Mayo Tapare and went to Madagali.

April 13th On Tuesday the last day of Ramadhan we saw the new moon, and that evening I gave my man Sa'id a short black gown.

(Marginal note: On the same day Atiku came back with a letter.)

April 14th On Wednesday the 1st of Shawwal we celebrated the Id al Fitr. I also went through the market with a view to repairing it.

April 18th On Sunday the 5th of Shawwal the Resident and Mr. Leonard arrived in Madagali.

April 19th On Monday the 6th of Shawwal the Resident arrested the Kadi Amin and Yaya and Risku, the Kadi Amin for his crime in selling a slave, and Yaya and Risku for imprisoning the young boy. He also ordered me to correct the Court Record Book.

On the same day I cleared Gabdo of guilt before the Resident, who told him not to do as he had been doing, or he would prevent himself being given his freedom.

I then took my leave of them.

In addition he increased the time I might keep people in prison by nine days. He also gave me £8 for road work.

April 20th On Tuesday the 7th of Shawwal the Christians left Madagali.

On the same day Malam Mukhtar returned me the Record Book.

April 21st On Wednesday the 8th of Shawwal I heard that a man in Madagali tried to get in to see the Christians but he did not succeed.

April 24th On Saturday the 11th of Shawwal Malam Umaru brought me the money I had given him to trade with, amounting to 200s. The profit was 100s. and I gave him 50s. as his hire out of the total amount of 300s.

April 27th On Tuesday the 14th of Shawwal I sent Malam Umaru on a journey to Bornu to buy me goods. I gave him 105s.

April 30th On Friday the 17th of Shawwal Allah Kyauta sent me a letter in which he mentioned the Christian Captain Reed.

On the same day in the month of Shawwal I sent Atiku to Yola with a letter saying I had appointed the Imam Ahmadu to the Madagali Court. I also mentioned the matter of a motor car.

On the same day I bought a horse from Ardo Suyudi for three cattle, that is a cow and a calf and another cow.

May 1st On Saturday the 18th of Shawwal I left Gubla and went to my house in Mayo Tapare.

May 2nd On Sunday the 19th of Shawwal I gave Dogari Kabaumi Udhwa a horse as a reward.

May 3rd On Monday the 20th of Shawwal I left Mayo Tapare and went to my farm at Wibengo, where I stayed during the day. Then I left in the afternoon, after ordering my horsemen to proceed to the farm which is behind Barai, while I went on and stopped at my house at Nyibango.

May 6th On Thursday the 23rd of Shawwal I said goodbye to Malam Ibrahim and Malam Hamman Sa'id. Their fee for reading the Koran was 15s.

May 7th On Friday the 24th of Shawwal I left my house at Nyibango and stopped at Mayo Tapare.

I spent 4 days on this journey.

May 9th On Sunday the 26th of Shawwal the pagans of Tur brought me 45 iron tokens valued at 11s. and I increased the amount by 30s. I gave my man Kaigamma Sa'id a ram as his wage. This was after the time I originally fixed owing to pressure of time.

May 16th On Sunday the 3rd of Siutorandu my female slave died during the night. On the same day I gave my people a calf.

May 20th On Thursday the 8th of Siutorandu I sent off Sarkin Tafarki with two letters, one to the Christian and the other to the Emir al Yemen, telling them about the payment of the tax and about giving Sa'id the duty of District scribe.

May 21st On Friday the 9th of Siutorandu Atiku returned from his journey to Yola, bringing a letter from the Christian Captain Reed, in which he said he was delaying his reply to my letter until he could visit me. As regards the matter of a motor car, he said I should inform the Emir al Yemen, and ask whether he also would permit me to have one. As to the visit of the Emir al Yemen to me, he said he did not know whether he would come or not.

May 22nd On Saturday the 10th of Siutorandu I sent Buba Kudeji to Yola and on the same day I left my house in Madagali and went to Gubla, and then I returned to my house in Mayo Tapare.

May 23rd On Sunday the 11th of Siutorandu I left my house at Mayo Tapare and went to Nyibango, where I spent one night.

May 24th On Monday I left there and went to Zu.

May 25th On Tuesday I left there and went to Wuro Alhamdu, where I spent one night.

Then I left Wuro Alhamdu and went to Nyiburi.

[May 27th] On Thursday the 15th of Siutorandu I received a letter from the Imam Ahmadu informing me he had received the post of Kadi.

On the same day a man of the Emir al Yemen came to me with a letter from the Emir asking for the witnesses in the case of the Kadi Amin.

May 28th On Friday the 16th of Siutorandu Hursu returned from his journey to Bau, bringing the money he had got from the sale of my horse, namely 160s. English and a black turban. He also gave me a silk mat and a fine piece of coloured cloth.

On the same day I dismissed the Emir al Yemen's man and gave him 5s.

On the same day I sent my horsemen to Sina.

May 29th On Saturday the 17th of Siutorandu Salma, a man of the Emir al Yemen, came to me with the Kadi Ahmadu and Malam Mukhtar. The Emir al Yemen had sent Malam Mukhtar back to me, but I refused to have him. I gave the Emir's man 60s. and a gown.

There was also a letter summoning the Yerima Abba.

June 1st On Tuesday the 19th of Siutorandu I sent off the man of the Emir al Yemen and Malam Hamman with the tax of the pagans and the Fulani, amounting to £100-13-0. I also sent Yerima Abba to follow him in to Yola.

June 2nd On Wednesday the 20th of Siutorandu I left my house at Nyiburi and went to Humuchi, where I spent two nights.

June 4th On Friday the 22nd of Siutorandu I left Humuchi and went to Maradi, where I spent one night.

June 5th On Saturday I left there and went to Wuro Alhamdu.

On the same day Eliasa returned from Mubi and said that the Christian had kept Malam Mukhtar back.

On the same day I gave Buba Marejo Wamgo Zigilia and he gave me 25s. and a calf. On the same day in the morning I sent Buba Kudeji to Yola.

June 9th On Wednesday the 27th of Siutorandu the Christian Captain Reed entered Duhu. I went and met him and then returned to Zu, where I spent the night.

June 10th On Thursday I returned to Madagali, and on the same day Mukhtar returned to Madagali.

June 11th On Friday the 29th of Siutorandu the Christian Captain Reed entered Madagali.

June 12th On Saturday the 1st of Dhu al Hijjah the Christian Captain Reed left Madagali accompanied by two of my people, namely Yerima Abd al Kerim and Sa'id. They went to the pagans of Kamale and Sina, and took from Kamale 32s. and 24 iron tokens, and from Sina 24s. From Sina Komde they took goods to the value of 20s. . . .

[June 16th] with which my man Sa'id returned on Wednesday the 5th of Dhu al Hijjah.

June 17th On Thursday the 6th of Dhu al Hijjah Malam Hamman and Buba Kudeji returned from their journey to Yola, bringing with them 187s. They informed me that the Emir al Yemen had ordered Mukhtar to wait until his relief came.

June 18th On Friday the 8th of Dhu al Hijjah I left Madagali and went to Mayo Tapare.

June 21st On Monday the 10th of Dhu al Hijjah we kept the feast of Al Adhdha.

June 22nd On Tuesday the 11th of Dhu al Hijjah Malam Dodo, Malam Mukhtar's relief, came to me, accompanied by one of the Emir al Yemen's men. He brought a letter telling me to make an effort to visit Yola on receipt of a letter to that effect.

June 25th On Friday the 14th of Dhu al Hijjah I left my house in Madagali and went to Mayo Tapare.

June 26th On Saturday the 15th of Dhu al Hijjah I left my house at Mayo Tapare in order to count cattle, and stopped at my house in Nyibango. On the same day Ardo Tughur and Gabdo returned from Mubi, and the latter informed me that he had received his freedom, both he and his family. On the following day I sent Ardo Humuchi to Yola in regard to this matter.

June 28th On Monday the 17th of Dhu al Hijjah I bought Ibrahim Bebel's horse for two cows. However, the second was a one-year-old.

June 29th On Tuesday the 17th [*sic*] of Dhu al Hijjah I left my house in Nyibango and went to Zu.

June 30th On Wednesday the 19th of Dhu al Hijjah I left Zu and passed through Duhu, counting cattle, and returned to Wuro Alhamdu. On the same day, the Christian Captain Reed sent me a letter ordering me to leave to Ardo Moda one of the farms of my land. On the same day also Yerima Abd al Kerim paid 40s. for Ardo Umaru's cow.

July 2nd On Friday the 21st of Dhu al Hijjah I left Wuro Alhamdu and went to my house in Maradi, and spent 2 nights there.

July 4th On Sunday the 23rd of Dhu al Hijjah I left my house at Maradi and met Baiki, who had returned from his journey to Yola, bringing two letters. I then passed through the village of the Fulani of Ardo Hauro and Mayo Wadu [Wandu] in order to count their cattle, and then I stopped at my house at Humuchi.

July 6th On Tuesday the 25th of Dhu al Hijjah I left Humuchi and went to my house at Nyiburi.

July 8th On Thursday the 27th of Dhu al Hijjah a letter from the Emir al Yemen arrived, ordering me to go in to him for the assembly of chiefs.

On the same day I left my house in Nyiburi and went to Humuchi and then stopped at Kuzum.

I then left there and stopped at Mubi, and then went to Kwagol and from there to Zummu.

From Zummu I went to Woderimo and from there to Fawa and Mayo Kulengi.

On Thursday I left there and went to Giri.

July 16th On Friday the 6th of Muharram I left my house at Giri and entered Yola. On the same day all the chiefs arrived.

July 17th On Saturday the 7th of Muharram I went to the station with all the chiefs to the place where they were to assemble, and I then went back to the Quarter.

July 18th On Sunday the 8th of Muharram I went to Yola and received from the Emir al Yemen 70s. on account of subsistence. Of this I gave my people 21s.

July 20th On Wednesday the 10th of Muharram I bought from Babadum three gowns for 580s. on four months' credit.

July 22nd On Friday the 12th of Muharram I bought from Hamma Yeru a striped shirt and a praying-mat for 47s.

July 24th On Sunday the 14th of Muharram Yakub returned from his journey to Ngaundere and told me that he had bought me 20 cows.

July 27th On Wednesday the 17th of Muharram the Governor [Sir Graeme Thomson] entered Yola and in the afternoon we all of us rode to meet the Governor at the assembly. He informed us of his intentions and we then took our leave of him on the same day.

July 28th On the next day I went to Yola and was caught in a heavy rainstorm.

July 30th On Friday the 19th of Muharram I went to Yola and was informed by the Emir al Yemen that the Christian had delayed my departure for a little while. He also gave me 70s., of which I gave my people 23s.

On the same day I gave the Emir al Yemen a horse.

August 3rd On Tuesday the 23rd of Muharram I left Yola, having spent 19 days there.

August 4th On Wednesday the 24th of Muharram I left Giri and went to Malabu. Thence I went to Woderimo, where I met the son of Ardo Humsi, who gave me a woollen mat. I then left there and went to Zummu, and then to Kwagol and Mubi, where I stayed two nights. From there I sent the Emir of Kwagol a horse in return for the calf he had given me.

August 10th On Tuesday the 1st of Tumbindu Haramji I left my house in Mubi and went to Kuzum and thence to Humuchi, where I stayed 2 nights. I then left there and went to Maradi, where Wakaltu gave me 6s. and Salman 2s. Ardo Yaya gave me three pieces of (word omitted) and some butter, and Sarkin Shanu gave me a woollen mat.

August 14th On Saturday the 6th of Tumbindu Haramji I left my house at Maradi and went to Wuro Alhamdu, where I stayed two nights.

August 16th On Monday the 8th of Safar I sent Yerima Bello, Sarkin Zongo and Yerima Abba to Yola on account of Yerima Abba's unruliness. I gave Yerima Bello 60s. for his food, Sarkin Shanu 20s. and Sarkin Zongo 10s. I gave Ahmadu, the Emir al Yemen's man 15s.

On the same day I left my house at Wuro Alhamdu and went to Zu, where I stayed one night. Then on Tuesday I left my house at Zu and entered Madagali, where I found that some of the people of Madagali had taken the part of Yerima Abba. They were Abba Bagiru, Barade

Umaru, Sairi, Ardo Suyudi, Jauro Abba Goga and others. So I told them not to appear before me, until their friend returned.

On the same day I gave my man Sa'id a gown.

(Marginal note: I spent one month and 23 days on my journey to Yola.)

August 20th On Friday the 11th of Safar Taimusu paid his debt to Koji, namely two gowns, four sheep and 5s., and Koji gave me two gowns and 3s.

August 22nd On Sunday the 22nd of Safar I gave a slave of Uba's a horse and his son a saddle cloth.

On the same day Taro came to me telling many lies against Baraya, and I want to fine him or turn him out of the town.

August 25th On Wednesday the 16th of Safar a letter arrived from the Christian Captain Reed ordering me to inform him of the names of the Kadi and of the two Muftis. On the same day I heard that Hamidu's female slave had run away from Gwoza and had come into my land. So I took her away from his brother Othman, and I intend to give her to her wife (*sic*).

August 29th On Sunday the 19th of Safar I left my house in Madagali and went to Mayo Tapare in order to marry my son Hasan to the daughter of Bulama Abba. I gave as her marriage present a cow, a female slave and 11 woollen mats. The cow, though, I borrowed from Hasan.

September 1st On Wednesday the 23rd of Safar at night I sent to the Malam in the village of Muvi some cloth, which had come from the sons of Hasan, namely 12 pieces of cloth, a woman's cloth, trousers and a fez.

During the night and from the time I arrived here I have been in pain and have had no rest.

On the 23rd of Safar I gave my wife, Zeitun by name, a girdle of nine ropes.

September 4th On Saturday the 26th of Safar one of the men of Muhammad Bello, the Emir al Yemen, arrived with a letter, in which they demanded witnesses in the case of Yerima Bello.

On the same day I sent Buba for my pay.

September 5th On Sunday the 27th of Safar I sent the witnesses whom they asked for from me. They are Dogari Kaka, Hamma Mai Bornu, the male and female slaves of Yerima Bello, Barkindo and others.

September 6th On Monday the 28th of Safar at night I gave the Emir al Yemen's man a white cloth and 5s.

On the same night Ajia's female slave ran away.

I gave Hamma the son of Mai Bornu a woollen mat and 2s. and I gave the female slaves of Yerima Bello three woollen mats.

September 7th On Tuesday the 29th of Safar one named Jumi Fummu said he intended to come and see me.

September 10th On Friday the 2nd of Haram Petel I sent the Wakili of Yola 15s. On the same day I left my house in Madagali and went to my house in Mayo Tapare.

September 12th On Sunday the 4th of Haram Petel I left my house at Mayo Tapare and went to Nyibango.

On Sunday the 4th of Haram Petel Malam Ahmadu the Mufti came back from Yola.

[September 13th] On the following day the Kadi Ahmadu quarrelled with Malam Abu Bakr on account of Malam Bakr's statement that he had told people that he did not agree with the Kadi Ahmadu's judgments, and with the number of people in prison. The Kadi Ahmadu blamed him for this, and then Bakr said he did not like the Mufti, and so he came to me at my village of Nyibango, where I made peace between them.

On the same day the Christian Captain Reed sent me Suduki with a letter about a schoolboy, who had run away.

September 17th On Friday the 10th of Haram Petel Ardo Tukur of Nyibango told the pagans of Muduvu, named Diaku, not to give Wakili Madagali any welcome, until Yerima Abba returns from Yola, and not to go to Baraya or Kaigamma Sa'id.

On the same day one of the pagans of Muduvu came to me—his name was Wacha—and said that there were two women with them, and that they intended to bring them to me.

On the same day Salman quarrelled with Bulama Gamdo, who he said was causing trouble among the pagans. They discussed the matter before me and it was proved that Gamdo lied and that he really was causing trouble.

On the same day I sent a letter to the Christian Captain Reed.

September 20th On Monday the 12th of Haram Petel the pagans of Muduvu brought me a calf and 50 iron tokens.

On the same day I left my house at Nyibango and returned to Mayo Tapare.

On the same day I received a letter from the Emir al Yemen, Muhammad Bello, asking me to send in my Jangali money.

On the same day I found that my date-tree had flowered.

I spent 8 days on my journey to Nyibango.

September 22nd On Wednesday the 13th of Haram Petel I left Mayo Tapare and went to Madagali.

September 25th On Saturday the 17th of Haram Petel I left my house in Madagali and proceeded to my house in Gubla. There I met Bula with the male and female slaves of Yerima Abba, and I kept them sitting down there until I could see what their intentions were.

September 28th On Tuesday the 20th of Haram Petel the pagans of Muduvu came to see me, after I had ordered them to do so.

October 3rd On Sunday the 25th of Haram Petel the Sarkin Katsina came to me regarding the matter of the Jangali and population count of my land.

October 4th On Monday the 26th of Haram Petel I wanted to pay the Jangali money of my land, namely 508s. I sent it by the hand of my scribe, Malam Dodo and my men and Sa'id.

October 5th On Tuesday the 27th of Haram Petel I left my house in Madagali and stopped at Zu for one night.

October 6th On Wednesday the 28th I left Zu and stopped at Wuro Al-hamdu. There I received news of the Resident, Mr. Browne (an error; it was Mr. Francis).

October 8th On the 1st of Rabi'a al Awwal I left my house at Wuro Alhamdu with the Resident and went to Madagali . . .

October 10th on Sunday the 3rd of Rabi'a al Awwal.

October 11th On Monday the 4th of Rabi'a al Awwal Yokodu Koro complained against me to the Resident and said that he had an accusation against me. He claimed I had said that I intended to give him £3 on account of the ransom of his female slave named Zamanei. Further, he complained against Malam Abu Bakr, with the result that the Resident got Abu Bakr arrested on the charge that he had whipped Ahmadu, and fined him without entering the case in the Court Record Book.

On the 4th of Rabi'a al Awwal Yokodu Koro made some very violent remarks, and was sent to the Kadi, who sentenced him to £2 fine and gave a judgment that his female slave Zamanei was free. Further, he ordered him to pay up Zamanei's property, namely a woollen mat, two pots and four sashes.

October 12th On Tuesday the 4th of Rabi'a al Awwal I said goodbye to the Resident after the midday prayer.

October 15th On Friday the 7th of Rabi'a al Awwal I left my house in Madagali and went to Mayo Tapare.

October 17th On Sunday the 9th of Rabi'a al Awwal my man Sa'id and Abbo returned from changing the money.

October 19th On Tuesday the 11th of Rabi'a al Awwal I left Mayo Tapare and went towards Gubla, and on the way met Buba, who had come back from Yola with my pay. He told me that my son Bello had won his case against Abba, and I gave Buba a shiny black gown, on hearing from him that Bello had returned with some Yola people.

October 20th On Wednesday the 12th of Rabi'a al Awwal the French people paid up the property of the Tur pagans and of the Bornu pagans. Those in my area received seven cows and 11 goats. On the same day I sent a letter to the Christian Captain Reed to inform him.

October 21st On Thursday the 23rd (*sic*) of Rabi'a al Awwal Yerima Bello returned from his journey to Yola and I gave him a black gown.

October 23rd On Saturday the 25th (*sic*) of Rabi'a al Awwal Samaki Yola, Yerima Abba, Sarkin Shanu and Sarkin Zongo arrived.

October 24th On Sunday the 16th of Rabi'a al Awwal I received a letter from the Emir al Yemen, Muhammad I, regarding the removal of the Kadi Ahmadu and his dismissal from his position.

October 26th On Tuesday the 18th of Rabi'a al Awwal Malam Hamman returned and said that Malam Dodo had had a great deal to say, but that Captain Reed would not agree to what he had written.

On the same day I sent to Yola and gave the Emir al Yemen, Muhammad Bello, 200s.

On the same day I received a letter from the Christian, the Captain, regarding a complaint made against me by Amin.

October 27th On Wednesday the 19th of Rabi'a al Awwal I left my house in Madagali and went to Gubla, where I spent one night.

On Wednesday night I gave it the name of Zangana, and on Thursday Yerima Abba and Samaki Yola left Madagali and I gave him 38s. and a white gown.

(Some pages of the MS, most probably two, are here missing.)

[December 5th] . . . the 5th of (Banjaru) Sakitindu I left my house in Madagali and stopped at my house in Sakia.

December 17th On Friday the 11th of Banjaru Sakitindu I left my house at Sakia and went to Madagali for the Friday prayers. On the same day I went on to Mayo Tapare, but I did not stop the night there, but went on to Sakia.

December 20th On Monday the 15th of Banjaru Sakitindu I left Sakia and stopped at Zu.

December 21st On Tuesday the 16th of Banjaru Sakitindu I left Zu and stopped at Wuro Alhamdu, and on the same day Buba came back from Yola with my pay. He informed me that my son Ahmad intended to return to Madagali, that he had controlled himself and petitioned the Emir al Yemen and asked him to return him to me.

On the same day Bello, the son of Sarkin Yaki, came to me.

December 23rd On the 29th (*sic*) of Banjaru Sakitindu I left Wuro Alhamdu on Thursday and stopped at Maradi.

December 25th On Saturday the 21st of Banjaru a messenger of Muhammad Bello, the Emir al Yemen, named Muhammad, arrived with a letter from the Emir al Yemen saying that Abba had come to him and kissed his feet and hands and wept and expressed his great repentance. The Emir al Yemen therefore sent him to me for him to show his repentance to me in the same way, and if I agree he asked me to leave him to live in my village of Wasfala.

December 26th On the 22nd of Banjaru Sakitindu I left Maradi and followed the Duhu road to see the bridge over the Mayo Wako. I then stopped at my house in Wuro Alhamdu.

December 28th On Tuesday the 23rd of Banjaru Sakitindu I left my house at Wuro Alhamdu and stopped at my house at Zu, where I spent one night.

December 29th On Wednesday I left my house at Zu and stopped at my house at Sakia.

This journey of mine lasted eight days.

December 31st On Friday the 25th of Banjaru Sakitindu I left my house at Sakia and went to my house in Madagali, where I spent two nights.

1927

January 2nd On Sunday the 27th of Banjaru Sakitindu I left my house in Madagali and went to the bridge over the Mayo Wako, where I stayed the day and then returned to Mayo Tapare.

January 4th On Tuesday the 29th of Banjaru Sakitindu I left Mayo Tapare and went to my house in Sakia.

January 7th On Friday the 2nd of Sumatendu Waube I left my house in Sakia and went to my house in Nyibango, where I stayed one night.

I heard that two of my female slaves in my house in Madagali, named Yutugimu and Gordi, very nearly managed to run away. They were, however, unable to do so.

January 12th On Wednesday the 7th of Sumatendu Waube Ardo Nyibango, Tukur, made his peace with me in regard to his offence of telling the pagans of something he should not have done. He gave me a cow and a calf, the latter of which I gave to my man Sa'id to take it to Sakia.

January 14th On Friday the 9th of Sumatendu Waube, while I was in my house at Nyibango, the Ardo of Wandei, named Hammawa, came down to me. I put him up in the house of my son Isa.

January 15th On Saturday the 10th of Sumatendu Waube I left Nyibango and went to my house in Sakia.

On the same day a messenger of the Emir al Yemen Muhammad Bello arrived with a letter ordering me to finish the General Tax of my land.

January 16th On Sunday the 13th of Sumatendu Waube I left Sakia and went to my house in Madagali.

January 19th On Wednesday the 14th of Sumatendu Waube I received a letter from the Christian Mr. Wilkinson containing a complaint against Kaigamma Sa'id. The cause of it was that a slave of Yerima Abba's [*sic*] complained against him. However, I know that this is a piece of trickery on his part. Further, Mr. Wilkinson ordered me to send for the pagan, who had killed a man by attacking him unawares.

January 22nd On Saturday the 17th of Sumatendu Waube I left my house in Madagali and went to my house in Sakia.

On the same day Malam Umaru, the mufti in place of Malam Ahmadu on the latter's dismissal, came to me.

January 27th On Thursday the 22nd of Sumatendu Waube Jauro came back from his journey to Yola with a letter from the Emir al Yemen of Adamawa, Muhammad Bello, ordering me to give Yerima Abba 20s. for the rent of his house.

January 28th On Friday the 23rd of Sumatendu Waube I left my house at Sakia and returned to my house in Madagali.

January 29th On Saturday the 24th of Sumatendu Waube Yerima Musa returned after being released from prison. With him was a man of the Emir al Yemen Adamawa, Muhammad Bello.

January 30th On Sunday the 25th of Sumatendu Waube I bought a length of striped cloth from a man named Umaru Jam for 10s.

February 5th On Saturday the 2nd of Wairordu Sumaye a Christian arrived at Madagali, named Mr. Wilkinson. Derebe made a complaint and recovered his daughter, and Umaru Adda made seven complaints, which were not proved. This was all a waste of time.

February 13th On Sunday the 10th of Wairordu Sumaye the Christian Mr. Wilkinson went to the pagans of Bukata, and on the same day I gave Makaji the Su'in road and told him not to accept anything from them.

February 14th On Monday the 11th of Wairordu Sumaye a man of the pagans of Jadko, named Ajatuku, came to me with 38s. and asked me to allow him to take the oath on their fetish in regard to the accusation against his wife of being a witch. If what Jalmari said was proved against him, then this money was to be recovered from me, just as previously I had returned money to him (? Arabic obscure).

February 15th On Tuesday the 12th of Wairordu Sumaye Buba came back from his journey to Yola with my pay. He also had a letter from the Ma'aji of Yola, in which the Ma'aji said that Baba Badum's debt was paid off in January.

On the same day Ture brought me 100s. from the Bororo.

February 15th On Tuesday the 12th of Wairordu Sumaye I heard that the pagans of Wibengo had made a complaint against Sinowa.

On the same day I left my house at Nyibango and returned to Madagali.

February 16th On Wednesday the 13th of Wairordu Sumaye the Christian Mr. Wilkinson went to Vizu after spending a night in Madagali on his return from Wanga.

February 18th On Friday the 14th of Wairordu Sumaye the Christian Mr. Wilkinson moved camp to Nyibango and I went with him and stayed in Nyibango three nights. He then passed on to Muduvu on Monday to see into the murder by the pagans of Muduvu of a Wadami man. On the same night I received a letter to the effect that the Resident would arrive in Madagali on Friday, if God will.

February 22nd On Tuesday the 19th of Sha'aban I gave Ardo Amin the rank named Bunu and gave him leave to collect all the "zakah" of the people of Madagali, all of them without exception, apart from the quarter of Khurga.

On the same day I ordered my son Yerima Bello to get ready to go to Mubi to meet the Resident and welcome him.

February 24th On Thursday the 21st of the month the Christian Mr. Wilkinson came down from the hill of Damai and Muduvu and made a boundary between them giving the grassy land to Damai and the wooded area to Muduvu. He also presented Arnado Sukur with a gown.

On the same day I left my house at Nyibango and returned to Madagali, while Mr. Wilkinson stopped the night and returned to Madagali on Friday.

February 25th On the same day the Resident entered Madagali.

February 26th On Saturday the 23rd of Wairordu Sumaye the Christian Mr. Wilkinson took my man Sa'id and kept him from the noon until the evening in connection with a matter of a chicken.

February 27th On Sunday the 24th of Wairordu Sumaye the Resident left Madagali, having spent two nights there.

March 1st On Tuesday the 26th of Wairordu Sumaye Malam Umaru returned from his journey to Bornu, bringing me wool for clothing, a saddle cloth and trappings for the saddle, kolas and a turban.

On the same day I left Madagali and went to Nyibango.

March 3rd On Thursday the 28th of Wairordu Sumaye I left my house at Nyibango with the Christian Mr. Wilkinson and spent the night on the Sukur hill.

March 4th On Friday the last day of Wairordu Sumaye Barade Bakari returned from his journey to Ngaundere and among the things he brought were 2080 frs.

On the same day we saw the new moon.

March 5th On Saturday in the month of Ramadhan we started the fast in the village of Sukur.

March 7th On Monday in the month of Ramadhan I left my house at Sukur and went to the pagans of Wula, where we spent 3 days.

March 9th On Wednesday we left there and came to Kurang, where we spent two nights.

March 11th On Friday we left there and stopped with the pagans of Kamale, where we spent three nights.

March 15th On Tuesday in the month of Ramadhan we left Kamale and went to Humuchi.

March 16th On Wednesday I went to Mr. Wilkinson's camp, and he arrested 11 men of the Humuchi pagans.

March 19th On Saturday the 15th of Ramadhan Barade Umaru fled to Mugudi on account of the case between him and Wafango.

On the same day we left Humuchi and came to the pagans of Garta, and the Christian Mr. Wilkinson burnt two houses of the Humuchi pagans.

March 21st On Monday the 17th of Ramadhan the Christian Mr. Wilkinson spent the night on the Kankela Hill.

On the same day Hamma Bulama Abba returned from his journey to Dikwa, bringing a silk cloth, which the Shehu of Bornu sent me.

March 25th On Friday the 20th of Ramadhan we left Garta and went to Sina.

March 27th On Sunday the 22nd of Ramadhan the Christian Mr. Wilkinson went to Sina Komde, where he spent one night. He returned with their chief Gada and brought him into my presence.

March 29th On the 24th of Ramadhan we left the Sina pagans and went to Kajiti, where we spent one night.

March 31st On Thursday I took leave of him and returned to my house in Zu.

April 1st Then the next morning, Friday, I returned to Madagali, having spent on this journey 31 days.

On the same day, a man of the Makaji pagans named A'ali brought a complaint against me on account of the goods he had given me in the matter of the "witch" business, the value of which was 50s. He, however, said that it was 70s. and I paid him what he said.

On the same day the Christian Mr. Wilkinson arrested two men of the Pellam pagans.

On the same day I returned to my house at Zu where I spent one night.

On Friday I left there and returned to my house in Madagali, having spent 31 days on this journey.

April 1st On Friday the 28th of Ramadhan I gave Barade Bakari a gown.

April 3rd On Sunday the last day of Ramadhan I gave Bunu, the Sarkin of the Madagali "zakah," a gown.

April 4th On Monday the 1st of Juldandu we celebrated the Id al Fitr.

On Monday the 1st of Juldandu I ordered Salman to give me the General Tax. He refused and was rebellious, so I took from him the pagans of my area of Mildu and drove him out of them.

April 5th On Tuesday the 2nd of Juldandu Dudugu came to me asking to be made head of the Zu pagans, and he gave me 18s.

April 6th On Wednesday the 3rd of Juldandu I left my house in Madagali and went to Mayo Tapare.

April 7th On Thursday the 4th of Juldandu a scribe of the Emir of Adamawa came to me to write up the cattle which had died.

April 8th On Friday the 5th of Juldandu I left my house in Mayo Tapare and went to my house in Madagali.

April 9th On Saturday the 6th of Juldandu I sent Dadandi with a letter to the Emir Adamawa, which he gave to Ardo Moda.

On the same day I left my house in Madagali and went to my house in Sakia.

April 10th On Sunday the 7th of Juldandu I made Labai head of the part of the land of Makar and gave him a gown. He gave me 55s. and a gown worth 15s.

April 12th On Tuesday the 9th of Juldandu Bairdu the Arnado of Chobali brought me two dollars and a pot of honey and I gave Tizi one of them as pay for the building work he had done and I also gave one to Barde Bakari.

April 15th On Friday the 12th of Juldandu I left my house in Sakia and went to my house in Madagali.

On the same day Ahmad claimed 5s. because Tizi put into his house a man named Bello for five months. I therefore took 5s. from Tizi.

On the same day a man of the Bororo Fulani brought me 18s.

On the same day we had rain.

April 16th On Saturday the 3rd (*sic*) of Juldandu I left my house in Madagali and went to my house in Sakia.

On the same day Ngurangala returned from his journey to Yola.

April 19th On Tuesday the 16th of Juldandu I ordered the young men at my gate to start cultivating my land. Ma'aji said that some of them refused to do it on the oath of God.

April 22nd On Friday the 19th of Juldandu I received news that Kachella Jadko had fled in the direction of Bornu.

On the same day I sent my female slaves with Hammad Jarma Bajam to Yola.

On the same day I left my house in Sakia and went to my house in Nyibango.

April 23rd On Saturday the 20th of Juldandu I heard that Kowa Dalile had fled to Mokolo.

On the same day Buba came back from Yola with my pay amounting to £13-11-0.

April 24th On Sunday the 21st of Juldandu I left my house in Nyibango and went to my house in Sakia.

April 25th On Monday the 22nd of Juldandu Dan Bornu came to me and said: "Which way has Kachella Jadko gone?"

April 26th On Tuesday the 23rd of Juldandu I got credit from Ahmadu Govi for two pieces of cloth valued at 32s. which I bought from him.

May 1st On the 29th of Juldandu the Christian Mr. Wilkinson sent for me to come to Bazza, and I left Sakia and stopped at Zu, spending the night there.

May 2nd Then on Monday I left Zu and stopped at my house in Humuchi.

May 3rd On Tuesday I left Humuchi and went to Bazza, where I talked with the Christian Mr. Wilkinson.

After taking my leave of him I returned to Humuchi on the 1st of Siutorandu.

On the same day I sent Buba Malabu to Malabu to express my condolences on the death of the Emir of Malabu. He took with him the money of the Sarkin Kasuwa with a letter to the Emir al Yemen and a letter to the Ma'aji of Yola.

May 6th On the 5th of Juldandu [*sic*] I left Humuchi and passed through the Humuchi {pagans} in order to collect their General Tax.

There Hursu came back from his journey bringing a tent, a white woollen mat and a fine coloured sheepskin for a saddle.

On the same day Yerima Abd al Kerim gave me a roll of cloth.

Then I went to Garta and took their tax and I stopped at Nyiburi.

May 7th On Saturday the 6th of Siutorandu Sarkin Yaki returned from his journey to Watani bringing three horses, a chestnut, a bay and a grey.

On the same day Mai Bornu's man, Bakr Dasin, came to see me.

May 8th On Sunday the 7th of Siutorandu I left Nyiburi and passed through the pagans of Kamale. Then I passed through the pagans of Pellam and talked to them about cultivating my farms. I then stopped at Wuro Alhamdu.

May 9th On Monday the 8th of Siutorandu, while I was in Wuro Alhamdu, Fadhl al Nar quarrelled with Kachella Aji. So I put Fadhl al Nar in charge of the pagans and Kachella Aji in charge of the Fulani.

On the same day I gave Waida a white shirt, as he set my mind at ease by swearing that he would not cause mischief with the pagans and would not exceed the limits I had set him.

May 11th On Wednesday the 10th of Siutorandu I left my house at Wuro Alhamdu and returned to my house at Sakia.

May 12th On Thursday the 11th of Siutorandu the Sarkin Dogari Yola came to me regarding the General Tax.

On the same day my house at Nyibango was burnt down, so I went to see what had happened, but nothing had been destroyed except the houses.

May 13th On Friday the 12th of Siutorandu Bulama Abba gave me a woollen mat because of the burning of my house, while Hursu gave me 4s. and Musa 2s. I then paid Musa 4s.

May 15th On Sunday the 14th of Siutorandu I left my house at Nyibango and stopped at my house in Madagali.

May 17th On Tuesday the 16th of Siutorandu I sent off the Tax of Madagali, £386.

May 18th On Wednesday the 17th of Siutorandu I left my house in Mayo Tapare and went to my house in Sakia. From there I sent Sarkin Hausawa Audu to Bornu to change some five-franc pieces.

May 21st On Saturday the 19th of Siutorandu Audu the Interpreter came to me bringing a letter from the Christian Mr. Wilkinson.

On the same day I left my house in Sakia and went to Madagali, and ordered the people of Madagali to repair the market. I stayed in the market a little while.

May 22nd On Sunday the 20th of Siutorandu I asked my man Sa'id what had prevented him from writing up my record book, and I told him that this was laziness on his part and that this made two offences he had committed.

May 27th On Friday the 25th of Siutorandu I left Sakia and went to my village of Nyibango.

On the same day I heard that Bello Nakura, the Sarkin Aiki, had come to Madagali to see about the road and had told my messenger that there was very little wrong with it.

May 26th On the 24th of Siutorandu while I was in Sakia Bula quarrelled with Aljuma with the result that Aljuma said that Bula had sent kolas in my house to the grandmother of Yusuf. I went into this matter and found that it was proved against Bula. The young slave said that Bula had given her 3 kolas and she had given them to the mother of Yusuf.

May 28th On Saturday the 26th of Siutorandu I left my house at Nyibango, stopped on the way at Sakia to get some shade, and passing through Madagali went on to Mayo Tapare.

May 29th On Sunday the 27th of Siutorandu Abd al Kerim returned from welcoming the Emir al Yemen of Adamawa, and on the same day I left my house in Mayo Tapare and went to Madagali.

May 30th On Monday the 28th of Siutorandu Buba Audu's messenger came to me with a letter from the Christian Mr. Wilkinson ordering me to arrest my protégé Kaji and Yerima Nana.

June 3rd On Friday in the month of Siutorandu Julde Laihaji (*sic*) I left my house in Madagali and went to Sakia.

June 5th On Sunday the 5th of Laihaji I left my house at Sakia and went to my house at Zu, and passing through it put up at Wuro Alhamdu for the night.

June 6th On the following day, Monday, I started off to meet the Christian Mr. Wilkinson and the Emir al Yemen of Adamawa at Michika. On the way I received a letter from them summoning me and Arnado Sukur and Wakaltu. So I met them.

(Marginal note: The Christian said that he did not forbid the pagans to cultivate my farms. He also said: "Why have you prevented Arnado Sukur from coming to me with his people?")

They appointed Ma'aji of Shellen Chief of Michika and Moda, and said that they had deposed the oppressors of the pagans.

I then went to my house in Humuchi.

June 7th On Tuesday the 7th of Laihaji I left my house in Humuchi and went to Michika and took my leave of the Christian Mr. Wilkinson and the Emir al Yemen Adamawa. He gave Arnado Sukur a gown to wear and a crown (presumably a fez is meant). Then I returned to my house at Maradi, which I reached after the time of the evening meal.

On the same day Mr. Wilkinson arrested a slave of mine, whom I had appointed to collect the tax outstanding from last year.

[June 8th] On Wednesday I left my house at Maradi and went to my house at Zu, and the following morning I went to my house in Madagali.

June 9th On Thursday the 9th of Laihaji I left my house in Zu and went to Madagali, and on the same day I went on to Mayo Tapare.

June 10th On Friday I celebrated the Id al Adhdha. I refused all the gifts that the pagans gave me, with the exception of the pagans of Waida and the pagans of Jiddere who are called Ubchi.

On the 10th of Laihaji I sent my Malam, Bayaji, to the Emir al Yemen Adamawa with two rams.

June 12th On Sunday the 12th of Laihaji I left Madagali and went to Sakia.

June 15th On the 15th of Laihaji Ardo Bebel came to me, while I was at Sakia. I summoned Ajia and he talked with him and I then fined Ardo Bebel two loads of millet.

June 17th On Friday the 17th of Laihaji I left Sakia and went to Madagali and attended the Friday prayers.

On the same day after sunset I left Madagali and returned to Sakia.

June 19th On the 19th of Laihaji I left Sakia and went to Zu.

June 21st On Tuesday the 21st of Laihaji I left Zu and went to Wuro Alhamdu.

June 22nd On Wednesday the 22nd of Laihaji I left Wuro Alhamdu and followed the boundary of my farm until I reached Bamaka, where I rested in the shade. I then returned to my house at Maradi.

June 24th On Friday the 24th of Laihaji I left Maradi and went to Bamaka, where I rested during the heat of the day. At Bamaka my horse broke loose and ran off as far as Mayo Wandu, where Usman caught it. It had broken loose from Badewi's charge with my saddle on it.

At Bamaka the Kadi Abba came along with Ardo Sanda and the son of Dade in connection with a complaint of Sanda's.

On the same day it appeared that Wakaltu had fled to French Territory with all his goods: five men, seven women, three boys, three girls, 20 sheep and goats and his horse.

June 25th On Saturday the 25th of Laihaji I left Maradi and stopped at Wuro Alhamdu.

June 26th On Sunday the 26th I left Wuro Alhamdu and went to Zu.

On the same day Musa Messenger arrived and passed on to Madagali, and refused to come to see me at Zu.

On the same day I got a girl from Guram named Muyidara, and I also got a girl of Ushewa named Asta, and I left her father his two sons. At the time, while I was at Zu, on Sunday the 26th of Laihaji, I intended to give Asta to my son to make her his concubine.

June 28th On Tuesday the 28th of Laihaji I left my house in Zu and went to my house in Sakia, where I spent three days.

July 1st On Friday the 1st of Muharram I left my house at Sakia and went to my house in Madagali.

July 2nd On Saturday the 2nd of Muharram I left my house in Madagali and went to my house in Mayo Tapare, where I stayed one night.

July 3rd On Sunday I left there and returned to my house in Madagali.

On the same day a letter arrived from the Christian Mr. Wilkinson containing a complaint by Waida regarding the daughter of the pagan. The other matter concerned the General Tax. Mr. Wilkinson ordered me to pay it in to Yola.

On the same day my concubine Awu ran away.

July 5th On Tuesday the 5th of Muharram I left my house in Madagali and went to my house in Sakia.

On the same day I received a letter from the Emir al Yemen Adamawa telling me that cases referring to German and French times should not be heard, if they were more than three years old.

July 8th On Friday the 8th of Muharram I left my house in Sakia and stopped at my house in Madagali.

July 12th On Tuesday the 12th of Muharram I left Madagali and went along the Wamga road, returning to my house in Sakia.

July 13th On Wednesday the 14th of Muharram Messenger Iya came to me with a letter from the Christian Mr. Wilkinson saying that a man of the Pellam pagans named Budanda had made a complaint against me regarding his wife, two cows, a woollen shirt and 10s. This was the man's tale.

On the same day I sent Dauda to Yola with £13-18-0.

July 15th On Friday the 15th of Muharram I sent Sa'adu and Buba Malabu to Mindif to express my condolences on the death of his daughter, and I gave them a horse to present to him.

On the same day I left my house in Sakia and went to Madagali, and on the same day I gave all my rice to my household.

July 16th On Saturday the 16th of Muharram Yerima Abba came to me. He had been in the direction of the Bororo and he told me that the Christian had ordered him to make a central place behind Goyo and the village of Michika.

On the same day I left Madagali and went along the road and returned to my house in Mayo Tapare.

On the same day the Christian sent a letter about the General Tax.

July 17th On Sunday the 17th of Muharram a letter came to me from the Emir al Yemen Adamawa, ordering me to make a population count of the whole of my land, all of it, and to collect the Jangali.

On the same day I went to see about the road work, and returned to my house in Madagali.

July 18th On Monday the 18th of Muharram I sent off the man of the Emir al Yemen Adamawa, Muhammad, with a letter making my excuses for the disobedience of his orders of which he accuses me.

July 19th On Tuesday the 19th of Muharram I left my house in Madagali and stopped at my house in Sakia.

On the same day Malam Dodo came back together with my son Mahmud Eliasa from counting the cattle. Mahmud informed me that Malam Dodo had written up 132 cattle less than the actual number and had taken from the owner 73s. as a reward for decreasing the number.

On the same day I collected the people of Madagali to do my cultivating for me and I intend to give them a horse, if I can manage it.

July 21st On Thursday the 21st of Muharram a letter came from the Christian Mr. Wilkinson, saying that Ghamiri had made a complaint against me. He ordered me to return the girl to her mother, but she rejected her parents and said to them that she would never return to the pagans.

July 22nd On the next day, Friday, the Kadi of Madagali, Abba, came into my presence, and she told him the same as she had told me. I therefore wrote a letter to the Judge of the North, Mr. Wilkinson.

July 23rd On Saturday the 23rd of Muharram I left my house at Sakia and went along the road to Wamgu [Wamga], where I sheltered during the heat, and then I returned to my house in Mayo Tapare.

On the same day I sent the Christian Mr. Wilkinson a letter containing the cattle count for my land.

On the same day I sent Tayau with a letter to give to Buba Albashi to be taken to the Emir al Yemen of Adamawa, Muhammad I. In it I told him about my wife, about the cattle count of my land and Isa's behaviour with the pagans of Bugel.

On the same day I summoned Adamayel and Buba Adama before me to answer for their offence in getting Malam Dodo to decrease their cattle by 43. I asked them about it and I then asked Malam Dodo and he told me as I have written.

On the same day the Christian Mr. Wilkinson sent me a letter and asked me where Kachella Jadko was.

July 24th On Sunday the 24th of Muharram I left Mayo Tapare and went along the Wamga road and returned to my house in Madagali, where I stayed one night.

July 25th On Monday I left there and went to my house in Sakia.

On the same day Adamayel sent me 40s. on account of his offence in decreasing the number of his cattle and I gave it to some people who were urging me to buy their horse.

July 28th On Thursday the 28th of Muharram Dauda returned from his journey to Yola.

July 29th On Friday the 29th of Muharram I left my house at Sakia and went to my house in Nyibango.

On the same day the Christian, who was in the direction of the Bororo, came to me and said that the reason for his coming was that he wanted to buy meat.

July 30th On Saturday the last day of Muharram Al Haji Mamma died.

July 31st On Sunday the 1st of Safar I left my house at Nyibango and went to my house at Sakia.

On the same day I sent Kauda on a journey to Yola with a letter.

August 5th On Friday the 6th of Safar I left my house at Sakia and went to my house in Madagali.

August 6th On Saturday the 7th of Safar I left my house in Madagali and went to look at the road work. I spent the day in the shade there, and then returned and passed on to my house at Mayo Tapare, and from there to my house in Madagali.

On the same day a letter came from Sardauna to say that two men had stolen two slave girls, Habibu and Basaitu, and he does not know who they are. One of them is called Bakari.

[From this point the dates are off by one day. If Saturday (August 6th) was the 7th of Safar, then the next entry, the 11th of Safar, would have been 4 days later or August 10th.]

August 9th On Tuesday the 11th of Safar I planted rice, but I do not know if it will grow or not.

August 12th On Friday the 14th of Safar two dogarai and a man of the Emir al Yemen of Adamawa came to me with a madman, who they said was a man of my land. In his letter the Emir ordered me to pay up the amount of the Tax of my land. He also asked for information as to the number of people who had emigrated to French Territory and the number who had immigrated from French Territory to my land.

August 14th On Sunday the 16th of Safar I left my house at Sakia and went to Madagali.

On that day I sent Musa with letters to the Christian Mr. Wilkinson.

August 15th On Monday the 17th of Safar the Christian Mr. Wilkinson sent Lawan Petel to me with 100s. and ordered me to collect 1000 cash bowls of flour and two calves.

August 17th On Wednesday the 19th of Safar I sent Eliasa with the Jangali money, amounting to £302-4-0.

On the same day I left my house in Madagali between the two hours of prayer of the sunset and the night and stopped at my house in Mayo Tapare.

On the same day Hamman Jam made his peace with me in the matter of his offence in refusing to give Maliki a letter I had written and refusing to do some work I told him to do.

August 19th On Friday the 21st of Safar I left my house at Mayo Tapare and went to the Rest House and then returned to my house in Madagali.

August 20th On Saturday the 22nd of Safar I went to the road and the bridge.

On the same day I paid my debt to a pagan named Foju for a short-sleeved gown. He received 14 dollars for it, leaving 6 dollars due, which I put off to the summer time.

On the same day the pagans of Silmi brought me 50s.

[These last dates are even more confused, though the last returns to the sequence above.]

August 21st On Sunday the 25th of Safar the Christian Mr. Wilkinson arrived in Madagali.

August 23rd On Tuesday the 27th of Safar two pagans of Webengo made a complaint against Sarkin Shanu. Ladan too complained against Baraya.

August 25th On Thursday the 27th of Safar I sent Tataraktu a slave-girl from my house, who belonged to the Webengo pagans. His wife gave me 32s. as her ransom.

On the same day Sarkin Lifida ruined the onions.

6. The Later History of the Diary: An Archival and Autobiographical Note

ANTHONY H. M. KIRK-GREENE

On my arrival at Yola as a new cadet in September 1950, I was inducted—if the term is not too formal for the leisurely and rather bored process—into my duties by the traditional method of sitting me down quietly in a corner of the office of the DO/Provincial Office—a sort of Private Secretary-cum-Adjutant to the Resident—and handing me an uncritical selection of "dead" files to peruse as background reading . . . preferably without my asking any questions. Several of these were brought out of the Resident's security cupboard: current files were either too much in use or considered too baffling for a mere cadet. History was safer ground, one hoped, than the politics of administration.

At the time, two of the Resident's files made a lasting impression on me. One was the draft history of the new (1926) Adamawa Province, largely reconstructed in 1936 from *Gazetteers* of Muri and Yola Provinces, compiled by J. A. Fremantle and C. O. Migeod and published in 1920 and 1927 respectively; this eventually formed the basis from which developed my *Adamawa Past and Present*, written on my early leaves and published in 1958. The other, though I was not to realize it at the time and quite forgot about its existence until I was caught up in the events of 1953, was the secret file containing the contemporaneous typescript translation of Hamman Yaji's diary.

On my posting from DO Numan on the Benue to Touring Officer Northern Area in July 1953, with headquarters at Mubi, I was warned by the Senior District Officer at Yola that trouble could be expected from the Kilba State Union centered on Pella. Trained and led by the Sudan United Mission, the young Kilba were chafing at the perceived iniquities of subordination to the Fulbe emirate hierarchy a hundred miles away in remote Yola. In the event, apart from a noisy but peaceful invasion of my compound one day by several hundred men, the Christian Kilba irredentists to the south gave no trouble. What trouble there was came—and it came within a matter of weeks of my taking up my post in Mubi—from Fulbe Madagali to the north, unexpectedly and out of the blue.

There, members of the Hamman Yaji family decided to demonstrate their dissatisfaction with the Lamido's decision not to recognize their claim in the emirate administration when the time came, as it now had, to appoint a new District Head of Madagali. Hamman Yaji had been succeeded in 1927 first by Hayatu, a great-grandson of Lamido Modibo Adama, with the subsequent *sarauta* of Lamido Mandara, and then in 1939 by Hayatu's eldest son, Hamman Gabdo, with the title of Marafa. Both were staunch opponents of the Hamman Yaji family (Kirk-Greene 1954a). In November 1952 the Lamido moved against the current District Head, Muhammadu Dan Galadima, and dismissed him; for several years the administration had suspected him of countless crimes. The appointment of Dahiru, son of the Galadima of Yola, in a mere acting capacity rekindled the hopes of the Hamman Yaji camp that maybe now was the time for the rule of Madagali to revert to his family or followers. Having engineered the support of Mubi and Madagali members of the NEPU (Northern Elements Progressive Union, the opposition party in the north) who were susceptible to an emotive protest against the new headquarters of the district being moved from Madagali to non-Fulbe Gulak, in Margi territory, the family members planned a vigorous demonstration in Mubi on August 29, 1953. When the Lamido was paying an official visit to Mubi accompanied by the Acting Resident from Yola, J. H. D. Stapleton, the three of us were immured by a hostile, lightly armed crowd in the District Head's compound. The Resident decided his duty was to stay with the Lamido and directed that mine, contrary to my argument that it was to remain at his side, was to escape however I could, make my way 120 miles to Yola at night, alert the Senior District Officer and the Assistant Superintendent of Police to the crisis, and return the next morning with as large a detachment of the Nigeria Police Force as we could muster and find transport for. Thanks to the efficiency of the Assistant Superintendent of Police, J. F. Ross, we were back in Mubi by dawn, a hundred strong. Half-jokingly on the lookout for bodies strung up *à la lanterne* as we entered Mubi in the morning mist (though there were, of course, no streetlights then), we were relieved to find that there was no need to storm the palace and rescue a gallant Resident and heroic Lamido from the hands of the mob. Indeed, John Stapleton was already back at my house, waiting hungrily for breakfast. The disturbance had quickly dissipated like the early harmattan, and the Hamman Yaji supporters had quietly slipped back to Madagali.

Although congratulations were handed out to those who had acquitted themselves well in what was officially described at the time as a "small but pungent riot," clearly our intelligence was at fault. (The opportunity was pointedly taken to allude officially to Hamman Yaji's "astounding record of oppression" and to Madagali Town "which, even today [26 years later] carries a depressing atmosphere of a slave town" [Provincial Annual Reports 1953].) In the face of the pressing Kilba problem, the rest of the Northern Touring Area had been consciously but dangerously undertoured over the previous eight months. I was now instructed to subject the northern area to a sustained period of intensive touring on horseback and, in the Mandara Mountains, on foot. But first I was given permission to go down to Yola and read the Hamman Yaji files, including the diary; this time it had far more relevance. Then, and over the next six months until I went on leave, I spent up to three weeks out of every four out on tour in the northern districts of Madagali, Michika, and Uba. To occupy often long lonely days in camp, I set about copying out (in microscopic and today sometimes barely legible handwriting, into an Adamawa NA Primary School exercise book, still extant) the whole of the diary; all the relevant pages from the Madagali District Note Book; and extensive extracts from the confidential historical files on the affair held in the Mubi office, especially the blow-by-blow accounts of 1927. These I added to notes I had made from the provincial reports going back to the capture of Yola in 1901, all painstakingly gathered, sorted and bound by W. H. Paul, Senior District Officer, and carefully preserved in the Residency library, to which I had had privileged access in 1951–52. Spending most of the next thirty weeks out on tour in the district and visiting several mountain-top villages which had not seen a European since W. R. Shirley and D. F. H. Macbride had visited them as TONAs in the 1930s, I was also able to carry out a number of oral interviews in Madagali, Sukur, Gulak, and Michika District relating to the history of Hamman Yaji and his family.

It is from the data recorded in my field notes between 1951 and 1954, especially for the period from September 1953 to March 1954—however unsatisfactorily set out in terms of the then non-existent technological aids of modern scholarship and however much I, then an apprentice administrator and now a demanding academic, perforce lament the absence of file references, etc.[70]—that this narrative has been derived. How many local files, District Note Books and touring reports on the area in the old TONA office at Mubi, lovingly compiled in the 1920s and 1930s by such deeply interested field administrators as E. A. Brackenbury, D. F. H. Macbride, W. O. P. Rosedale, J. Hunter Shaw, W. R. Shirley and S. H. P. Vereker, have survived and can today be easily consulted in the National Archives or at Arewa House, Kaduna, is not easy to say. Recent scholars working on the history of Adamawa and its environs—Martin Njeuma, Sa'ad Abubakar, and Bawuro Barkindo—suggest that while many of the Provincial files and some of the divisional ones have been preserved, the record at the lower administrative level of the district is less complete. If the local TONA documentation has been retained, my fieldwork of 1953–54 stands open to confirmation or challenge; if it has not, then we are left with the proverbial half loaf, prepared

70. As a crumb of comfort, and in no way an excuse, the historian Robert Heussler was resolutely (and less pardonably, I would argue) as uncommunicative in his generous use of files in both the National Archives, Kaduna and the Colonial Records Project papers in the Rhodes House Library, Oxford, copiously cited throughout his important *The British in Northern Nigeria* (1968), as to indicate nothing more exact as a source than the follow-up researcher's dead-end of "K." and "CRP" respectively.

with stale flour by a then-amateur baker. For these reasons, the account as presented in the ultimate local official records of 1921–27, amplified by intensive field work some 40 years ago and the scholarly observations of Prof. James H. Vaughan, is offered here, however raw its original form, pending a more extensive, and welcome, research project. At least the heart of the matter—the translation of Hamman Yaji's remarkable diary—is now for the first time made available for historians to consult and consider.[71]

There remains the question of why, as a practicing academic since 1957 and the author of a number of books and articles on Nigerian history published since 1954, I have taken nearly forty years to make my copy of this unique diary available to other scholars. The story is almost as replete with refusals, delays and smokescreens as that of the Yola Provincial Administration's cunctatory handling of Hamman Yaji. To continue in the autobiographical mode, when in 1955, in keeping with Colonial Regulations, I submitted draft articles on the Northern Touring Area of Adamawa which the Historical Society of Nigeria wished to consider for publication, I was advised by the Civil Secretary's office in Kaduna that parts of the text should be withheld and other parts deleted because such comments were considered untimely by the colonial government in light of the recentness of the Hamman Yaji family fracas at Mubi in 1953. Furthermore, some of the material I had unearthed was held to be the kind of record that "should be kept in the archives of Government offices" and was never intended for publication (Civil Secretary Kaduna GEN.110/35, 17 January, 1956)—a comment applicable, in the event, to a lot of the Colonial Office files in the PRO since the introduction of the 30-year rule. This ukase from on high also restricted any further work on what I had titled "A Biographical Sketch of Hamman Yaji, with Excerpts from his Unpublished Diary." Ten years later, with the colonial government no longer in authority, I again sought approval to write up the diary, this time from my academic base at Ahmadu Bello University; now it was the Premier's office's turn to refuse my request, considering it liable to be "viewed with disfavour" and "easily misconstrued" (PM 215/T/3, 3 June 1964). With the fall of civilian government in 1966, and the civil war over, it seemed worth returning to the charge. This time, after my request had been referred to the Interim Common Services Agency, the Federal Military Government approved that the National Archives should authorize the University of Ibadan to release a photocopy of the diary. To my delight, the text supplied by the University of Ibadan Library in 1970 was a photocopy of the very same file I had read in the Resident's office at Yola in 1951 and copied verbatim in 1953.

In 1972 D. J. M. Muffett, who likely had access to the diary when the Northern Regional Government was preparing its submission to the Willink Commission on Minorities in 1957–58 and had been Resident of the short-

---

71. Asma'u Garba Saeed (see chapter 2) tells me that Sheikh Hayatu Sa'id also kept a diary, probably while in exile at Buea, but that it was lost after his death.

lived Northern Cameroons Under United Nations Administration in 1960–61,[72] was now teaching at Duquesne University. He asked whether I would care to contribute to a version of the diary which he had in mind to publish (his putative title still arguably "inappropriate"!) (personal correspondence; January 22, February 22, and March 14, 1973). But by then I was already committed to another cooperative project on the diary, having begun a collaboration with Jim Vaughan, then associate professor of anthropology at the University of Cincinnati, in 1967. On my recommendation, Prof. Vaughan had undertaken fieldwork among the Margi of Madagali at Gulak in 1959. No sooner had we worked out a division of labor than new commitments overtook us both, with Vaughan moving to Indiana University and I to research in East and Central Africa. Sometime later, after I had approached Prof. John Lavers of Bayero University, Kano, to make sure we were not treading on any local scholars' toes, I was invited by Dr. Bawuro M. Barkindo of Bayero University—who was completing his doctorate on the history of the neighboring Sultanate of Mandara—to collaborate in his project of a full-length biography of Hamman Yaji. While welcoming the idea, both Vaughan and I felt it was a proposal which would be more appropriately handled by a Nigerian scholar than by expatriates. It was not until 1987, when we had accomplished our respective research priorities, that Vaughan and I were able to work together on the diary for a term at Oxford and get the project into final shape. In the belief that the original Hamman Yaji diary would be enhanced by a commentary from a Nigerian scholar, we invited Dr. Barkindo to contribute an afterword. Although, to our pleasure, he accepted this invitation (letter of July 3, 1991), it unfortunately turned out that his new post with the National Boundary Commission left him no free time to provide such a contribution during the succeeding twelve months. We understand that Ahmed Musa from the History Department at Maiduguri was writing his final-year dissertation on Hamman Yaji in 1992–93. Since 1990 we have been greatly supported by the enthusiastic encouragement of Prof. Paul Lovejoy of York University, Toronto, in making this text available to a wider world of scholarship, particularly in Nigeria, as part of his major *Primary Texts Relating to the Sokoto Caliphate* project. Finally, in 1992, we were able to discuss the diary with Judy Sterner, on her return from fieldwork in Nigeria. She drew our attention to the brief quotation from the diary by Walter E. A. van Beek in his paper on domestic production among the Kapsiki (Geschiere and Konings 1989:619–620) and to the confirmation established by herself and Nicholas David that the conversion of the Islamic to the Christian calendar dates in the diary compared with the dates of the moon's eclipses using the Voyager 2.1 program. She added the following current (1991) Sukur version of the death of Hamman Yaji:

72. This curious administrative unit was created after a United Nations plebiscite in 1960 in which the British Cameroons refused to join Nigeria. It was terminated after a second plebiscite in 1961. For the dynamics of that transition in the Madagali area and the importance of the ghost of Hamman Yaji, see Vaughan 1964.

He was stopped by the Europeans who captured him and poisoned him. When he died he fell spread-eagled with his arms outstretched. When you go down to the town [Madagali] you see wooden crosses that Europeans have put up in memory of his death.

Glossary

aflas = unknown meaning; as in "I paid my debt of 90s. to Malam Mansur: 40s. of this was the cost of 'aflas' (?) and the rest I had borrowed from him."

ajami = Hausa or Fulfulde written in Arabic script

alkali = (Hausa) judge

ardo = (Fulfulde) chief, district head (a Fulbe)

arnado = (Fulfulde) pagan village head

arne = (Fulfulde) pagans

bangirma = respect to those in sanctioned authority

Beit-el-Mal = (Arabic) Native Authority Treasury

bobori = tree; Sterculia tomentosa (setigera?)

bunu = (Fulfulde ?) a rank

chimajo = (Fulfulde) unofficial tax

dogari (pl. dogarai) = (Hausa) Native Authority policeman

fadanci = institutionalized flattery

Fatihah = (Arabic) opening chapter of the Koran

golombi = tree; Stereospermum kunthianum

hadiths = (Arabic) stories or traditions of the Prophet

haraji = (Hausa) poll or head tax

hijrah = (Arabic) the flight of the Prophet, at least an event which occurred in 1345.

Id al Fitr = (Arabic) a religious feast day

Id al Adhdha = (Arabic) a religious feast day

jangali = (Fulfulde) tax on cattle

jauro = (Fulfulde) village head

jekadu = official representatives

ka'abah = (Arabic) the holy black stone at Mecca

kachella = (Kanuri) head slave, a title of the slaves, also the leader of a caravan

kadi = (Arabic) judge, same as *alkali*

kaigamma = (Kanuri) title

kiblah = (Arabic) direction of prayer

lamido = leader

ma'aji = (Hausa) treasurer

ma-ga-takarda = personal scribe

mai = (Kanuri) king

malam = (Hausa) teacher

maliki = (Arabic) Islamic law

mufti = (Arabic) judge's assistant, assessor

Muwatta = the title of Imam Malik's collection of Hadiths

nasara a kan arna = "victory over the pagans"

nasara = European (from Nazarene, i.e., Christian)

riga = gown

Salat al Fitr = (Arabic) same as Id al Fitr

salsala = chain armor

sarauta = (Hausa) government or chieftaincy

Sarkin Kasar Arewa duka wanda ya fi sarakuna duka = "Lord of all the North who is above all other kings"

Sarkin Musulmi = "Leader of the Faithful"

Sarkin = (Hausa) chief or head

sheikh = (Arabic) religious leader

Ta Ha = (Arabic) the 20th chapter of the Koran

talakawa = commoner

tasa = measuring bowl

wakil or *wakili* = representative of the Lamido

wanda ya kashe alkafirai = "Slayer of the Infidels"

Wata'a = (Arabic) a book title

waziri = (Hausa from Arabic) vizier

Yerima = (Kanuri) prince

zakah = unknown meaning; as in "I gave Ardo Amin the rank named Bunu and gave him leave to collect all the 'zakah' of the people of Madagali, all of them without exception, apart from the quarter of Khurga."

zaure = courtyard

zuwa ga wanda Allah ya ba shi karama = "To him to whom Allah has given the spirit of cordial generosity"

References

Abubakar, Sa'ad
   1977. *The Lamibe of Fombina: A Political History of Adamawa, 1809–1901.* Zaria: Ahmadu Bello University.
Al-Hajj, Muhammad A.
   1971. "Hayatu bin Sa'id: A Revolutionary Mahdist in the Western Sudan." In *Sudan in Africa.* Yusuf Fadl Sasan, ed. Khartoum: Khartoum University Press.
Anonymous
   The Madagali District Note Book. Unpublished manuscript.
Aymèrich, J. G.
   1931. *La Conqûete du Cameroun.* Paris: Payot.
Barth, Heinrich
   1857. *Travels and Discoveries in North and Central Africa.* vol. 2. New York: Harper and Brothers.
Barkindo, Bawuro M.
   1989. *The Sultanate of Mandara to 1902: The History of the Evolution, Development and Collapse of a Central Sudanese Kingdom.* Stuttgart: F. Steiner.
van Beek, Walter E. A.
   1992. "The Dirty Smith: Smell as a Social Frontier among the Kapsiki/Higi of North Cameroon and North-Eastern Nigeria." *Africa* 62:38–58.
   1989. "Transformations in Kapsiki Social Formation." In *Conference on the Political Economy of Cameroon—Historical Perspectives.* vol. 2. Peter Geschiere and Piet Konings, eds. Leiden: African Studies Centre.
Denham, Dixon
   1826. *Narrative of Travels and Discoveries in Northern and Central Africa.* London: John Murray.
East, Rupert M.
   1935. *Stories of Old Adamawa.* Zaria: West Africa Publicity.
Frantz, Charles
   1981. "Fulbe Continuity and Change under Five Flags atop West Africa." *Journal of Asian and African Studies* 16:89–115.
Gorges, Edmund Howard
   1927. *The Great War in West Africa.* London: Hutchinson.
Great Britain Colonial Office
   1928. "Report by His Britannic Majesty's Government to the Council of the League of Nations on the Administration of the British Cameroons for the Year 1927" (Colonial No. 34). London: His Majesty's Stationery Office.
Heussler, Robert
   1968. *The British in Northern Nigeria.* London: Oxford University Press.
Ikime, Obaro
   1984. *Groundwork of Nigerian History.* Ibadan: Published for the Historical Society of Nigeria by Heinemann Educational Books.
Kirk-Greene, Anthony H. M.
   1953. Field Notes.
   1954a. "The Madagali Patrol of 1921." Unpublished.
   1954b. "A Note on the History of Madagali." Mimeographed.
   1958. *Adamawa Past and Present.* London: Oxford University Press.

1960. "The Kingdom of Sukur: A Northern Nigerian Ichabod." *The Nigerian Field* 25:67–96.

1988. "Examinees, Examiners and Examinations: The Hausa Language Requirements of the Northern Nigerian Government, 1902–1962." In *Studies in Hausa Language and Linguistics: Essays in Honour of F. W. Parsons*. Graham Furniss and Philip Jagger, eds. London: Kegan Paul International Association with the International African Institute.

Le Vine, Victor T.
1964. *The Cameroons: From Mandate to Independence*. Berkeley: University of California Press.

Lemoigne, J.
1918. "Les pays conquis du Cameroun Nord." *L'Afrique Française: Bulletin Mensuel du Comité de l'Afrique Française et du Comité du Maroc* 28 Renseignements Coloniaux et Documents supplément (7–8): 94–114 et (9–10): 130–55.

Lethem, G. J.
Lethem Papers, Rhodes House Library, Oxford (Brit. Emp. s. 276).

Lovejoy, Paul E., and J. S. Hogendorn
1990. "Revolutionary Mahdism and Resistance to Colonial Rule in the Sokoto Caliphate, 1905–06." *Journal of African History* 31:217–44.

Lugard, Fredrick John Dealtry, Baron
1970 [1917]. *Political Memoranda: Revision of the Instructions to Political Officers on Subjects Chiefly Political and Administrative*. No. IX, "Native Administration" (3rd ed.). London: Cass.

Meek, C. K.
1931. *Tribal Studies in Northern Nigeria*, vol. 1. London: Kegan Paul, Trench, Trubner.

Migeod, C. O.
1972 [1927]. "Gazetteer of Yola." In *Gazetteers of the Northern Provinces of Nigeria*, vol. 2. A. H. M. Kirk-Greene, ed. London: Frank Cass.

Moberly, F. J.
1931. *Military Operations: Togoland and the Cameroons, 1914–1916*. London: H. M. Stationery Office.

Mohammadou, E.
1981. "L'Implantation des peuls dans l'Adamawa (Approche chronologique)." In *Contribution de la Recherche Ethnologique à l'Histoire des Civilisations du Cameroun*, vol. 1, pp. 229–247. Claude Tardits, ed. Paris: Centre National de la Recherche Scientifique.

Nadel, S. F.
1942. *A Black Byzantium*. London: Oxford University Press.

Njeuma, M. Z.
1978. *Fulani Hegemony in Yola (Old Adamawa): 1809–1902*. Yaounde: Centre for Teaching and Research.

Oakley, R. R.
1938. *Treks and Palavers*. London: Seeley Service Co.

Provincial Annual Reports
1953. Adamawa.

Report on the Cameroons, 1924.

Report on the British Sphere of the Cameroons, 1922 and 1923.

Rosedale, W. O. P.
Rosedale Papers. Rhodes House Library, Oxford (Mss. Afr. s. 582).

Rowling, C. W.
1930. Marghi District Assessment. Unpublished manuscript.

Rudin, Harry
    1968 [1938]. *Germans in the Cameroons, 1884–1918.* Hamden, Conn.: Archon Books.
Saeed, Asma'u G.
    1982–85. "The British Policy towards the Mahdiyya in Northern Nigeria: A Study of Arrest, Detention and Deportation of Shaykh Said b. Hayat, 1923–1959." A biographical note. *Kano Studies* 2:95–119.
Strümpell, Kurt
    1912. "Die Geschichte Adamauas nach mündlichen Überlieferungen." Sonderabzug aus *Mitteilungen der Geographischen Gesellschaft in Hamburg* Bd. XXVI, Heft. 1 (49–107). Hamburg: L. Friederichsen.
Tomlinson, G. J. F., and G. J. Lethem
    1927. *History of Islamic Political Propaganda in Nigeria.* London: Waterlow.
Ubah, C. N.
    1976. "British Measures against Mahdism at Dumbulwa in Northern Nigeria 1923: A Case of Colonial Overreaction." *Islamic Culture* 50:95–110.
Vaughan, James H.
    1964. "Culture, History, and Grass-Roots Politics in a Northern Cameroons Kingdom." *American Anthropologist* 66:1078–1095.
    1977. "Mafakur: A Limbic Institution of the Margi." In *Slavery in Africa.* Suzanne Miers and Igor Kopytoff, eds. Madison: University of Wisconsin Press.
    1980a. "Margi Resistance to Fulani Incorporation: A Curious Resolution." In *Studies in Third World Societies* 11:95–106.
    1980b. "A Reconsideration of Divine Kingship." *Explorations in African Systems of Thought.* Ivan Karp and Charles S. Bird, eds. Bloomington: Indiana University Press.
Documents and Letters in the Kaduna National Archives
    Civil Secretary Kaduna GEN.110/35, 17 January 1956.
    DNA 20/10/Vol.III/266, 8 September 1970.
    NAK 28/A/29.
    NAK 30/A/31.
    NAK 31/A/32.
    PM 215/T/3, 3 June 1964.
    Public Record Office, London, CO.583/164/441/29.
    SNP 10/2 95p/1914.
    SNP 10/3 373p/1916.
    SNP 17 12577.
    SNP circular letter, K.5621/12, 4 October 1927.
    SNP pamphlet, MP.K.5669/3.
    SNP[K] 5621/4, 29 September 1927.

Index

Accession by Hamman Yaji, 9

Accusations, 20–21, 79, 84, 101, 119, 133, 136, 143

Adamawa (as emirate, province and state), 1, 2, 4, 4n10, 6, 7, 8, 10, 17, 22, 23, 23n34, 24, 25, 27, 29, 30, 36, 37, 38, 40n60, 41, 44, 146, 148, 149

Administration of justice, 62, 80, 81, 82, 83, 84, 85, 86, 95, 96, 99, 100, 101, 102, 103, 104, 105, 106, 107, 110, 111–12, 114, 115, 125, 126, 127, 131, 133, 136, 137, 142, 143, 144

Administrative meetings: with Resident, 82, 91, 113, 124, 126, 133, 136–37; with Emir al Yemen, 74, 75, 77, 97, 104, 113, 124–25, 130, 141

Admonition from Europeans, 6, 74, 91, 97, 99

Adultery, 75, 86

Africans frequently mentioned: Atiku, 52, 53, 55, 83, 84, 96, 99, 101, 106, 111, 117, 118, 119, 121, 125, 126, 127; Bakari Duhu, 58, 59, 61, 62, 63, 64, 66, 67, 69; Dadandi, 79, 87, 90, 91, 92, 102, 104, 105, 107, 108, 109, 110, 111, 114, 116, 117, 118, 126, 138; Emir al Yemen (also Emir of Adamawa and Emir of Yola), 6n14, 10, 17n29, 18, 27n46, 56, 60, 61, 74, 75, 76, 77, 82, 87, 92, 94, 97, 99 (death of, 99, 100, 104, 105, 106, 112, 113, 114, 118, 122, 124, 125, 127, 128, 129, 130, 131, 132, 133, 134, 135, 138, 139, 141, 143, 144, 145) (see also Lamido); Emir of Kano, death of, 69; Emir of Malabu, 81, 97, 139; Emir (also Sultan and Lamido) of Mandara, 56, 59, 94, 100, 147; Emir of Marua, 70, 109; Emir of Moda (also Ardo Moda), 68, 78, 129, 138; Emir of Mubi, 58, 69, 89, 96, 97; Emir of Rei, 71, 78, 107; Emir of Uba, 13n24, 52, 68, 91, 93, 95, 97, 100; Fadhl al Nar, 60, 62, 63, 64, 65, 66, 68, 69, 70, 71, 72, 73, 74, 81, 93, 140; Hausawa (also Hausawa Audu), 57, 60, 61, 89, 90, 92, 94, 95, 96, 103, 104, 105, 106, 109, 112, 140; Jadko, 81, 95, 136, 139, 144; Lamido, 5, 6, 7, 8, 10, 26n43, 27, 27n46, 27n49, 28, 29, 30, 31, 34, 35, 36, 39, 147 (see also Emir al Yemen); Mai Bornu, 85, 87, 88, 99, 101, 104, 107, 109, 110, 122, 131, 140; Malam Mukhtar, 84, 85, 90, 91, 92, 101, 112, 117, 118, 121, 126, 128, 129; Malam

Umaru, 89, 91, 92, 101, 107, 108, 110, 111, 112, 119, 120, 121, 123, 124, 125, 126, 135, 137; Modibbo Adama, 6n15, 6, 7, 147; Muhammad Bello, 131, 132, 134, 135; Othman, 80, 81, 84, 87, 101, 102, 110, 112, 113, 114, 131; Sa'id, 74, 76, 77, 81, 87, 90, 92, 93, 95, 102, 111, 112, 115, 116, 124, 126, 128, 131, 132, 133, 135, 137, 140; Sa'id ibn Hayatu (also referred to as Mallam Said), 16, 16n27, 17, 25n42, 30n51, 38, 149n70; Shehu of Bornu (also Shehu and Emir of Bornu), 5, 74, 76, 78, 87, 109, 137; Usman dan Fodio, 6n15. See also Kin and affines

Age of Hamman Yaji, 85

Ammunition, 124. See also Cartridges

Armour, 51

Arrest and removal, 1, 14, 19, 20, 32–36; planning, 31–32; reasons for, 14, 15, 16n26, 17, 20, 25n41

Arrests, 56, 62, 67, 69, 75, 77, 79, 80, 81, 84, 85, 86, 89, 94, 114, 115, 119, 121, 126, 133, 137, 138, 141

Automobiles. See Motor car

Boat, 97

Bornu, 5, 12, 15, 28, 31, 32, 70, 75, 78, 80, 89, 90, 92, 94, 98, 101, 103, 104, 106, 107, 108, 109, 110, 111, 112, 114, 118, 119, 120, 121, 122, 123, 126, 133, 137, 139, 140

Boundaries, 59, 61, 62, 85, 95, 104, 110, 113, 117, 142

Boundary adjustments by Europeans, 66, 69–70, 74, 75, 76, 77, 79, 88, 89, 102, 117, 136

Bribery allegations, 20, 21n30, 40

British Administration: structure of, 10; first contact with, 24, 74; viewed by Hamman Yaji, 14–15, 20, 24–27; fears of Hamman Yaji, 29–30

Burning of houses, 53, 58, 59, 65, 120, 137; by Europeans, 87, 140

Cameroon (Republic of), 2–3

Cameroons (Northern), 2, 10, 22, 23n34, 24, 31, 40, 41n36, 150, 150n71

Cameroun (French), 2, 16, 26, 30, 40

Caravan, 70

Cartridges, 51, 53, 54, 58, 61, 68, 69, 70, 73, 86, 90, 114. See also Ammunition

Cattle, difficulty of indexing, 19

tance of, 4, 14; relations with Fulbe, 6, 19; complaints against Hamman Yaji, 28

Mosques built, 78, 121

Motor car and motor-car, 18, 19, 25*n43*, 26, 91, 104, 113, 118, 126, 127

Mubi, 10, 12, 14, 23, 23*n34*, 28, 31, 32, 34, 38, 40, 41, 42, 43, 53, 54, 56, 59, 63, 65, 67, 68, 77, 79, 80, 82, 84, 85, 86, 91, 92, 94, 96, 97, 98, 99, 101, 102, 107, 108, 109, 111, 113, 114, 117, 118, 119, 123, 124, 125, 128, 129, 130, 136, 146, 147, 148, 149

Murders, 70, 101, 114, 115, 125, 126, 136; son of Hamman Yaji suspected, 75

Native Authority (NA), 10, 35, 39, 41, 42, 148

Ngaundere, 10, 51, 52, 54, 130, 137

Nigeria (*also* Northern Nigeria), 1, 8, 10, 16, 25, 39*n59*, 40, 41, 44, 150, 150*n71*

Note to reader from Hamman Yaji, 121

Oral history, collection of, 92

Orders by Hamman Yaji, 54, 80, 82, 83, 85, 93, 94, 95, 110, 117, 119, 120, 121, 122, 123, 125, 127, 132, 136, 138, 139, 140

Orders from Europeans to others, 86, 88, 90, 99, 117

Orders to Hamman Yaji: from Europeans, 53, 55, 56, 57, 62, 65, 66, 67, 68, 71, 75, 77, 79, 82, 83, 84, 85, 87, 88, 89, 91, 92, 93, 96, 102, 113, 116–17, 121, 123, 126, 129, 131, 135, 139, 141, 142, 143, 145; from Emir al Yemen, 129, 131, 135, 143, 145

Parenthetical summations by translator, 54, 55, 57, 58, 59, 60, 61, 62, 65, 66, 67, 69, 72, 74, 75, 76, 77, 82

Partition by Europeans, 8, 10, 22

Pay from Hamman Yaji to others, 79, 102, 113, 115, 127, 138, 140

Pay or remuneration to Hamman Yaji, 55, 56, 64, 76, 83, 92, 99, 117, 120, 130, 131, 133, 134, 136, 139, 145

Police. *See* Arrests

Praise from superiors, 113, 123

Prayer and praying, 74, 78, 80, 91, 106, 109, 112, 116, 120, 121, 122, 130, 133, 134, 142, 145

Prison, 83, 89

Prisoners, European taking of, 71. *See also* Slaves and slavery

Prophet, 109, 121, 122; Moses, 106

Qur'an (*also* Quran). *See* Koran

Raids: by Europeans upon montagnards, 70, 71, 72, 87, 137; by Hamman Yaji, 51, 52, 53, 54, 56, 57, 58, 59, 60, 61, 62, 63, 64, 65, 66, 67, 68, 69, 70, 71, 72, 73, 74; by

Hamman Yaji with Europeans, 72; by montagnards upon Europeans, 81; by montagnards upon Fulbe, 52, 60, 65, 66, 67–68, 70, 83, 85, 88, 89, 98, 112, 115; by montagnards upon other montagnards, 72, 73, 74, 87, 118; by other Africans upon montagnards, 51, 53, 78, 89

Rain, 57, 62, 65, 88, 93, 102, 110, 114, 116, 117, 118, 130, 139

Record book and record-book, 118, 126, 133, 140

Rei, 10, 79, 102, 103, 107, 115, 123

Religious practices, 52, 57, 69, 73, 76, 80, 93, 96, 99, 100, 106, 111, 112, 114, 121, 126, 129, 138, 141. *See also* Prayer and praying

Rest Houses, 55, 56, 63, 76, 77, 79, 82, 83, 86, 90, 91, 104, 113, 116, 117, 145

Revolt in Madagali, incipient, 130–31

Rifles (*also* guns), 51, 52, 59, 61, 63, 67, 69, 70, 72, 90, 100, 124

Riot of 1953, 146–47

Rivers, 66, 76, 83, 106; the Yedseram, 2, 3*n6*, 4, 5, 6, 12, (inferred, 97), 98; the Benue, 4, 5, 6, 22, 36, (inferred, 97), 146; the Gori, 76; the Julaiwa, 76; the Lammukara, 76; the Galbije, 91; the Nyibango, 108; the Talwarchira, 116

Salt, 108, 118

School, 61, 74, 93, 99, 112

Scribe, 68, 73, 94, 96, 102, 111, 115, 118, 127, 132, 138

Sentencing, 58, 83. *See also* Imprisonment; Fines

Slaves and slavery, 1, 6–7, 12–13, 12*n23*, 13, 13*n24*, 14, 15, 18, 19, 20, 23–24, 24*n35*, 26, 28, 35, 43–44, 51, 52, 54, 59, 60, 61, 63, 66, 67, 68, 69, 70, 71, 72, 74, 75, 76, 78, 79, 80, 81, 82, 83, 84, 85, 90, 92, 93, 94, 95, 99, 100, 101, 103, 104, 105, 106, 108, 111, 112, 115, 119, 122, 123, 125, 126, 127, 131, 132, 133, 135, 139, 141, 144, 145; capture of, 53, 54, 57, 58, 59, 60, 61, 62, 63, 64, 65, 66, 67, 68, 69, 70, 71, 72, 73, 74

Sokoto, 6, 14, 25, 29, 36, 39, 40, 41, 42, 150

Sugar, 108

Taxes, 53, 60, 64, 65, 66, 67, 68, 71, 78, 81, 82, 84, 88, 89, 90, 91, 92, 97, 101, 103, 110, 111, 112, 113, 116, 117, 121, 127, 128, 135, 138, 139, 140, 141, 142, 143, 145. *See also* Jangali tax

Tea, 97

Tours within Madagali area, 87, 88, 89, 90, 91–93, 94–96, 97–99, 100–101, 103–104, 105–107, 108, 109–10, 111, 112, 113–14, 114–16, 117, 118–19, 120–22,

JAMES H. VAUGHAN is Professor Emeritus of Anthropology at Indiana University and since 1959 has made several trips to Madagali District to conduct research. His principal interest has heretofore been in the Margi, a montagnard society.

ANTHONY H. M. KIRK-GREENE was Special Lecturer in the Modern History of Africa at the University of Oxford from 1967 until his retirement in 1992. Before that he was Professor of Government at Ahmadu Bello University, Zaria, and from 1950 to 1960 had been a District Officer in Nigeria. He is the author of numerous publications on Nigerian history and politics, and is currently writing a history of British colonial administrators in Africa.